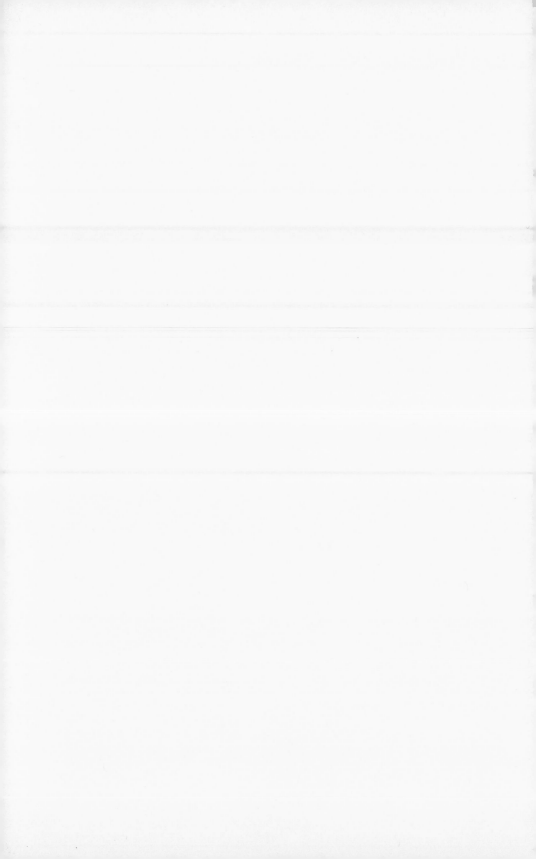

Plato's Poetics — The Authority of Beauty

PLATO'S POETICS,

The Authority of Beauty

Morriss Henry Partee

University of Utah Press
Salt Lake City
1981

Copyright 1981 by Morriss Henry Partee
ISBN 0-87480-197-4
University of Utah Press, Salt Lake City, Utah 84112
Printed in the United States of America

Library of Congress Cataloguing in Publication Data

Partee, Morriss Henry, 1938–
 Plato's poetics.

 Bibliography: p.
 Includes index.
  1. Plato.   2. Poetry.   3. Aesthetics.   I. Title.
 B398. P6P37   801′.93   81-3332
 ISBN 0-87480-197-4   AACR2

IN MEMORIAM

Douglas N. Morgan
1918–1969

Contents

Preface

Once upon a time — so the ancient Indian tale goes — four blind men came upon an elephant and attempted to describe the beast. One blind man felt the elephant's leg and pronounced the elephant to be an immovable log. Another, feeling the elephant's tail, was moved to declare that this rope-like being was a light and airy creature indeed. A third man, coming upon the ear, maintained that the beast was like a fan. The fourth touched the animal's broad side, and therefore declared the elephant something without beginning or end.

The commentators on Plato's aesthetics give us an obvious parallel. Those who stress his expulsion of the poets would make him a surly log. Those who emphasize his doctrine of poetic inspiration find a rope which would enable them to ascend to heaven. The ones who use Plato to stress the ethics of poetry have made the ear into a fan to brush away immoral and trivial poems. Those who declare that no conclusion is possible maintain that he presents only a blank wall. One might legitimately extend the analogy further. Some men, despairing of finding the truth of the elephant, turned away and began feeling each other's limbs. They declared, "Why, Plato just modifies the thought of Pythagoras," or "Plato's importance comes from his being a forerunner of Aristotle." Even less intelligently, some, repelled by the rough and hairy exterior, began to touch their own, much smoother, bodies. They exclaimed, "My goodness, Plato is a modern critic," and "Plato is really a poet wrapped in a philosopher's skin." And a few unfortunates never even got to the elephant.

Instead, they found limbs broken in the elephant's wake, and accordingly declared that the elephant, while great, had little relevance to any proper study. Clearly, there are many pitfalls for those in search of this mighty creature.

Another safari must nevertheless set forth. Plato's struggle with poetry has produced one of the most important statements of aesthetics in the history of Western culture. But despite the brilliant work done in classical philology in the past fifty years, Plato has never assumed his proper role integral to the tradition of literary criticism. Too often critics have passed over Plato's aesthetics with a testimony to his philosophical greatness in metaphysics, ethics, and logic, slighting his literary criticism as misguided and contradictory. Aristotle has generally been recognized as the father of criticism for two reasons. First, the *Poetics*, for all its ambiguities, gives a single text for consideration. Second, Aristotle's methodical and clear-sighted analysis of epic and drama gives a fairly satisfying statement about the nature and use of poetry. No such order exists in Plato's dialogues. This study of the poetics of Plato has therefore a twofold task. First, I shall attempt to establish which of Plato's scattered comments, if any, represent his own serious thought. Obviously, what Plato said often differs from what he really meant. Second, this book will attempt to delineate Plato's efforts to reconcile his magnificent poetic power and his love of poetry with his commitment to unyielding philosophical integrity.

While almost every full-length study of Plato will include some commentary on his theory of art, his poetics have never been fully outlined. For instance, one half of Carleton L. Brownson's *Plato's Studies and Criticisms of the Poets* simply lists Plato's citations of various poets. Only the latter half seeks to determine Plato's own thought. John Warry's *Greek Aesthetic Theory*, treating both Plato and Aristotle, considers Plato's theory of beauty rather than of art. Again, Rupert C. Lodge's *Plato's Theory of Art* relies heavily on Plato's forerunners to relate his philosophy generally to various aspects of his aesthetics. My study, on the other hand, begins with the texts themselves, in particular those devoted to poetry. Only after listening to Plato speak for himself am I willing to generalize about his aesthetics. Eric A. Havelock's *Preface to Plato* has suggested the necessity for a reevaluation of language and poetry in Greek thought; I have found this book invaluable in directing my thought on Plato's poetics.

My discussion of Plato is addressed to those who feel the attraction of his spirit, yet confess to a frank bewilderment when confronted with the variety of his poetics. Plato unequivocally banishes poetry in the same dialogue that pays tribute to its usefulness in education. He argues that philosophy must be presented clearly and directly, yet he chooses the ambiguous dialogue form to convey his thought. When questing after truths of man and nature, Plato displays a dazzling facility in citing relevant lines of poetry. Obviously he relishes both the form and content of the words. Yet when discussing poetry specifically, he either banishes the art or limits it to the immediately didactic. Still, no one would seriously argue that Plato himself preferred bad didactic poetry to the noble offspring of the poetic mind.

Despite the cross-purposes and varied approaches to philosophy throughout the dialogues, Plato takes a consistent underlying stance toward poetry and its criticism. He loves poetry in all its forms, and in particular the beauty of language. The beauty of all harmonious physical objects — if properly regarded — can lift the soul to a vision of true beauty. But alone among the various forms of earthly beauty, language cannot for Plato raise man above physical appearances. Beauty in language presents a danger, for words are the only means by which we can communicate ideas. And Plato is too concerned with the substance lying behind his words to trust any human means of expression. The poet in Plato feels language so powerfully that the philosopher in him would attack the inherent beauty of all poetry. Man cannot resist abusing this powerful tool.

But only the brave — or the foolhardy — dare claim certainty about Plato's thought. The philosopher's forceful dialogues defy definitive analysis; his wingèd words elude the hands which would capture "the essential Plato." He simply refuses to be categorized. Throughout his life Plato expended enormous energy in mocking those who sought dead authority rather than living thought. We must follow Plato's spirit, not the literary residue of his questing mind. He challenges and prods us to be philosophers rather than passive, drudging scholars or critics. He is honest enough to dismiss the ability of his own dialogues to embody truth. Explicitly, both his guise of Socratic ignorance and his condemnation of poetry, books, and sophistic authority testify to his misgivings about the direct human communication of knowledge. And implicitly, his use of the dialogue form asserts that eternal truth cannot reside in human writings. Plato confronts us and bemuses us. He insists that we think for ourselves and seek truth as actively and as passionately as he does himself.

Plato's bold condemnation of poetry surely represents one of the most fearless and selfless acts of the intellect. He is a master poet himself and of all philosophers one of the greatest lovers of poetry. We must accept his sincerity in *Republic X*, but we dare not stop with his literal word here or anywhere. Plato may never have resolved in his own mind the problems involved in communicating the truth in all its beauty and purity. Thus, to claim a definitive inquiry into his poetics would evoke Plato's contempt for such pompous nonsense. But coming after him in these latter days, we can with awe trace some of the paths this gigantic mind has hewed for us.

The prolegomena to this study has appeared as "Plato's Banishment of Poetry," in the *Journal of Aesthetics and Art Criticism*. Part of Chapter II appeared in the same journal as "Inspiration in the Aesthetics of Plato." "Plato's Theory of Language," published in *Foundations of Language*, formed the basis for Chapter VI. An earlier version of Chapter VII can be found as "Plato on the Rhetoric of Poetry," in the *Journal of Aesthetics and Art Criticism*, and a part of Chapter III appeared in *Philological Quarterly* as "Plato on the Criticism of Poetry." I wish to acknowledge the kind permission of these journals to reproduce this material here.

I would especially like to thank my wife Donna for her constant encouragement and very real practical assistance in the preparation of the manuscript and the book.

Plato's Poetics — The Authority of Beauty

I

The Quest
for Unity
amid Multiplicity

He who would not be frustrate of his hope to write well hereafter in laudable things, ought himself to be a true poem, that is, a composition and pattern of the best and honorablest things — not presuming to sing high praises of heroic men, or famous cities, unless he have in himself the experience and the practice of all that which is praiseworthy.

John Milton, *Apology for Smectymnuus*

There can be little doubt that Plato had grave reservations about the value of poetry.[1] Unlike Aristotle and most later aestheticians, Plato views poetry as a process rather than as an object for rational analysis. He advances no legitimate method for interpreting this energy, for the flow comes too close to the transient world of becoming. Plato's praise of poetic inspiration stems from his recognition of the inhuman beauty of this energy. But the social, communicative nature of verbal representation inextricably ties any particular

[1] I have discussed the danger of dismissing Plato's argument against poetry in "Plato's Banishment of Poetry"; taking a contrary position in "Plato's Theory of Art: A Reassessment," Robert W. Hall feels that the *Republic* does allow for "the craftsman who through educated right opinion can create an object which is both beautiful and correct" (p. 82). The reader may refer to the Bibliography for the facts of publication pertaining to texts, translations, commentaries, and other sources cited.

[1]

bit of poetry to the world of sense impressions. While he believes that passive exposure to harmonious objects can instill harmony in the soul, language demands an active involvement of the mind. Thought for Plato does not depend on language, and indeed attention to any particular discourse is likely to distract the dialectician from his pursuit of higher wisdom. Language is didactic on every level down to the letter and sound; poetry of course shares this quality. The coherently rational universe of Plato gives little space to statements which are neither true nor false.

Plato is unalterably opposed to dramatic recitals. Censorship or outright banishment are the only ways to handle such representations of men in action. And as his argument progresses in *Republic X*, he rejects anything recognizable as lyric or epic poetry as well. Elsewhere a few glancing references link the true poet and philosopher. Favorable citations of excerpts of poetry and pious evocations of the Muses abound throughout the dialogues. But while Plato accepts wise sayings of the ancients for analysis, he adamantly refuses to allow an extended example of language any role in education of the youth. The mature philosopher needs no such enjoyment or enlightenment. Poetry, gripping the emotions as it does, cannot make a legitimate appeal to the rational part of the soul. Homer must leave the well-governed Republic, and Plato advances there no new band of enlightened poets or even philosophers to take the place of the old poets.

The *Republic X* gives us Plato's most thorough discussion of poetry and its effects. Here he condemns all currently existing art both for its confusing of the intellect and for its corrupting of the emotions. At least Plato *thinks* that he has banished all dramatic poetry (*Republic X* 595a).[2] And shortly thereafter all other forms of poetry join the drama in exile (*Republic X* 606e–08b). His

---

[2] Quotations from Plato throughout this book refer to Stephanos numbers. Although I have preferred Hackforth's reading in *Plato's Phaedrus* and Francis Cornford's in *The Republic of Plato*, I have generally followed Jowett's four-volume translation, *The Dialogues of Plato*. I have freely amended these translations, however, against the standard Greek text, *Platonis Opera*, ed. John Burnet.

sincerity and finality here cannot be questioned with impunity. A critic can have little justification for ignoring or explaining away his arguments on grounds irrelevant to the dialogue. Plato's extreme position in the last book of the greatest repository of his thought represents his boldest, if perhaps his most distressing, conclusions. "An author possessing Plato's skill in composition is not likely to blunt the edge of what he is saying by allowing his thought to stray away from it at the end." [3]

Plato certainly does not always express this malevolent antipathy toward poetry. In passing illustrations he will even glorify art. But he consistently applies the same strictures to poetry that he places on language throughout his dialogues. For Plato, thought precedes language. Rhetoric, poetry, reasoned discourse, all must primarily point toward rather than claim to embody truth. Plato would and does condemn even his own dialogues should anyone regard them as objects of beauty and meaning in themselves. The dialogues and all acceptable uses of language must be taken as guides for thought; only then will verbal discourse be a clear asset to a good society.[4] But the *Republic* seems pessimistic about the possibility of poetry's admittance, for memorized poetry is as fixed as the written word is.

The extreme diversity of interpretations of Plato's aesthetics suggests that any one simple statement will be inadequate. Plato treats poetry's effect on society throughout the bulk of the dialogues; his scattered and theoretical aesthetics can be brought together only with an effort, and historically, few critics have been willing to try. Because of the indirect presentation, critics can select that part most useful to them. Sir Thomas Elyot cites Plato to defend poetry in the *Governour* and to attack poetry in the *Defence of Good Women*.[5] The most vociferous attacker of poetry in the Elizabethan Age,

[3] Eric A. Havelock, *Preface to Plato*, p. 3.

[4] See Richard L. Nettleship, *Lectures on the Republic of Plato*, pp. 340–54.

[5] *The Boke Named the Governour*, ed. H. H. S. Croft, I, 121–22; *The Defence of Good Women*, ed. Edwin J. Howard, pp. 13–14. I have discussed this curious ambivalence in my "Sir Thomas Elyot on Plato's Aesthetics."

Stephen Gosson, cites his aesthetics as superficially as does the great
bishop of Hippo, St. Augustine.[6] Only a larger view than these
can be judicious. Whereas Aristotle will separate his aesthetics from
a metaphysical scheme and put the results in one specific place,
Plato's aesthetics occurs in the context of his immediate and pressing
concern for man as a social and political creature.[7]

The lack of critical unanimity should surprise no one. Plato
gives us inherent problems in approaching any topic in his dialogues. Generally, Plato was not a system-builder; his manner of
presentation itself allows the critic wide latitude. In addition, the
mask of the dialogue form compounds the ambiguity introduced by
the changing thought of Plato's long and productive life. His
thought may indeed represent a unity, but this unity possesses many
facets. More specifically, Plato never considers poetry by itself. He
always presses toward some other conclusion: the beauty of poetic
process, the ignorance of rhapsodes, the education of the youth. The
scattered sayings concerning inspiration, the uses of poetry, and the
nature of poetry itself only grudgingly give up the heart of Plato's
aesthetics.

While his direct thought runs counter to accepting poetry,
Plato's tacit attitude toward beauty and art indicates a real ambiguity in his mind. Except in *Republic X*, he approvingly quotes
Homer, Hesiod, and other poets; traditional wisdom receives great
respect. A solemn thinker with a pedestrian style and a reasoned

---

[6] *The Schoole of Abuse*, ed. Edward Arber; *Basic Writings of Saint
Augustine*, ed. Whitney J. Oates, 2:42.

[7] A. E. Taylor, in *The Mind of Plato*, judiciously states Aristotle's de-
pendence on Plato:

> The formal reverence which Aristotle expresses in his writings for his
> predecessor was combined with a pugnacious determination to find him
> in the wrong on every possible occasion. Yet, in spite of the carping and
> unpleasantly self-satisfied tone of most of the Aristotelian criticism of
> Plato, the thought of the later philosopher on all the ultimate issues of
> speculation is little more than an echo of the larger utterance of his
> master, and it is perhaps as much by inspiring the doctrine of Aristotle
> as by his own utterance that Plato has continued to our own day to exer-
> cise an influence in every department of philosophic thought, which is not
> less potent for being most often unsuspected. [p. 19]

prejudice against poetry could be dismissed as a misguided phi-
listine.[8] But "Plato is not merely the well-read, appreciative student
of Greek literature, the able critic of the poetic art, the admirer of
the noblest poets in Greece; he is himself a poet in the truest sense
of the word, a dramatic artist of surpassing skill. He has given to
his philosophy all the charm and grace of poetry. His dialogues are
themselves dramas, in form, in fullness of scenic setting, in characterization, in dignity of expression. In his greatest works he shows
himself first, the literary artist and second, the philosopher." [9] It is
little wonder that Sir Philip Sidney says Plato, "of all *Philosophers*,
I have ever esteemed most worthie of reverence; and with good
reason, since of all *Philosophers* hee is the most *Poeticall*." [10] But
felicity of expression does not transform a philosopher into a poet.
Plato himself asserts — without much explanation or proof — the
identity of the true poet with the philosopher. Just as the philosopher serves the state in all his actions, so must this ideal poet. Plato
consistently subordinates all known human discourse to the immediate needs of the state. Only the new and seductive spirit of philosophy totally escapes condemnation.

1

A STATEMENT OF THE PROBLEM

Establishing Plato's attitude toward aesthetics is of course only
a small part of the general problem of interpreting Plato. Plato
harrows a vast field of knowledge, of which aesthetics occupies a
limited space. Despite his extensive familiarity with poetry and his

[8] Paul Shorey, in *Platonism: Ancient and Modern*, feels that Plato's very
brilliance has repelled some people: "Men grow weary of the very perfection
of Plato, the polished surface of the unfailing literary art, the mastery of an
inevitable dialectic, the sense of intellectual adequacy or superiority, the perfect reasonableness, the entire absence of pseudo-science and a technical and
system-building terminology for the mind to play with, the ironical evasion of
unprofitable discussion of ultimates in symbolism and myth" (p. 23).

[9] Carleton L. Brownson, *Plato's Studies and Criticisms of the Poets*, p. 77.

[10] *The Prose Works of Sir Philip Sidney*, ed. Albert Feuillerat, 3:33.

obvious love of art, Plato spends remarkably little time with poetry
itself. He certainly refuses us an easy — and therefore shallow —
grasp of his thought. The dialogues are easy to love, baffling to try
to understand.[11] Throughout his varied dialogues he prods rather
than clarifies. Whitehead's famous overstatement that all philosophy is only a footnote to Plato serves to remind us that lesser
thinkers have attacked, embraced, misinterpreted, but seldom ignored this giant. Unfortunately for the history of literary criticism,
Plato's scattered statements on aesthetics lend themselves to great
misrepresentation.

Confusion in Plato's mind does not necessarily follow from
variety. His honesty will not allow him to impose a foolish consistency on intractable material. Shorey argues that Plato's changes
of opinion and emphasis indicate only his growing maturity:

> Plato repeatedly refers in a superior way to eristic, voluntary
> and involuntary, and more particularly to the confusion, tau-
> tology, and logomachy into which the vulgar fall when they
> attempt to discuss abstract and ethical problems. Some of these
> allusions touch on the very perplexities and fallacies exemplified
> in the minor dialogues. They do not imply that Plato himself
> had ever been so confused. Why should we assume that he
> deceives us in order to disguise his changes of opinion, or
> obliterate the traces of his mental growth? Have we not a right
> to expect dramatic illustration of so prominent a feature in
> the intellectual life of the time, and do we not find it in the
> *Laches, Charmides, Lysis,* and the corresponding parts of the
> *Protagoras?*[12]

[11] Whereas Rupert C. Lodge's monumental study *Plato's Theory of Art*
relates Plato's aesthetics to previous Greek philosophy, my primary concern
is with the dialogues themselves. Paul Friedländer, in *Plato: An Introduction,*
trans. Hans Meyerhoff, sanctions my approach when he says, "Plato may have
been well versed in the systems of earlier thinkers. According to ancient
tradition he was well acquainted with Herakleitean Kratylos, so we can
assume that he was at least familiar with this trend of thought. One thing is
certain, though invariably ignored: his philosophy did not grow out of earlier
systems" (p. 21).

[12] Paul Shorey, *The Unity of Plato's Thought,* p. 13. See also Renford
Bambrough, "The Disunity of Plato's Thought Or: What Plato Did Not
Say," pp. 295–307.

Monroe Beardsley would support Shorey's thesis on the rigor of Plato's thought.[13] While no one would dare make him a systematic philosopher on the lines of Aristotle, Kant, or Hegel, Plato does not significantly modify his stance on poetic inspiration between the *Ion* and the *Laws*. "There is no question that Plato regarded art as a serious and dangerous rival to philosophy — this is a theme that remains constant, from the very early *Ion* to the very late *Laws* — but beyond this there is much disagreement." [14]

Nevertheless, the surface of Plato's aesthetics in particular generates a great deal of friction.[15] His praise of poetic inspiration seems to conflict with his mistrust of poetry itself. Even between books *III* and *X* of the *Republic*, Plato appears to shift in his attitude toward poetry.[16] Infinitely responsive to nuances, Plato does not wish to formulate a tightly integrated philosophical system. He rejects false order even more forcefully than disorder and chaos. We must not plod through his literal words, but follow the larger sweep of his thought to find the truth Plato sought. As Douglas Morgan has said of Plato's consistency, "There really is no Platonic 'architecture' to study, for (as I read him; the issue has long been disputed among philosophers) Plato was not a system builder in the Teutonic manner. He was rather, through and through, a level-headed Golden Greek, looking with clear and steady eyes at the ugliness and agony around him, calmly analyzing meanings and tracing implications. Profoundly discontented with every partial

---

[13] *Aesthetics from Classical Greece to the Present*. Yet he sanely warns that we must not insist upon the unity of Plato's thought "to the point where we ignore important suggestions that he may not have succeeded in reconciling with his other views" (p. 31).

[14] Kenneth Dorter, "The *Ion*: Plato's Characterization of Art," p. 65.

[15] For example, Plato condemns dithyrambic poetry as merely pleasurable in *Gorgias* 502, the writers of dithyrambs being ignorant imitators in *Apology* 22c; yet in *Republic III* 394b and *Laws III* 700b, he finds this form of poetry highly praiseworthy.

[16] See William Chase Greene, "Plato's View of Poetry," p. 29; J. Tate, " 'Imitation' in Plato's Republic," pp. 16–23, and "Plato and 'Imitation,' " pp. 161–69; R. C. Cross and A. D. Woozley, *Plato's Republic: A Philosophical Commentary*, pp. 270–88.

answer, he honestly tried to think things through." [17] His discontent
made him a poet, his search for answers a philosopher. The variety
of Plato's thought does not so much suggest a philosophical limita-
tion as witness to his concern for the most complete answer possible.
Out of this conflict between preference and duty comes Plato's
aesthetics.

The ambiguity inherent in the dialogue form further compli-
cates the problem of interpretation. Every citation of Plato's strictures in one place can be countered by an example elsewhere of his
oft-expressed love of the poets. The *Laws* has been taken to modify
the position expressed in the *Republic*. The *Laws*, a work of his
last period, would admit poetry into the state as a necessary evil —
always under the proper safeguards.[18] But whether through the
voice of the Athenian or of Socrates, Plato never recognizes an
example of poetry to contain a truth immediately useful to man.
Any preserved saying or bit of traditional lore must submit to philosophical analysis; sustained discourse is dangerous (*Republic VI*
487bc). Since poetry speaks to a body of listeners, language can
fruitfully be interpreted only for its direct social relevance. Plato
views the cosmos as a whole — that which is not immediately useful
may be harmful.[19] Thus the *Republic* would deny dramatic readings even to the Guardians.

Furthermore, Plato gives no extended statement on poetry in
any dialogue. His explicit discussion of poetry occupies only a
minor place in his questioning of the communication of knowledge
and wisdom. He cites poetry frequently to illustrate his views on
education and politics. The *Ion* gives an explicit consideration to
the criticism of poetry, but this dialogue, exposing only one clearly
erroneous method of interpretation, makes a very limited statement
on poetry itself. The *Protagoras* sets forth a brilliant (and ironic)

---

[17] *Love: Plato, the Bible, and Freud*, pp. 5–6.

[18] *Literary Criticism: Plato to Dryden*, ed. Allan Gilbert, pp. 55–56.

[19] For the argument that the dialogues may not represent Plato's literal
thought, see Allan Gilbert, "Did Plato Banish the Poets or the Critics?,"
pp. 1–19.

example of Socrates' ability to criticize language. But Plato dismisses the analysis as useless frivolity.

Plato insists that poetry presents a dangerous beauty rather than instructive harmony or eternal truth. And in Plato beauty and truth can be legitimately linked only in the realm of the dialectic, not in the verbal creations of man.[20] "The lovers of sounds and sights are fond of fine tones and colors and forms and all the artificial products that are made out of them, but their mind is incapable of seeing or loving absolute beauty" (*Republic V* 476b). The *Ion* and Book *X* of the *Republic* suggest that poetry is everywhere a mechanical imitation of physical or human reality. Art misleads the unwary by distorting the true reality lying behind the literal and the physical. Man cannot rise beyond his earthbound existence solely by contemplating mundane reality. Harmonious surroundings may encourage harmony in the soul;[21] indeed, "the life of man in every part has need of harmony and rhythm" (*Protagoras* 326b). One cannot partially respond to beauty: the *Symposium* suggests that the entire soul becomes possessed with a divine love. But all examples of art contain some admixture of this present world. Art, by demanding attention, asserts some worth for man and physical phenomena. Thus Plato will not discuss poetry independently of man's understanding of ultimate knowledge. Recognizing the attraction of art and poetry, Plato nevertheless does not propose that this power can be harnessed for man's good.[22]

The *Republic* provides the cornerstone for an evaluation of Plato's most representative thought.[23] Only when other dialogues offer significant counterevidence can one discount the reasoning in the *Republic*. Defenders of Plato have lamented the massive au-

[20] See Gilbert Murray, "Prolegomena to the Study of Greek Literature," *Greek Studies*, pp. 22–43.

[21] See *Republic III* 410, *VII* 531, *Timaeus* 47.

[22] See John G. Warry, *Greek Aesthetic Theory*, p. 54.

[23] In *Plato: An Introduction*, Friedländer states, "A survey of the total body of his writings must place the *Republic* in the center of his entire literary production. In fact, it is legitimate to consider most of the earlier dialogues as a preparation directly leading to the *Republic*" (p. 9).

thority of this dialogue. John Warry says, for example, "It is unfortunate that the sections of the *Republic* in which Plato deals with poetry and fine art represent his fullest and most systematic treatment of the subject, since a comparison with other dialogues makes it quite clear that they do not contain his considered opinion." [24] Nevertheless, an evaluation of comparable passages in other dialogues such as the *Ion* and the *Phaedrus* shows that Plato does not really modify his position in the *Republic*. Instead, the dialogues which ironically praise poetic inspiration stand under the judgment of Plato's serious assessment of poetry's role in the state. Plato never discusses poetry apart from its service to man, and without strong support, we can hardly separate what Plato himself did not.

Despite the unsystematic presentation of Plato's ideas, a definite pattern of antipathy emerges. [25] Ironic praise, mockery, denigration of its interpreters abound throughout the dialogues. Only negative evidence — his refusal to banish poetry dogmatically from every conceivable situation — supports Plato as a friend of the poets. Earthly beauty does have the power to stir the emotions, but only absolute beauty can grip the entire rational soul (see especially *Phaedrus* 249de, 254). Optimally, poetry could stir emotions for a good cause as well as for a bad. Plato's explicit strictures obviously do not imply an insensitivity to poetry. There is no reason inherent in Plato's philosophy why the spirited part of man could not respond to a purified poetry. The properly disciplined emotional element in man ($\theta\upsilon\mu\omega\epsilon\iota\delta\acute{\epsilon}\varsigma$) lies closer to the rational element than to the appetitive (*Republic IV* 441a).

But Plato stubbornly maintains that philosophy and reason do more than poetry to make the state run smoothly, and that there

[24] Warry, *Greek Aesthetic Theory*, pp. 64–65.

[25] Vernon Hall, Jr., in *A Short History of Literary Criticism*, correctly notes Plato's rejection of poetry: "From every point of view he took, pedagogical, metaphysical, ethical, or political, Plato arrived at the same sobering conclusion — poetry is dangerous. The puritan streak in him even, we suspect, found melancholy satisfaction in giving up what he loved. For Plato loved poetry, or he would not have feared it so" (pp. 1–2). But Plato's love of beauty denies any puritan element in him, and his uncompromising honesty testifies against any "melancholy satisfaction" in banishing poetry.

is a constant danger that poetry may incite violent emotions in the citizens. The emotions cannot be trusted to influence the course of the soul; there is no faculty for judging in man except for the rational, reasoning element. The appetitive and the passionate elements have little to do with the lover of learning (φιλομαθὲς) or the lover of wisdom (φιλόσοφον): "Every one sees that the principle of knowledge is wholly directed to the truth, and cares less than either of the others for money or fame" (*Republic IX* 581b).

2

THE CENTRALITY OF THE *REPUBLIC*

Scholars today usually avoid all or at least some of the issues in the *Republic X* in their attempts to make Plato more sympathetic to art. One approach would directly question the purpose of the *Republic*, the only dialogue which seems to condemn poetry totally. The most popular vitiation of the argument of this dialogue holds that the *Republic* is an ideal state, a kind of utopia. This interpretation stresses that poetry deals with the emotions of real and fallible human beings. Thus, Plato dismisses art lest the portrayal of reality shatter the ideal like a grubby finger destroys a soap bubble. In a perfect state no imperfection can exist. Darnell Rucker reasons that "Neither the legislator nor the philosopher nor the poet has the same role in the *Republic* as he has in an actual state; and these differences in role are consequent upon the difference between an ideal and an actuality." [26] G. M. A. Grube likewise agrees that Plato is legislating for an ideal republic, a pattern laid up in heaven. "In such a state no one has ever claimed a place for Pericles, Themistocles, or indeed for any statesman that has ever lived. Why should an exception be made for the poets?" [27] But one might argue that Plato does provide for enlightened rulers — the philosopher–kings — yet he specifically excludes all poets. And Plato would vio-

[26] "Plato and the Poets," p. 167.
[27] *Plato's Thought*, p. 189.

lently object to his Republic's being considered less real than the decaying political organization of Athens in its decline. Great though Athenian statesmen had been, Plato, like Machiavelli, could see the degeneration of past grandeur all around him. Clearly, radical and relevant proposals were needed.

The argument stressing the *Republic* as visionary but impractical likewise reasons that, as the state itself, the ruler of the commonwealth must be independent of the actual world. The philosopher–king needs almost a physical isolation, as in More's *Utopia*, to guard him from the rigors of a real state. One might argue that "The philosopher in our world, as Plato says in the *Apology* and Socrates exemplifies, must exist in a private station. Short of the institutionalization of the education process of the Republic, the philosopher–king could not hope for the necessary support from the institutions and the citizens of his city." [28] Indeed, Plato is always mindful that philosophers were often ill-treated in the city-state (*Republic V* 488a–501e, *Apology* 23b, *Sophist* 216cd) and frequently alludes to their otherworldliness (*Theaetetus* 174). But the philosopher's present ills and seeming dreaminess are only the appearances that the ignorant can see. [29]

The argument that the Republic is an ideal state has by no means found universal acceptance. Cross and Woozley argue that "the *Republic* . . . grew out of what Plato regarded as pressing moral and political problems, and it sought to provide an answer to these problems in the way of a programme of reform." [30] Eric A. Havelock explicitly attacks this view as a present-day fallacy: "On the overall issue, Plato is accommodated to modern taste by arguing that the programme of the *Republic* is utopian and that the exclusion of poetry applies only to an ideal condition not realizable in the recognisable future or in earthly societies. One might reply that even in that case why should the Muse of all people be selected for exclusion from Utopia?" [31]

[28] Rucker, "Plato and the Poets," p. 167.
[29] See *Gorgias* 508–9, *Republic VII* 517.
[30] Cross and Woozley, *Plato's Republic*, p. xiv.
[31] *Preface to Plato*, p. 7.

Plato's seriousness can be seen in his consistent demand that poetry and all discourse be subordinate to reason and thought in the proper education of youth. From the *Ion* to the *Laws* Plato insists that poetry be judged in terms of the knowledge it embodies, the wisdom it imparts. The great political figures in Athens' past offer the same danger to the Republic that poetry does: the weight of authority may detract from the force of active reasoning. Besides, most good statesmen act only through "right opinion" (*Meno* 99a). And in the *Republic* Plato says, "Opinion without knowledge is always a shabby sort of thing. At the best it is blind. One who holds a true belief without intelligence is just like a blind man who happens to take the right road" (*VI*, 506c). Even right opinion, sanctioned in the *Meno*, cannot be trusted here.

The greatest danger in making the Republic an ideal is that the interpretation denies Plato's carefully considered analysis of knowledge. Our distinction between ideal and real is not Plato's. The *Republic* states that "a measure of such things which in any degree falls short of reality is no measure at all" (*VI* 504c). "The assertion that theory comes closer than practice to truth or reality is characteristically Platonic. The ideal state or man is the *true* state or man; for if men, who are in fact always imperfect, could reach perfection, they would only be realizing all that their nature aims at being and might conceivably be." [32] Plato intends the *Republic* to describe a system better than that of any actual or foreseeable state. But his attack on poetry is from the standpoint not of politics, but rather of ethics. The dialogue deals as much with education as with the state. "Were it not for the title, it might be read for what it is, rather than as an essay in utopian political theory. It is a fact that only about a third of the work concerns itself with statecraft as such." [33] If Plato says emphatically that poetry should be banished from the ideal state, then his criticism applies even more strongly to any less-than-perfect state. If poetry is a necessary evil in a real

[32] Cornford, *The Republic of Plato*, pp. 175–76.

[33] Havelock, *Preface to Plato*, p. 3. Richard Kraut speaks of the psychology of the rulers in the *Symposium*, the *Phaedrus*, and the *Republic* in his "Egoism, Love, and Political Office in Plato," pp. 330–44.

state, it must be excluded from a more perfect commonwealth. A necessary evil is still an evil.

To Plato the philosopher is a realist in the widest sense of the word. As opposed to the benighted politicians who must compromise their convictions, a true philosopher works in both the world of appearances and the world of higher realities. Plato himself went to Syracuse in order to advise Dionysius. And one must agree with Plato that Socrates lived and died more triumphantly than did the tyrants who were superficially successful in this world of shadows. Otherwise, Plato would insist that the *Phaedo* be rejected from a proper state because of its description of an unjust punishment.

Moreover, Plato stresses that the true philosopher is constantly engaged with the world. The awakened philosopher will not be allowed to remain in the upper world of the Forms: "they must not be allowed, as they now are, to remain on the heights, refusing to come down again to the prisoners or to take any part in their labors and rewards, however much or little these may be worth" (*Republic VII* 519d). The vision of absolute virtue and beauty makes the philosopher effective: "Remember how in that communion only, beholding beauty by the proper means, he will be enabled to bring forth, not images of beauty, but realities (for he has hold not of an illusion but of a reality), and bringing forth and nourishing true virtue to become the friend of God and be immortal, if mortal man may" (*Symposium* 212a). Even at the moment of greatest remove from the physical world, Plato makes the philosopher bring forth the realities of true virtue. The poet, on the other hand, is likely to produce only "images of beauty."

Admittedly, the Republic is not to be found among actual states, but then, the true philosopher does not live on the same plane with ordinary men. In his search for justice, Socrates states: "When we set out to discover the essential nature of justice and injustice and what a perfectly just and a perfectly unjust man would be like, supposing them to exist, our purpose was to use them as ideal patterns: we were to observe the degree of happiness or unhappiness that each exhibited, and to draw the necessary inference that our own destiny would be like that of the one we most resembled. We did not set out

to show that these ideals could exist in fact" (*Republic V* 472cd).
He recognizes that theory can never be completely realized in practice, for action always comes less close to truth than thought. He
asks, "Is our theory any the worse, if we cannot prove it possible
that a state so organized should be actually founded?" (*V* 472e).
Plato even proposes practical measures to implement establishing
this state (*Republic VII* 540d–541b). The *Republic*, then, is an
honest and courageous attempt to cut through the confusion inherent in any society already realized.

Socrates proposes that the philosopher–king may be effective
even in an actual state. The philosopher, in companionship with
the divine order, will first reproduce that order in his own soul:

> Suppose, then, he should find himself compelled to mold other
> characters besides his own and to shape the pattern of public
> and private life into conformity with his vision of the ideal, he
> will not lack the skill to produce such counterparts of tem-
> perance, justice, and all the virtues as can exist in the ordinary
> man. And the public, when they see that we have described
> him truly, will be reconciled to the philosopher and no longer
> disbelieve our assertion that happiness can only come to a state
> when its lineaments are traced by an artist working after the
> divine pattern. [*Republic VI* 500de]

The philosopher's role is to create a humanity true to its highest
possibilities, not to pander to the confused emotions of ignorant
men. The guide of the philosopher, the true artist, should be the
ideal model of virtue. He is a lover of truth and reality. The institutions described in the *Republic* will certainly be the best, if they can
be realized. And Plato rather sanguinely states that "to realize
them, though hard, is not impossible" (*VI* 502b). A true utopia,
a "nowhere" such as Sir Thomas More's, may be a social satire, a
skeptical attack on existing institutions. The *Republic*, however, is
no flight of the imagination; the dialogue represents Plato's attempt
to suggest the Form of the state.

Therefore, one cannot dismiss the attack on poetry in the *Republic* merely on the basis of its presenting an ideal state. If a critic
is justified in dismissing any part with which he happens to dis-

agree, there is no limit to the material he can ignore. The *Republic* is neither an impossible ideal nor a blueprint for a possible state; its contribution is both to politics and to ethics. Like Aristotle, Plato identifies the good of the individual with that of the state. A. E. Taylor comments on the purpose of this dialogue: "It has sometimes been asked whether the *Republic* is to be regarded as a contribution to ethics or to politics. Is its subject 'righteousness,' or is it the 'ideal state'? The answer is that from the point of view of Socrates and Plato there is no distinction, except one of convenience, between morals and politics. The laws of right are the same for classes and cities as for individual men. But one must state that these laws are primarily laws of personal morality; politics is founded on ethics, not ethics on politics." [34] Plato proposes a guide for man to order his life, not a utopian scheme for intellectual amusement. He intends his precepts concerning ethics to be universally applicable no less than does Kant. Few men may follow the categorical imperative, but human failings do not render the principle less true. So while any thoughtful discussion of the *Republic*'s applicability to our humdrum existence is valuable, one must still consider whether Plato seriously and consistently attacks poetry in this dialogue and elsewhere.

3

THE RELEVANCE OF OTHER DIALOGUES

Another method of making Plato a patron of the arts would attack not the purpose of the *Republic*, but Plato's seriousness in banishing poets.[35] These apologists claim that Plato condemns only the abuse of poetry. The *Laws* thus represents Plato's awakening to the necessity of poetry in human life; the *Ion* becomes an exposé of contemporary Greek criticism. Stressing the *Ion*, Allan Gilbert

[34] *Plato: The Man and His Work*, p. 265.

[35] Gavin Ardley thinks that such a dialogue as the *Republic III* makes a jest; the dialogues suggest that one must never be too serious about any writings ("The Role of Play in the Philosophy of Plato," pp. 226–44).

argues that "Plato attempted to banish the bad critics that the poets might appear as they truly were and are, even if only to the fit audience who can discern their nature as artists." [36] This line of reasoning is attractive, for Plato's main thrust in the *Ion* certainly appears to be against the stupidity of the rhapsodes. Then, too, Plato's constraints on poetry are, for the most part, balanced by his frequent citations of poetry. Finally, the *Republic II* and *III* as well as the *Laws II* and *VII* primarily censure immoral poetry. If some poetry were moral, Plato would have to allow its presence in the well-run state.

Unfortunately, grave difficulties beset each of these arguments. Nowhere in the *Ion* does Plato accept poetry as a guide to proper conduct. Instead, we have only an ambiguous praise of the source of poetry, the Muse. This divine source of inspiration plays no integral role in Plato's discussion of knowledge or virtue. Surprisingly, Plato almost never mentions poetic inspiration in the context of his examination of poetry. He quotes poetry often, but seldom pauses to consider the poetic worth, the beauty of any passage. The quotations usually illustrate some point about conduct. Next, the dialogue form may not express Plato's final position. Again, if we dismiss whatever we please in the dialogues simply because of the tentative nature of Plato's reasoning, we have little hope of understanding any of his thought. Finally, if other dialogues accept the possibility of moral poetry, the *Republic X* certainly denies that any poetry Plato knew would fulfill the requirement. Plato's final comment on poetry in the most complete exposition of his thought surely takes precedence over the trivial *Ion* and the important but pedestrian *Laws*.[37]

Besides considering the theory of poetic inspiration, critics may emphasize the dialogues which admit some ethical uses of poetry. Indeed, only the *Republic X* seems to deny even the possibility of good poetry. Plato's strictures in the few places where he directly

---

[36] "Did Plato Banish the Poets or the Critics?," p. 19.

[37] See A. E. Taylor, *Plato: The Man and His Work*, p. 38, and Paul Shorey, *What Plato Said*, p. 355.

considers poetry seem overweighted by his overall attitude toward
the art of the ancients. Professor Gilbert comments on the *Laws*:
"Since the form of the dialogue is still employed and no speaker can
be identified with the author, it is impossible to say that Plato's
opinions are absolutely laid down. I find it impossible to think that
the Athenian who takes the chief part, for Socrates no longer
appears, is Plato himself, or at least represents more than aspects of
Plato's mind. The comic picture of eminent generals and statesmen
solemnly reciting bad verses is hardly to be explained as the serious
opinion of a man who knew and loved Homer as Plato did." [38]
Plato has already admitted in the *Republic X* that Homer is "the
first and greatest of the tragic poets." But truth must not be sacri-
ficed for personal satisfaction: "if the dramatic poetry whose end
is to give pleasure can show good reason why it should exist in a
well-governed society, we for our part should welcome it back, being
ourselves conscious of its charm; only it would be a sin to betray
what we believe to be the truth. You too, my friend, must have felt
this charm, above all when poetry speaks through Homer's lips"
(*X* 607d). Of course Plato is charmed. But he does not on that
account accept disruptive poetry into a well-run state.

Rather than question the *Laws*, however, most critics agree that
here Plato offers a serious theory of art. Warry states that "in the
Laws, which, though it lacks the literary power of the *Republic*,
offers us a far saner and more practical version of an ideal State,
no automatic criterion of poetry and art is offered. Instead, tragedy
and comedy are cautiously admitted, subject to reservation." [39]
Grube agrees that "by far the most mature, as well as the most
complete, discussion of art is to be found in the *Laws*, where it
should be noted we are no longer dealing with the ideal state." [40]
Any variation in the perfect Republic must be for the worse. The
less visionary *Laws*, however, would seem to allow as much poetry
as needed to regulate the souls of imperfect men.

[38] *Literary Criticism: Plato to Dryden*, ed. Allan Gilbert, p. 55.

[39] Warry, *Greek Aesthetic Theory*, p. 64.

[40] *Plato's Thought*, p. 196.

But Plato's treatment in the *Laws* is at heart almost exactly the same as in the *Republic*. Both admit only praises of noble men and of gods; neither dialogue allows evil to be presented by poetry. Both the *Republic III* 400 and the *Laws VII* 810 allow poetry to stimulate harmony in the young. And even the *Republic X* 607a states that "we can admit into our commonwealth only the poetry which celebrates the praises of the gods and of good men." The *Laws* would require the poet to "present in his beauteous and well-wrought rhythms and harmonies the gestures and accents of men who are wise, strong, and altogether good" (*II* 660a). The major difference between the dialogues is that the *Republic* defends this restriction philosophically while the *Laws* is more concerned with implementing the selection of such noble poetry. The art Plato seems to accept is not actually poetry, however, but philosophical and didactic discourse.

Plato's attack on poetry grows immediately out of his response to abuses in the Athenian education.[41] A lover of poetry is tempted to say that Plato objects only to the memorized education described in *Protagoras* 325d–26b. The position is attractive: Plato does indeed defend the right of philosophy to exist against the unreasoned espousal of poetry. His comments about poetry arise from this defense of reason at a time when poetry was the blindly accepted arbiter of conduct. Plato will use myth fluently and profoundly for his own purposes, so he tacitly admits at least the possibility of useful imaginative works.[42] To censor blatantly vicious works and to insist on intellectual analysis of poetry is a far cry from condemning poetry altogether as an inherent evil for all times. Yet ultimately his rhetorical overstatement in defense of philosophy remains unbalanced by any significant tribute to poetry elsewhere in the dialogues.

Poetry must make its way through the battlefield of Plato's war with imitation. He wavers between viewing poetry as an imperfect

[41] See Beardsley, *Aesthetics*, pp. 24–25, and Havelock, *Preface to Plato*, pp. 3–19.

[42] See Ludwig Edelstein, "The Function of Myth in Plato's Philosophy," pp. 463–81.

imitation of the ideal and as a faithful imitation of the mundane. Both forms are dangerous, and either offense would be enough to merit poetry's expulsion from an intelligent society. The *Cratylus* (439ab) asserts that servile attention to an image cannot substitute for a study of the reality behind that copy. To examine an imitation when reality can be grasped is at best irrelevant and at worst damaging to the soul.[43] The *Republic* applies this principle directly to poetry. This dialogue presents or suggests the Form of the absolutely perfect state. Starting from this elevated point, representations of human traits from the old bitter world are necessarily illegitimate. Thus, no matter how good or bad the workmanship, poetry cannot justify its existence as imitation.

But imitation in a different sense is integral to Plato's ethics. A man's imitation of the Good is not only beneficial but imperative. "Whenever imitation is condemned, the inconsistent manifold it implies is condemned with it." [44] Since there can be no inconsistency in the perfect state, imitation of actions or things loses its curse altogether. The *Laws*, which does not attempt to delineate the Form of the perfect state, permits imitation in poetry to a correspondingly greater extent. In such works as the *Laws*, *Ion*, and *Phaedrus* — none of which assumes the Good to be achieved —

---

[43] William K. Wimsatt and Cleanth Brooks state, in *Literary Criticism: A Short History*,

> Plato has confronted the very difficult problem of the relation between formalism and illusionism in art and, in line with the austerity and subtlety of his basic mathematical view of reality, has expressed his mistrust of the realistic trends of his day and has cast a perennially influential vote in favor of some kind of visual formalism. If this part of his theorizing does not go far in telling us about the nature of poetry, at least it offers a prototype for theories of "stylization" or "detachment" which have never since in the history of poetics been altogether submerged. In what is no doubt its excess of detachment Plato's theory offers an approach by contrast to — as indeed it was historically the point of departure for — the more empirically weighted and warmer theory which we shall encounter in the next chapter. [p. 20]

Since their next chapter deals with Aristotle, these authors clearly find Plato less appealing than his successor. I would argue that to find Plato's aesthetics cold and detached misses the point of the dialogues altogether.

[44] Katherine E. Gilbert and Helmut Kuhn, *A History of Esthetics*, p. 30.

Plato recognizes the weakness of real individuals. By presenting man in all his complexity, poetry glorifies man's inadequacy to an inadmissible extent. Plato speaks of the whole society in the *Republic*; his primary concern is for the perfect state rather than with imperfect individuals. But if the individual living in a less perfect world is to imitate good or bad, he certainly must choose the former. When Plato talks of the world of appearance, he permits imitation of the Good. Here imitation moves toward rather than away from the Forms.

The foregoing discussion has suggested that Plato's dialogues present the modern reader with a thorny and multifaceted statement on poetry. Only the *Republic X* specifically excludes all poets from the commonwealth, and even here Plato opens the possibility of admitting poetry in the proper form. But he refuses to call this beautiful language "poetry," and its function is obviously different from that which he normally associates with poetry. The absence of any extended discussion of good poetry demands an inquiry into why Plato denied the worth of all poetry, even that which he loved. Clearly, to Plato poetry is dangerous; otherwise he would not be so vehement. And he regards the problem as basically insoluble. All discourse must present truth clearly and directly; even dialectical discussions are ultimately restricted — the rulers in the *Republic* should be aware of possible abuses (*Republic VII* 537e).[45] Plato has no faith in man's discretion about poetry. Allegory is especially forbidden to children; by the omission of approval later in the *Republic*, he presumably would extend his strictures to adults as well. In other words, all language — particularly the beautiful form called poetry — must present a wholly unambiguous statement. Yet the *Cratylus* declares that language springs from an imitation of reality; it can never embody this reality. Thought precedes the expression; characteristically Socrates will say, "to reach what is now in my thoughts would be an effort too great for me" (*Republic VI* 506e; see also *Timaeus* 19). At best, language can point to the original truth. Any attention to language (which poetry insists we pay) exalts a blind imitation.

[45] See also *Republic VI* 500 and *Theaetetus* 174.

As the following chapter will show, Plato is not thinking about the nature of poetry when he discusses inspiration. He never denies that poetry has almost irresistible charm. But inspiration in Plato serves only to explain the existence of beauty. The Muse — a metaphor for the Good — chooses this way of communicating with man, of linking man's questing soul with the absolute. Man cannot actually create poetry; he can only passively respond to its attraction. An analysis of the *Ion* will show that Plato responds too immediately to beauty to allow an analytic treatment of static poetry elsewhere. The true poetry is not an object, but a process.

II

Inspiration
and
the Muse

The lunatic, the lover, and the poet
Are of imagination all compact.
One sees more devils than vast hell can hold;
That is the madman. The lover, all as frantic,
Sees Helen's beauty in a brow of Egypt.
The poet's eye, in a fine frenzy rolling,
Doth glance from heaven to earth, from earth to heaven.
And as imagination bodies forth
The forms of things unknown, the poet's pen
Turns them to shapes, and gives to aery nothing
A local habitation, and a name.

A Midsummer Night's Dream V. i. 7–17

I have tried to show in the preceding chapter that there are two major errors in interpreting Plato: taking him too seriously and not taking him seriously enough. Plato will use irony and humor often, but only when words fail to do justice to the enormous complexity and seriousness of his thought. Perhaps all interpretations of Plato differ simply in their degree of willful misunderstanding. Great men seldom have great followers, for genius either drives lesser minds into servile imitation or stimulates stronger minds to independent inquiry. Plato himself never solidifies his living thought into sterile categories. His comments on love and beauty represent a lucid and vigorous theme of his philosophy. But his half-serious praise of poetic inspiration leaves us unsatisfied, particularly since this concept is usually accompanied by a devastating attack on man's ignorance and presumption. We must always listen for Plato's mocking and ironic laughter as we attempt to assign his concept of inspiration to its proper role in the drama of his philosophy.

A great deal of the confusion about Plato's aesthetics stems from his ironic and often ambiguous comments on poetic inspiration, or enthusiasm (ἐνθουσιασμός). Some critics, perhaps fresh from a reading of *Republic X*, think that Plato views poetic inspiration as a form of insanity, one more element in a general skepticism about the worth of poetry.[1] Others, impressed with the poetic qualities of the dialogues and with the praises of beauty, use the comments to suggest that Plato links poet with philosopher as a divine creator of beauty.[2] Where such diverse opinion abounds, the few facts available are especially precious. One such fact is that nowhere in the dialogues does Plato discuss the relationship between poetry as inspiration and poetry as imitation. Inspiration is a mute response to beauty or the Muses; the creation of poetry itself is another matter. He never discusses a possible relationship between man's passive receptivity of poetic infusion and man's own conscious ability to create poetry. As agent of the Muse, the poet pours out beautiful words. Yet when relying on his own ability, the poet produces imitation of one sort or another. A second fact is that Plato never explains how a man — poet or philosopher — can communicate truth and beauty directly to another mind. He asserts that

[1] See Rupert C. Lodge, *Plato's Theory of Art*, pp. 139–43; A. E. Taylor, *Plato: The Man and His Work*, pp. 38–40; Katherine Gilbert and Helmut Kuhn, *A History of Esthetics*, pp. 24–26.

[2] See Carleton L. Brownson, *Plato's Studies and Criticisms of the Poets*, pp. 13–15; J. A. Stewart, *The Myths of Plato*, ed. G. R. Levy, pp. 344–57; John G. Warry, *Greek Aesthetic Theory*, pp. 68–82. G. M. A. Grube's statement in *Plato's Thought* is typical: "Not only the inspiration of the poet, but the beauty of the work he produces, is freely admitted in the *Ion*, and there is here no quarrel between philosophy and poetry, so long as poetry does not, like the poets in the *Apology*, lay any claim to knowledge" (p. 182).

such images may be transmitted, but he does not recognize any vehicle to accomplish this communication. An examination of Plato's treatment of inspiration in the *Ion* will help delineate the boundaries of his magnificent yet frustrating conjectures.

This chapter will explore the serious themes underlying Plato's ironic statements on inspiration. Too often scholars fail to see the limits of Plato's approval of divine possession. Darnell Rucker, for instance, emphasizes that Plato praises inspiration and condemns only art which unjustly pretends to knowledge. "Socrates does not attack Ion's ability as a rhapsode in the *Ion*; he attacks Ion's claim to knowledge of the topics of his recitations. So long as the poet makes no claim to knowledge of those things he is inspired to say (or make), Plato has no quarrel with him as a poet." [3] In light of Plato's careful qualification, however, one cannot accept a total seriousness in his praising of inspiration. The *Ion* does indeed attack only the unlearned rhapsode directly. But the theory of poetic inspiration, far from praising the poet, chiefly testifies to poetry's charm. And Plato never questions the effects of poetry. More typically he questions how dangerous are these effects to the intellect.

Before an analysis of the *Ion*, a statement of Plato's general attitude toward possession will help establish the context of his theory of divine inspiration. Although his comments on poetic enthusiasm have influenced poets and the friends of poetry throughout the course of Western thought, Plato himself makes very little of the subject. Indeed, this minor motif runs counter to Plato's serious investigation of poetry. The *Phaedrus*, which cites the poet favorably, mentions four kinds of madness. The subjects of the dialogue are love and rhetoric; only one short section (245a) mentions poetry at all. Similarly, the *Symposium* 205c touches on the poet on its way to an exposition of Absolute Beauty. The passages are frequently attacks on the poet's knowledge, poetry being praised in a backhanded manner. The *Phaedrus* 245a would make the poet a "divine madman," several degrees below the inspired philoso-

---

[3] "Plato and the Poets," p. 170.

pher. Here Plato does attribute the same sort of greatness to poet and to philosopher. But more typically in Plato the philosopher is one who knows rather than one who is "inspired."

Two other dialogues are even less favorable in their attribution of divine inspiration to the poet. The *Apology* 22bc states that "there is hardly a person present who would not have talked better about their poetry than they did themselves. Then I knew that not by wisdom do poets write poetry, but by a sort of genius and inspiration; they are like diviners or soothsayers who also say many fine things, but do not understand the meaning of them." This passage, dripping with Socratic irony, is hardly matter on which to build a significant praise of inspiration. The *Laws* shows little development or refinement of those concepts expressed early in Plato's thoughts on poetry. Here the poet responds freely to inspiration, but the art itself is imitative. Lacking knowledge, he contradicts himself by presenting men of disparate temperaments (*IV* 719c). The poet cannot, therefore, be a legislator, for a legislator must not give two rules about the same thing. These passages about inspiration say little about what poetry is. Plato stresses the poet's ignorance even while accepting his divine calling.

Plato admits that beauty in all its forms has a profound effect on the soul. He stresses, however, that only the beauty of virtue and of knowledge does not lead to the impure enjoyment of pleasure. Except for the early training and discipline of the soul through harmony, poetry does not lead directly to an understanding of proper conduct. The poet cannot possess knowledge of what he does unless he becomes a philosopher too. The poet himself is usually the passive agent of the Muse; the inexplicable beauty of poetry comes from its divine origin. But when Plato looks at the poet's own contribution to the process, he finds the poet only an untrained and untrainable agent. Plato's doctrine of divine inspiration applies more to his theory of love than to his concept of poetry. The *Phaedrus* and the *Symposium* suggest an affinity between the soul and beauty with which the doctrine of the Forms does not completely agree. References to poetic inspiration, however, are almost a dead end; Plato does not attempt to integrate this inspiration with his explicit thought on poetry and language.

1

The *Ion* and Inspiration

The *Ion* gives us one of Plato's two distinct theories of poetic inspiration. This dialogue, as well as the *Apology* and the *Laws IV*, makes the poet a passive agent of the Muses. Here Plato glowingly describes poetry, while at the same time he declares the poet ignorant both of the nature of poetry and of his personal contribution. Plato directly relates only passive inspiration to the origin of poetry itself.[4] On the other hand, the *Symposium* and the *Phaedrus* represent the poet as only slightly inferior to the philosopher in his access to absolute knowledge. This poet, infused with a love of wisdom, may toss off true images of beauty. But he is not so much a creator of poetry as he is an aspiring soul. These dialogues of love and beauty show individuals of all sorts as they move silently and separately up toward the divine. But a dialogue such as the *Ion* will mention inspiration as part of a discussion of education and ethics. Here, the divine moves down through the man, the end result being poetry or some other social response. Thus, Plato considers the type of inspiration which produces poetry not in the context of man's aspiration, but only within a consideration of mundane human knowledge.

In brief, the *Ion* states that the majority of people — including the professional critics in Athens — understand neither themselves nor poetry. This dialogue consists of a discussion between Socrates and the rhapsode Ion. This reciter of Homer, flushed with his recent success, claims to be a great interpreter of poetry, the poet in turn being a repository of knowledge and common sense. Socrates shows immediately, however, that Ion's concept of interpretation as repetition of Homer's words is totally inadequate. Socrates readily admits the ability of Ion to move his audience, but he asserts that

---

[4] I disagree, therefore, with Beardsley's combining the types of inspiration when he says, "the artist may have his own insight into the nature of ideal beauty, even though his effort to bring it to earth and establish it here may require an inspired state in which he does not fully know what he is up to, but is taken hold of and used, so to speak, by some creative forces poetically or conventionally called the Muses" (*Aesthetics from Classical Greece to the Present*, p. 44).

the rhapsode does not work by art, but by his unconscious link with the poet and with the Muse behind the poet. Socrates then proves that poetry cannot be used directly as a source of knowledge. Each man in his own field can judge the authority of poetry far better than can the rhapsode.[5] Thus, the *Ion* contains two themes: the nature of divine inspiration and the interpretation of poetry in terms of its direct relevance to the world.

Presenting Plato's fullest statement on poetic inspiration, the *Ion* illustrates his mistrust of poetry and of those who claim to originate it.[6] As a presupposition for the dialogue, Plato has decided that the beauty of poetry cannot be explained solely in terms of a human creator. But more important, he thinks that almost no one interprets poetry correctly. Thus, very little of the dialogue actually deals with inspiration; the work concerns more the inadequacy of so-called interpretations of poetry by the majority of Athenian citizens. The rhapsode Ion is obviously unintelligent, and, on the surface, Socrates merely proves him to lack understanding of his craft.[7] This attack on poet and audience leaves open the possibility for a correct interpretation of poetry, but Plato's argument against stupidity cannot be generalized into any sort of acceptance of poetry elsewhere.[8] While the beauty and attractiveness of poetry are beyond human ability and comprehension, the misuses of poetry are all too obvious.

The comment on aesthetics in the *Ion* deserves a qualified but sincere respect. The philosopher's later dialogues do not show any significant development of the position initially stated in this rela-

---

[5] Cf. *Republic II* 370, *Laws VIII* 846–47.

[6] See Paul Shorey, *What Plato Said*, pp. 96–99.

[7] Jerrald Ranta, in "The Drama of Plato's *Ion*," speaks of the dramatic form in which Socrates corresponds to the Eiron, Ion to the Alazon (pp. 219–29).

[8] Eric A. Havelock, in his *Preface to Plato*, states that "those who thought in prose and preferred prose — that is the philosophers, who were intent upon constructing a new type of discourse which we can roughly characterize as conceptual rather than poetic were driven to relegate the poetic experience to a category which was non-conceptual and therefore non-rational and non-reflective" (p. 156).

tively slight dialogue. Although the *Ion* and the other dialogues containing passages on inspiration do not attack all poetry, Plato's ambiguous praise suggests the irrelevancy of poetry to human intellect and ethics. The attack on Ion's stupidity foreshadows the later attack on Homer himself in *Republic X*. Plato's linking of rhapsode and poet in the earlier dialogue indicates that poetry, springing from nonrational sources, cannot direct human conduct in a good commonwealth. Yet the topics of discussion are entirely different. The *Ion* speaks of the beauty issuing from poetic inspiration, the *Republic* of the effect of poetry on the audience. The *Ion* concerns primarily the source of art — the Muse — and the content of poetry — beauty. Neither poetry nor literary criticism as we know it today falls under direct attack at this point. The dialogue therefore allows by omission the possibility of tolerance toward poetry. The *Republic*, on the other hand, directly examines poetry itself. Here, poetry is treated as significant, a powerful force possibly for good, probably for evil. Explicit morality and knowledge provide the standards for poetry, thus condemning all but the simplest and most direct language. The more systematic treatment of poetry in the *Republic* and in the *Laws* must have more overall influence on our interpretation of Plato's aesthetics than the brief *Ion*.

First, the effect of inspiration on the poet and the rhapsode: Plato's skepticism about the traditional gods has unfortunately led critics to dismiss his references to the Muses as wholly ironic. His offhanded introduction of these deities as the source of poetry simply reflects his general insistence that poetry consists of beauty, is indeed a reflection of absolute beauty. Plato's discussion of the Muses, set within an attack on false interpretations of poetry, presents a distinction between inexplicable beauty and the practical application of human language. Far from mocking the Muses, he assigns them the same nebulous status that the gods enjoy.[9] No matter what the context, Plato almost always refers to the Muses favorably.[10] Like

[9] See Agathon's speech, *Symposium* 197.

[10] Euthydemus 275, *Phaedrus* 262, *Laws III* 682.

the wise men of antiquity, they represent symbolically a tradition to
be respected. Accordingly, Plato does not analyze their exact role
here or later.[11]

The *Ion* itself focuses primarily on the rhapsode's value as critic
and teacher. Ion wishes to accept Homer's words as living thoughts,
not realizing that the proper response to poetry cannot be passive
acceptance.[12] But no language, not even poetry, can embody knowledge or aid directly in understanding reality. Ion's inability to speak
well about poets other than Homer suggests that he lacks any real
understanding of his profession or of his relationship to the Muses.
He knows the words of Homer, but he asserts rather than understands the words' applicability to various subjects. Socrates denies
Ion any personal skill to project this great beauty, for the gift which
he possesses of "speaking excellently about Homer" is not an art,
but a divine power or ability ($\delta\acute{v}\nu\alpha\mu\iota\varsigma$). To prove that Ion's craft
is unconscious, Socrates uses an analogy of a magnet: "there is a
divine power moving in you, like that contained in the stone which
Euripides named a magnet, but which is commonly known as the
stone of Heraclea. This stone not only attracts iron rings, but also
imparts to them a similar power of attracting other rings; and sometimes you may see a number of pieces of iron and rings suspended
from one another so as to form quite a long chain. All of these rings
receive their power of suspension from the original stone" (*Ion*
533de). The poet, then, is only the medium for this divine power.
Neither the passive poet nor his mindless follower, the rhapsode, can
claim a special virtue for his own contribution to poetry.

On the human level, then, the *Ion* strips the poet and the
rhapsode of their false claims to special knowledge and authority.
Socrates shows Ion that rhapsodes are only "interpreters of interpreters" (*Ion* 535a). The poet acts not by art, but by divine gift.
The poet interprets the divine maker; the rhapsode interprets the
poet. A critic in the modern sense of the term has no role at all.

[11] See *Meno* 99, *Lysias* 214.

[12] See Havelock's chapter, "The Psychology of the Poetic Performance,"
in *Preface to Plato*, pp. 145–64.

The *Ion* merges the function of the rhapsode and the critic. More-over, the rhapsode is certainly no model for the temperate citizens to follow. Ion, when interpreting Homer, acts bewitched; in his imagination of the events — the reliving — he acts as if his senses have left him.[13] And, as in the education of the Guardians of the *Republic*, self-possession is an essential virtue.[14] Plato likes clear moral examples, and there is no way of telling whether the madness of the rhapsode and the poet is temporary artistic madness or simply insanity.

Whereas the elevated philosopher of the *Symposium* and the *Phaedrus* moves toward knowledge, the inspired poet of the *Ion* makes no effort as an individual. For Socrates, the poet's work is primarily social; he need have no personal acquaintance with knowledge. The inspiration of the Muses goes first to the poet, then out into the chain of people related to the poet:

> For all good epic poets say their beautiful poems not by skill [τέχνης], but because they are inspired and possessed, and in the same manner, the lyric poets do likewise. And as the Corybantians when they dance are not in their right mind, so the lyric poets are not in their right mind when they make their beautiful songs. Yet when they fall under the power of melody and rhythm, they are inspired and possessed; like Bacchae who draw milk and honey from the rivers when they are under the influence of Dionysus but cannot do so when they are in their right mind. [533e–34a]

The lyric poets even claim the divine frenzy, for "they tell us that they bring songs from honeyed fountains, culling them out of the gardens and dells of the Muses: they, like the bees, winging their way from flower to flower" (*Ion* 534ab). The poet has little or no

[13] Havelock warns against our limiting Plato's antipathy toward poetry only to the drama; we should not forget "that in Greek practice epic recital equally constituted a performance, and that the rhapsodist apparently exploited a relationship to his audience analogous to that of an actor" (*Preface to Plato*, p. 9).

[14] For examples of this pervasive theme, see *Republic IV* 441–42 and *Phaedrus* 246ff.

conscious control over this art. Yet there are some preconditions to the creation of poetry: the poet must be receptive to "the power of music and rhythm." Plato has no direct criticism, then, for the enraptured poet in the gardens of the Muses.

Nevertheless, the *Phaedrus* denies the possibility of a neutral response to true inspiration.[15] For Plato knowledge consists of the universals, whereas poetry deals with particular skills. The universals of any sort are the province more of the lover of wisdom than of the maker of poetry:

> The soul of a man may enter into the life of a beast, or from the beast return again into the man. But only the soul which has seen the truth may enter into human form. A man must understand the language of Forms, passing from a plurality of perceptions to a unity gathered together by reasoning. This understanding is a recollection of those things which our souls beheld aforetime as they journeyed with their god, looking down upon the things which now we suppose to be, and gazing up to that which truly is. [249bc]

This form of rapture encourages the man to seek the universals; such flights of the spirit enable him to perceive a vision of being. Men vary, however, in the steadiness of their inquiry. Of the four truly possessed men, only the philosopher seeks constantly for communion with the higher realm.[16]

Thus, the *Phaedrus* explicitly links poet and philosopher in a way the *Ion* only implies. In addition, the two dialogues present the comments on poetic inspiration in radically differing contexts. The *Ion* asserts a division of human activity, each man doing what he is most suited for. Inspiration in the *Ion* requires a passive response from a man, any man, whereas the *Phaedrus* shows men in various stages of noble aspiration. The *Ion* looks down from the Muse to

---

15 Beardsley even has Plato allowing the artist to imitate the beautiful: "From this point of view he could be said to belong with the greatest creator of all — the *demiourgos* who put the world together" (*Aesthetics*, p. 41).

16 A close analysis of the *Phaedrus* can be found in Herman L. Sinaiko, *Love, Knowledge, and Discourse in Plato*, pp. 22–118.

the poet to the audience's earthly bedazzlement with poetry's beauty. The *Phaedrus* looks upward from man's partial grasp of truth and beauty to his search for the ultimate:

> And therefore it is right that the soul of the philosopher alone has wings: for she, so far as may be, is ever near in memory to those things which make a god divine. And he who employs these memories correctly is always being initiated into perfect mysteries, and he alone becomes truly perfect. Standing aside from the busy doings of mankind, and drawing nigh to the divine, he is rebuked by the multitude as being out of his wits, for the many do not realize that he is inspired. [249cd]

Plato is always aware of the vulgar popularity of the poets and the general contempt for the philosopher. So in the highest rapture possible, he depicts the philosopher as misunderstood. The poet of the *Ion* contributes nothing to the ascent of his soul; the Muse takes total possession of him. The philosopher, however, clings to his memory as a guide back to the higher realm.

There is no inherent reason within Plato's philosophy why the poet's inspiration should not be akin to the philosopher's. Both involve perception of universals. Yet Plato himself never makes this connection with respect to any discussion of poetry. Poetic inspiration in the *Ion* explains only the delightful effect of poetry; the poet himself does not move toward knowledge. More typically in Plato, understanding of the universals precedes man's true reproduction and communication of these Forms. In a sense, the philosopher's drive toward beautiful truth comes from the same source as the poet's aspiring to truthful beauty:

> Mark therefore the sum and substance of all our discourse touching the fourth sort of madness: to wit, that this is the best of all forms of divine possession, both in itself and in its sources, both for him that has it and for him that shares therein; and when he that loves beauty is touched by such madness he is called a lover. Such a one, as soon as he beholds the beauty of this world, is reminded of true beauty, and his wings begin to grow; then is he fain to lift his wings and fly upward; yet he has not the power, but inasmuch as he gazes upward like a bird, and

cares nothing for the world beneath, men charge it upon him that he is demented. [*Phaedrus* 249de]

A lover of wisdom will produce beautiful utterances — there is nothing pinched and crabbed in Plato's vision of this world's beauty. Yet these temporal words are only incidental to man's thrust toward his proper end. In keeping with his favorable attitude toward the source of this infusion, Plato gives the Muses Calliope and Urania to the philosopher, for these are the "twain whose theme is the heavens and all the story of gods and men, and whose song is the noblest of them all" (259d). Thus philosophy, the "sweetest utterance," and the supreme poetry can be identical.[17]

The philosopher is enraptured, ravished of all earthly senses, by his perception of the divine, a state necessary for all good poetry. If man could see true beauty, "pure and clear and unalloyed," he could rise above the pollutions of the flesh. The *Symposium* allows the disciplined lover of wisdom not only to perceive beauty immediately, but also to generate realities. This god-like creator stimulates true excellence in others (212a). Plato gives all three requirements for true inspiration and true poetry here: possession and elevation beyond the earthly, beneficent teaching, and knowledge of realities in the creator of beauty. But the lover of beauty has long since passed the stage of any human poetry, and the realities now grasped by the man lie only in the higher realm.

The *Ion* admits only the rhapsode's rapture, not his perception of realities or his value as teacher. The partially sincere praise of the Muse in the dialogue comes close to condemnation of the poet. With passive inspiration, both rhapsode and poet can appreciate beauty and receive credit for its existence. But Plato categorically denies knowledge to be a prerequisite for this sort of art:

For the poet is a light and winged and holy thing, and there is no invention in him until he has been inspired and is out of his

---

[17] *Cratylus* 406a states, "The name of the Muses and of music would seem to be derived from their making philosophical enquiries (μῶσθαι)." See also *Symposium* 205.

senses, and the mind is no longer in him. When he has not
attained to this state, he is powerless and is unable to utter his
oracles. Many are the noble words in which poets speak concerning the actions of men; but like yourself when speaking
about Homer, they do not speak of them by any rules of art:
they are simply inspired to utter that to which the Muse impels
them, and that only; and when inspired, one of them will make
dithyrambs, another hymns of praise, another choral strains,
another epic or iambic verses — and he who is good at one is
not good at any other kind of verse: for not by art does the poet
sing, but by power divine. Had he learned by rules of art, he
would have known how to speak not of one theme only, but
of all; and therefore the god takes away the minds of poets, and
uses them as his ministers, as he also uses diviners and holy
prophets, in order that we who hear them may know them to
be speaking not of themselves who utter these priceless words
in a state of unconsciousness, but that the god himself is the
speaker, and that through them he is conversing with us.
[534bcd]

Against Ion's mindless self-satisfaction, Plato makes two important
points. First, poetry is truly beautiful and cannot be completely
appreciated or interpreted. Second, the poet in the act of creating
loses conscious control of his art; he must stand outside of his particular human existence in order to grasp the general truths. Lacking knowledge, this poet — like the poet in the *Republic II* — can
produce only one type of poetry.

2

THE MUSES AND THEIR POWER

A word about the Muses and their power is now in order.
Possession for Plato in contexts other than those discussing poetry is
almost always beneficent, for then man is entirely involved, his
soul in harmony.[18] But this involvement must be individual, not
social. And basically, the dialogues view poetry as public. The

---

[18] See *Phaedrus* 235.

Muse can be the source of good effects. As an influence from the divine, the Muse can help regulate human conduct, a point Plato does not allow in the *Ion*. Pleasure is the first and natural response to poetry, but such ephemeral happiness must not paralyze the soul. When the Muses speak through the intermediary of language, mere pleasure is apt to result. But harmony and music in all its forms correct the discord in the soul as the "intelligent votary of the Muses" knows (*Timaeus* 47d). According to the *Laws*, to prevent various forms of violence we must use three things: fear, law, and right reason, thus "turning humanity away from that which is called pleasantest to the best, using the Muses and the gods who preside over contests to extinguish their increase and influx" (*VI* 783ab).[19]

For the most part, however, the Muse of poetry does not so much regulate the soul as possess it. Man's response is involuntary.[20] The inspired philosopher, the lover of wisdom — moves dynamically toward absolute involvement with knowledge. The inspired poet — the lover of beauty and words — exists statically in his rapture. Whereas the philosopher's vision is personal, poetic possession when revealed to the vulgar can inflame a whole crowd:

> Do you know that the spectator is the last of the rings which, as I am saying, receive the power of the original magnet from one another? The rhapsode like yourself and the actor are intermediate links, and the poet himself is the first of them. Through all these the god sways the souls of men in any direction which he pleases, and makes one man transmit to another. Thus there is a vast chain of dancers and masters and undermasters of choruses, who are suspended, as if from the stone, at the side of the rings which hang down from the Muse. And every poet has some Muse from whom he is suspended, and by whom he is said to be possessed, which is nearly the same thing; for he is taken hold of. And from these first rings, which are the poets, depend others, some deriving their inspiration from Orpheus, others from Musaeus; but the greater number are possessed and held by Homer. Of whom, Ion, you are one, and are possessed by

[19] Also *Laws II* 653 and *II* 665.

[20] Even Socrates is swept away when he begins to produce words (*Phaedrus* 238).

Homer; and when anyone repeats the words of another poet you go to sleep, and know not what to say; but when any one recites a strain of Homer you wake up in a moment, and your soul leaps within you, and you have plenty to say. For not by art or knowledge about Homer do you say what you say, but by divine inspiration and by possession; just as the Corybantian revellers too have a quick perception of that strain only which is appropriated to the god by whom they are possessed, and have plenty of dances and words for that, but take no heed of any other. And you, Ion, when the name of Homer is mentioned have plenty to say, and have nothing to say of others. You ask, "Why is this?" The answer is that you praise Homer not by art but by divine inspiration. [*Ion* 535a–36c]

Like the dormouse in *Alice in Wonderland*, the rhapsode falls asleep easily. But he is awake enough to grasp the irony that Socrates is not praising his skill: "I doubt whether you will ever have eloquence enough to persuade me that I praise Homer only when I am mad and possessed" (536d). Ion and his fellows claim to be interpreting the poets faithfully, but they in fact only mechanically parrot words. They undeservedly enjoy a reflected glory. Plato's attack on Ion himself does leave poetry and the poets untouched directly. But still we are dismayed that Plato does not explicitly disassociate the rhapsode's improper public spectacle from the ideal listener's sensitive and individual response to beauty in words.

The nonrational ability of poet and rhapsode finds expression in other dialogues. Just as Plato considers poetry itself in terms of truth or falsity, so the personal contribution of the maker of poetry is judged in terms of rational and nonrational. Plato's serious analysis of poetry in terms of surface texture or its obvious statement echoes his theory of the source of poetry. Both poet and poetry are judged according to their function within the state. Poetry has no deeper level for interpretation, just as the poet's creative spirit cannot operate on diverse levels. The *Ion* has suggested that the creative mind and the created poetry possess a certain unity, an identical embodiment of beauty. But Plato does not tell us how inspiration is transformed into creation within the poet's mind. This creation, perhaps like the action of the demiurge of the *Timaeus*, lies beyond our rational appreciation.

Plato's doctrine of inspiration makes the poet divine and yet mad. The metaphorical term "madness" is pejorative; the adjective "divine" prefixed to it merely increases the ambiguity. Along with prophecy and the purging of evil, poetic inspiration represents a noble madness:

> There is a third form of possession or madness, of which the Muses are the source. This seizes a tender, virgin soul and stimulates it to rapt passionate expression, especially in lyric poetry, glorifying the countless mighty deeds of ancient times for the instruction of posterity. But if any man come to the gates of poetry without the madness of the Muses, persuaded that skill alone will make him a good poet, then shall he and his works of sanity with him be brought to naught by the poetry of madness, and behold, their place is nowhere to be found. [*Phaedrus* 245a]

The creation of poetry lies outside the province of human skill. And since Plato will not elsewhere discuss the human generation of poetic beauty, we must not generalize this comment in the *Phaedrus* into a significant statement of Plato's aesthetics. Even here the inspiration of the inferior muses lacks the power of that enthusiasm given by the Muses of philosophy or by a yearning toward the reality of the absolute.

Nevertheless, individual or silent rapture can often be justified. Plato does not always condemn seemingly irrational and subtle acts. Socrates himself listened to a mysterious voice.[21] Plato will ignore for a moment the misuses of poetry to pay tribute to the "delicate and virgin soul" who approaches the Muse with humility. A vision of the impersonal dialectic provides a more certain guide to useful and beautiful action than does the Muse, however. The earth-bound soul, already in obscurity, as the cave image suggests, can no more follow the Muse's call than catch a will-o'-the-wisp.[22] The

[21] *Apology* 31, 40; also *Cratylus* 396e, *Phaedrus* 242.
[22] *Republic VII* 514ff.

bright vision of knowledge remains the justification of man's journey out of the cave of ignorance. This end takes precedence over the force which propels man outward. To focus upon and to enjoy the experience of seeking would deny the purpose of the quest.

Plato attacks presumption wherever he finds it, particularly among public figures. "The criticism of the *Apology* is concerned with content only, not form, and the poets are blamed for what they taught or failed to teach, not for their method of teaching." [23] Plato attacks the poets and rhapsodes as he does the sophists — for presuming to knowledge they have no right to claim. Socrates flatters the poets ironically by admitting that they can make some fine speeches: "They are like diviners or soothsayers who also say many fine things, but do not understand the meaning of them" (*Apology* 22). If the poet cannot explain his work, he obviously has little contact with the dialectic and thus little appreciation of the end to which poetry might possibly lead. Therefore, he can point only indirectly and thus confusingly to the truth.

On the human level, Plato insists upon a distinction between the creator and the interpreter of poetry. Knowledge alone gives the versatility to understand poetry. Making no contribution of his own, the critic-rhapsode depends entirely on the poet. And the poets themselves certainly are no critics: "There is hardly a person present who would not have talked better about their poetry than they did themselves" (*Apology* 22b). Plato is too much a lover of beauty to claim that the bystanders could declaim as good poetry as the poets. But as in the *Ion*, he says that the art of poets is not that of reason. Just as people should be careful in defining the virtues, they must not attribute false qualities to poetry. The poets are condemned only because "upon the strength of their poetry they believed themselves to be the wisest of men in other things in which they were not wise" (*Apology* 22c). That poets could possibly claim knowledge of everything suggests the awesome respect the Greeks must have given them.[24]

[23] Warry, *Greek Aesthetic Theory*, p. 59.
[24] R. R. Bolgar, *The Classical Heritage*, pp. 17ff.

Later dialogues do not significantly modify the attitude expressed in the *Ion* toward the poet's inspiration. Throughout, Plato has defined the most important part of man as mind; in particular, the reason.[25] Any delight in the merely physical or in the emotions runs contrary to the best interests of reason. Man in producing poetry always performs a negative function; he is the channel for the Muse.[26] Plato's last dialogue asserts the ignorance of the inspired poet even more definitely:

> The poet, according to the tradition which has ever prevailed among us, and is accepted of all men, when he sits down on the tripod of the muse, is not in his right mind; like a fountain, he allows to flow out freely whatever comes in, and his art being imitative, he is often compelled to represent men of opposite dispositions, and thus to contradict himself. And he cannot tell whether there is more truth in one thing that he has said than in another. [*Laws IV* 719c]

This free response to the Muse lacks a necessary discipline; the true poet must alter and evaluate the formless data presented by the physical world. Plato would have the poet make a clear statement concerning the truth. He generally disapproves of those people who make indiscriminate statements about nature.[27] After all, a poet and a sophist have the common ground of persuasion and pleasure without true wisdom.

Plato does not judge poetry apart from the speaker, word apart from action. Just as he has insisted that poetry contribute immediately to virtuous actions, he suggests that virtuous actions will encourage acceptable poetry. The *Laws*, like the earlier part of the *Republic*, allows only prayers and encomia. Both dialogues attempt to describe a state better than that currently in existence. Plato himself might not actually like unmusical, though virtuous, croakings. But he knows that he should. His insistence on moral poetry

---

[25] *Republic IV* 431–43.

[26] W. J. Verdenius, *Mimesis*, p. 4.

[27] *Sophist* 253.

always dominates his love of beautiful language. "Those who are themselves good and also honorable in the state, creators of noble actions — let their poems be sung, even though they be not very musical" (*Laws VIII* 829d). Plato's instinctive love of poetry forces him to recognize that sober-sided generals are unlikely to create beautiful songs. Poetry is to be the reward of the noblest alone, and an unauthorized poet cannot chant, "even if his strain be sweeter than the songs of Thamyras and Orpheus; but only such poems as have been judged sacred and dedicated to the gods" (829de).[28] A man is what he says; virtuous words come only from virtuous men.

3

THE COMMUNICATION OF KNOWLEDGE

Plato leaves the process of communication ambiguous. The *Meno* considers two sorts of men — those who individually aspire to wisdom, and those who operate effectively within society. Practically, right opinion can guide correct action. Experience shows that great men may lack knowledge and still accomplish worthwhile deeds. But knowledge comes only when the individual responds by binding his opinion to recollection. These same statesmen may have non-distinguished offspring; virtue sometimes cannot be transmitted even to one's children. Yet we must praise those who succeed in actions or in words. "Then we shall also be right in calling divine those whom we were just now speaking of as diviners and prophets, including the whole tribe of poets. Yes, and statesmen above all may be said to be divine and illuminated, being inspired and possessed of the god in which condition they say many grand things, not knowing what they say" (99cd). Poetry must not be accepted as teaching, for such words are only the production of one with the right instinct for the art. Indeed, no communication of facts can be termed teaching. Only the response, the leap to recollection, can link a man with permanent, true knowledge.

[28] Cf. *Laws II* 669.

The impulse to seek knowledge comes from the gods rather than from man. Nothing man can do will increase this virtue; Plato assigns no freedom in man to increase his store of excellence. Man's proper action lies in returning to knowledge instead of accepting the partial knowledge he possesses:

> Virtue is neither natural nor acquired, but an instinct given by the god to the virtuous. Nor is the instinct accompanied by reason, unless there may be supposed to be among statesmen some one who is capable of educating statesmen. And if there be such a one, he may be said to be among the living what Homer says Tiresias was among the dead, "he alone has understanding; but the rest are flitting shades"; and he and his virtue in like manner will be a reality among shadows. [*Meno* 99e–100a]

Thus Plato partially explains the differences of worth in the world among various forms of activity. Certainly, Plato would never deny that some actions are better and more useful than others. To possess understanding involves the ability to inculcate virtue; such knowledge cannot be passively held. But Plato does not discuss man's communication with man; one cannot look to the individual man to gain a general wisdom. If virtue and excellence cannot be taught even by direct exposition, surely the ambiguous language of poetry will have still less beneficial effect.

When Plato speaks of truly inspired poetry, he does not make clear the boundaries between creator, created, and audience. Interpretations of poetry consist of seeking its literal meaning, of responding immediately to the one speaking. Nothing inherent in poetry leads to the proper criticism. Correct criticism is almost as mysterious as true creation, and poetry itself is an enigma. Like later critics, Plato recognized ambiguity to be at the heart of poetry. But for him, ambiguity is confusion. There is more than one level to poetry; complexity in poetry is a result of the extent to which the poet wishes to keep his wisdom to himself. Socrates declares that the poet makes sense, expresses his respect accordingly, then typically turns on him:

> Only the poet is talking in riddles after the fashion of his tribe. For all poetry has by nature an enigmatic character, and it is

by no means everybody who can interpret it. And if, moreover, the spirit of poetry happens to seize on a man with a begrudging temper who does not care to manifest his wisdom but keeps it to himself as far as he can, it does indeed require an almost super-human wisdom to discover what the poet would be at.

[*Alcibiades II* 147b]

Plato then declares Homer to be "the wisest and most divine of poets," indeed a philosopher, and proceeds to discuss whether one can know a thing badly. The more complex or begrudging of temper the poet, the more one must probe to seek his meaning. The example emphasizes the demands which literary criticism places on the critic. Plato's willingness to analyze poetry suggests that he did not view proper criticism as impossible, yet he is never satisfied with his analysis.

The foregoing discussion of the Muse and inspiration has shown that throughout the dialogues Plato sharply distinguishes the individual's inspired perception of beauty from the poet's inspired flow of words. The *Ion* gives the poet no real art or knowledge. The maker of words can only channel divine inspiration. Plato knows that some poets have felt a true and philosophical enthusiasm, but they are more philosophers than poets when they do. He does not speak of the conscious creation of poetry or any truly beautiful language. Plato consistently uses visual, not auditory, metaphors for the ultimate wisdom, the goal of man. Therefore, while all men — including the poets — have the possibility of seeing beauty absolute, Plato does not tell us how a man can speak of this vision.

4

THE DIVISION OF LABOR

The discussion of poetry as knowledge in the *Ion* brutally ignores the praise of inspiration. As in *Republic X*, the poet, speaking as he does to all men, speaks well for none. Plato here attacks a particularly Athenian way of interpreting poetry. But the issues he raises are not altogether dead for the modern reader. Even today there are two forms of analysis hiding under the term "interpretation." We have both "oral" and "critical" interpretation. Plato condemns an over-generalized application of the former, while ignoring the possibility of the latter. The interpreters of poetry do not so much follow in time as coexist with the spirit of the poet. Perhaps influenced by his own artistry, Plato agrees with Ion that no distance exists between creator and interpreter. Ion obviously cannot "analyze" poetry — for him interpretation means repeating of the words of Homer. Socrates states that Ion is "obligated to be continually in the company of many good poets, and especially of Homer, who is the best and most divine of them; and to understand him, and not merely learn his words by rote, is a thing greatly to be envied. And no man can be a good rhapsode who does not understand the meaning of the poet. For the rhapsode ought to interpret the mind of the poet to his hearers, but how can he interpret him well unless he knows what he means? All this is greatly to be envied" (530bc). The interpreter's function is to convey the poet's mind to the listener. After all, the mind is the highest part of man, the only part which has the possibility of being communicated with the clarity Plato sought. But the intermediary, the rhapsode, must understand the poet, lest the transmission be garbled past recognition.

Plato thus opens the *Ion* with important distinctions between art and other forms of human activity, not with a praise of divine inspiration. The poet is never a good critic, nor can an actor-rhapsode do more than play his particular role. The general application of the particular truth of poetry requires a different analysis from that given by these artists. Ion attempts to praise poetry by a shallow and subjective response: Homer sings "incomparably better" than any other poet. But pathetically unconscious of his own limitations, Ion cannot explain why Homer is different from other poets. Moreover, the rhapsode cannot shift the ground to a more tenable position. Socrates asks:

> Would you or a good prophet be a better interpreter of what these two poets say about divination, not only when they agree, but when they disagree?
>
> *A prophet.*

And if you were a prophet, would you be able to interpret them when they disagree as well as when they agree?

Clearly. [531b]

Similarly, an arithmetician can better judge a poet's comments on math, or a physician judge statements on diet. In a real sense, Ion's intelligence is limited to the words of the poet. He can summon up only Homer's sayings on any given topic. Like many modern examples of scholarship, his work is all footnote and no text, all authority and no wisdom.

Ion has claimed competence far beyond what the *Republic* would recognize in any individual. Plato feels that far more specialization is necessary. In the *Republic* he states that no two people are born with the same abilities. Innate differences fit them for the various occupations. For this reason, a man will do better keeping to one trade rather than working at many. An efficient state is impossible without this division of labor: "Obviously work may be ruined, if you let the right time go by. The workman must wait upon the work; it will not wait upon his leisure and allow itself to be done in a spare moment. So the conclusion is that more things will be produced and the work be more easily and better done, when every man is set free from all other occupations to do, at the right time, the one thing for which he is naturally fitted" (*Republic II* 370bc).[29] And indeed, Plato explicitly condemns in the *Republic* the sort of extravagant claims Ion makes: "No man is to be two or more persons or a jack of all trades; this being the reason why ours is the only state in which we shall find a shoemaker who cannot also take command of a ship, a farmer who does not leave his farm to serve on juries, a soldier who is not a tradesman into the bargain" (*III* 397e).[30]

---

[29] See *Republic II* 374, *III* 394–95, *IV* 423, 433, 435, 441, 443, and *V* 453; also, J. R. S. Wilson, "The Argument of *Republic IV*," pp. 111–24.

[30] The *Laws* continues the sanctions against multiple skills: "If any stranger profess two arts, let the wardens of the city chastise him with bonds and money penalties, and expulsion from the state, until they compel him to be one and not many" (*VIII* 847ab).

Ion, here foreshadowing Wordsworth and romantic criticism, claims a function for his art distinct from the actions of other men. Socrates has proven Ion to lack a particular or specialized ability such as that of the charioteer, the physician, or the fisherman. Yet the rhapsode would still want to teach all men their respective crafts. Ion thinks that the rhapsode should be knowledgeable on what people should say generally:

> *Soc.* Ion, select for me passages which relate to the rhapsode and the rhapsode's art, and which the rhapsode ought to examine and judge of better than other men.
>
> *Ion.* All passages, I should say, Socrates. [539e]

Socrates immediately reminds the rhapsode that he has already confessed ignorance about some skills. Ion correctly senses that he can speak like a variety of people, but neither he nor Socrates enunciates a distinction between man being a general human and man being a specific artisan. Although no one can perform all tasks, one can know to some extent how a person will talk. Ion says, "he will know what a man and what a woman ought to say, and what a freeman and what a slave ought to say, and what a ruler and what a subject" (540b). Ion does not realize, however, the distinction between imitating people's actions within a limited framework of art and, on the other hand, legislating what a person should do in the actual world. Ion ignores the distinction between copying a specific action or speech and understanding its general significance.

Plato thinks that each skill has a distinct body of knowledge which promotes effectiveness. But he also allows a suggestion of a man's possessing various sets of human knowledge. A well-rounded, complete man assumes his true humanity not by attaining a vast sensitivity of spirit, but by acquiring various bodies of knowledge. Ion claims that he might know what a general ought to say, and Socrates agrees: "Why, yes, Ion, because you may possibly have a knowledge of the art of a general as well as of the rhapsode; and you may also have a knowledge of horsemanship as well as of the lyre, and then you would know when horses were well or ill managed" (540d). A poet cannot pursue his verbal craft without some understanding of human events, for words — especially those gripping to the human soul — must be comprehensible in terms of man's experience with the world. But Ion's judgment on horses — his ability to ascertain the relevance of the poet's words — would come from his knowledge of horses, his judgment of the lyre from knowledge of the lyre.

Ion remains in an untenable position, however, as he declares the rhapsode to be a leader of men instead of a follower. He claims direct relevance of his art to the actions of men. Ion cannot see any essential differences between the ability of the general and of the rhapsode. A good rhapsode would also be a good general even though a good general is not necessarily a good rhapsode.[31] But Socrates quickly exposes Ion's weak reasons. In an ad hominem argument which foreshadows that of *Republic X*, Plato scornfully denies that either Homer or Ion could be a general: "You have literally as many forms as Proteus; and now you take all manner of shapes, twisting and turning, and at last slip away from me in the disguise of a general, in order that you may escape exhibiting your Homeric lore" (541e–42a). The dialogue ends on Ion's acceptance of the role of a divine madman. To accept inspiration is nobler than to claim knowledge which he lacks. Like poet and sophist, the rhapsode has unthinkingly extended the proper boundaries of his lesser art. The *Ion*, then, has considered both the source and the interpretation of poetry. No position has been taken toward poetry itself except that of an indirect attack on poetry's value to teach.

5

THE *ION* IN PERSPECTIVE

Far from exorcising the troublesome spirit of poetry, Plato conjures up a host of vexing issues. One reason for our dissatisfaction

---

[31] The *Statesman* repeats that every ordinary occupation has its own distinct body of knowledge. Thus generalship or military tactics constitutes a science (304e). But the dialogue also argues that the true statesman possesses

with inspiration in these dialogues is inherent; we want Plato to give us a definite program. But he is exposing inconsistency and ignorant pretense in the interpretation of poetry. Having punctured the idea of poetry as knowledge, Plato places his paean to poetry's beauty before our bedazzled eyes. We may infer with trepidation the positive statement that poetry presents beauty rather than truth. But Plato would clearly not be content with this facile dichotomy. Less satisfying still, the philosopher insists that each man possesses a particular skill and that for all practical purposes he becomes that skill. Lacking a Form for mankind, Plato has each artisan correspond to the Form of the craftsman of his particular discipline. This man can speak and judge only on his own discipline; he is a craftsman first, and a human second.

Plato fails to explain how poetry can flow accidentally from man aspiring after ultimate truth and beauty. The truly divine madness of *Phaedrus* and the *Symposium* and the blank receptivity of the *Ion, Apology,* and *Laws* have little in common, yet in some unspecified way, both influences result in poetry. Behind Plato's theory of poetry as divine madness lies his concept of philosophy as the true poetry. But Plato cannot — or will not — give us an example of this mysterious entity of philosophy-poetry. Indeed, the next chapter will show that Plato regards all examples of poetry as partial and tentative philosophical statements rather than as soul-stirring language and music.

When not picking apart the pretensions of poets and their interpreters, Plato will admit that the poet has a craft of his own. All purposeful human activity — including that of the poet — can result in praiseworthy art. "All creation or passage of non-being into being is poetry or making, and the processes of all art are creative; and the masters of arts are all poets or makers. They are not called poets, but have other names; only that portion of the art which is separated off from the rest, and is concerned with music and meter, is termed poetry, and they who possess poetry in this

---

an understanding of all lesser disciplines. As noted later here, ch. IV, sec. 1, Plato insists that the rulers of the Republic have a detached knowledge of all other occupations.

sense of the word are called poets" (*Symposium* 205bc). But again, Plato has no time to show how the intellect can be welded into the music and harmony. In any event, the *Ion* should warn us against attributing conscious artistry to this noble craftsman of words and music.

On the positive side, Plato has punctured a great sphere of nonsense concerning the interpretation of poetry. The ability to create or to use words does not enable one to comment on specific crafts or specific human situations. Before he can correctly analyze the relevance of poetry, the interpreter must possess enough intellect to generalize the particular words lying in his mind. Oral interpretation or acting has a place in Plato's philosophy — these skills provide a necessary link between poet and audience. But such sensitive responses to the surface of poetry must not be confused with probing the content or the relevance lying behind the words.

Moreover, Plato's distinction between two sorts of inspiration holds a great deal of potential. Just as a man cannot be happy by seeking happiness itself, so the poet cannot write great poetry with this mundane intention primary to him. Fame is indeed the last infirmity of noble mind. W. H. Auden commented that the man who delights in playing with words will be a poet before the man who burns with a message for all mankind. But while a player with words may write clever comedies, he is not likely to hit randomly on a great statement of the human predicament. The *Phaedrus* and the *Symposium* declare that a poet must have vision — an active intellect and sensitivity to go beyond the world of nature. The poet will write as a natural outpouring of his spirit, not by narrow fidelity to man's actions and the rules of art.

Plato intends the other sort of inspiration, blind receptivity, to help explain the emotional impact of poetry. Ultimately, man's communication with the Muses and with his fellows cannot be explained. We can only guess the origin of poetic inspiration, just as we can only seek with humility the source of wisdom and beauty. Moreover, there exists a powerful emotional response in an audience exposed to poetry. Here, as throughout, Plato admits the attraction of poetry, its undeniable ability to affect both masses and individuals. Yet he feels that the unexplainable presents a potential danger. The realm of the emotions is for reason an uncharted and unchartable area. Disinterested curiosity — in Matthew Arnold's sense — can never emerge from an orgy of passion. The reasoning soul thrusts only toward the good; the aroused emotions may mire as well as free the mind. The next chapter will show that Plato recognizes the usefulness of some purified examples of poetry for elementary education. The reason of tender youth may temporarily need strengthening by exhortation to virtue.

III

On the
Literal Interpretation
of Poetry

Now this overdone, or come tardy off, though it makes the
unskillful laugh, cannot but make the judicious grieve; the
censure of which one must, in your allowance, o'erweigh a
whole theatre of others. O, there be players that I have seen
play, and heard others praise, and that highly, not to speak
it profanely, that, neither having the accent of Christians nor
the gait of Christian, pagan, nor man, have so strutted and
bellowed that I have thought some of Nature's journeymen
had made men and not made them well, they imitated
humanity so abominably.

Hamlet III. ii. 22–38

In the previous chapter I have suggested that Plato's attitude
toward inspiration does not bear directly on his analysis of poetry.
Man's ascent toward absolute beauty and truth remains an individual flight. There is some possibility that the aspiring soul may
incidentally leave behind poetic words or faithful representations of
true beauty. But Plato does not give us an example of poetry which
presents such beauty, nor does he explain how the philosophic
individual can communicate with individuals still unenlightened.
Plato expresses his powerful and instinctive love of poetry by a wry
admission of the inexplicability of poetry's beauty. But we must
avoid the temptation to extend his theories of inspiration and the
power of the Muse to his comments on poetry itself.

Plato respects antiquity, its traditions and wisdom, but, more strongly, he demands an intelligent response to the past. Admiring references to poets and their sayings fill the dialogues; wise sentences from the poet may prove invaluable aids to further inquiry. But the penetrating mind of Plato accepts or dismisses a saying according to the direction his argument leads him. He makes little distinction in function among Muse, poet, and rhapsode — all are part of the transmission of the inexplicable beauty and mystery of things to mankind. The business of the philosopher — the aware and responsive individual — cannot wait on such ephemeral, sporadic, arbitrary impulses.

As previously noted, the Muse receives courteous, if sometimes ironic, reference throughout the dialogues. And, for the most part, Plato refers to ancient poets with deference, an admiration based on extensive familiarity. But his respect has limits.[1] Neither Muse nor allusion shows Plato directly considering the use and nature of poetry. Plato's citation of poets forms an integral part of the fabric of the dialogues. The early dialogue *Lysis* shows the pattern for his later citation and analysis. After paying his respects to the great

---

[1] The ancient traditions in themselves might be permitted, but the effect of these tales on children requires that we banish them from the good state. The Athenian says,

> At Athens there are tales preserved in writing which the excellence of your state, as I am informed, refuses to admit. They speak of the gods in prose as well as verse, and the oldest of these narratives relate that the primitive realities were the heavens and such. And not far from the beginning of their story they proceed to narrate the birth of the gods, and how after they were born they behaved to one another. Whether these stories have in other ways a good or a bad influence, I should not like to be severe on them, because they are ancient; but, looking at them with reference to the duties of children to their parents, I cannot praise them, or think that they are useful, or at all true. Of such ancient accounts I have nothing more to say; and I should wish to say of them only what is pleasing to the gods. But as to our modern scientists and their theories, I cannot let them off when they do mischief. For do but mark the effect of their words: when you and I argue for the existence of the gods, and produce the sun, moon, stars, and earth, claiming for them a divine being, if we would listen to the aforesaid philosophers we should say that they are earth and stones only, which can have no care at all of human affairs, and that all religion is a cooking up of words and a make-believe. [*Laws X* 886bcde]

poets and thinkers of the past, he proceeds to incorporate their wisdom into his own argument. He cites a poet, approvingly, on the objects of love and desire, then he proposes to take another subject "and see what the poets have to say; for they are to us in a manner the fathers and authors of wisdom" (214a).[2]

Dialogues before the *Ion* give little warning of the barrage that was to be loosed on poetry. Plato seems to accept gracefully the high honor accorded dramatists in Athens. Yet there are pretenders who pollute the landscape with vapid verses. Plato raises a question about learning to use arms; the honor given poets provides a useful analogy. A master of the art of war in Lacedaemon should be able to make his fortune among other nations, "just as a tragic poet would who is honored among ourselves; which is the reason why he who fancies that he can write a tragedy does not go about wandering in the neighboring states, but rushes straight down here, and exhibits at Athens; and this is natural" (*Laches* 183ab). This casual illustration suggests that poets always perform with an audience immediately before them; the functions of poet and rhapsode are not clearly distinguished. Temporal fame and honor go to the poet. Curiously enough, Plato never shows the poet composing by himself for his own pleasure.

Poetry must be judged by its effects, but this judgment must be founded on truth, not subjective pleasure.[3] Even the wise old men cannot be the final arbiters. People naturally choose according to their intelligence and literary sophistication. Very small children prefer puppet shows, older children advocate comedy, and the educated will generally prefer tragedy. The Athenian states that he believes "we old men would probably have the greatest pleasure in

---

[2] *Meno* 81 and *Laws III* 682 give sincere praise to the poets; *Protagoras* 316, *Republic II* 366, *Timaeus* 40, and *Theaetetus* 152, 179, refer ironically to their greatness.

[3] Cf. *Laws II* 653c: "The discipline of pleasure and pain which, when rightly ordered, is a principle of education, has been often relaxed and corrupted in human life." The festivals of the Muses and Apollo help improve education. The *Laws II* 668 agrees that truth, not pleasure, is the test of good art; pleasure is not altogether excluded, however (*Laws II* 658).

hearing a rhapsode recite well the *Iliad* and *Odyssey,* or one of the Hesiodic poems, and would easily award the victory to him. But who then would truly be the victor? That is the question. Clearly you and I will have to declare the true winner to be those who are preferred by men of our own age. Our customs [ἔθος] are by far superior to any which at present exist anywhere in the world" (*Laws II* 658de). This argument is not so much directed at Homer as toward the quality of judgment required to respond correctly to his poetry. As in the *Republic,* Plato always faces the problem of the proper interpretation of poetry. Youth, lacking knowledge, are inferior judges. Plato admits that "the worst of authors will say something which is to the point" (*Phaedrus* 235e).[4] So there is no inherent reason why sufficient maturity will not enable man to appreciate poetry correctly, but in the *Republic* Plato does not recognize poetic sophistication. Poetry that does not cause involvement is not really poetry at all, and involvement with the poetry of this world injures the mind all too often.

Not only does Plato honor the poets by frequent allusion elsewhere, but he sets an example through dialogues of poetic power. Running counter to his own restrictions on poetry, perhaps unconsciously, Plato delights in presenting dramatic situations. The *Republic* itself is set on a long walk.[5] And even the later dialogues have the question and answer form which demands going beyond the surface meaning of the words. Plato's own mind becomes more transparently revealed in later dialogues as explicit statement supercedes the presentation of opposing views. But he does not suggest a corresponding change in his attitude toward poetry. The *Republic,* coming at the highest point of Plato's literary and philosophical

[4] *Phaedrus* 258 states that there is no disgrace in the mere fact of writing. Plato would criticize only bad compositions. Socrates and Phaedrus propose to inquire into what constitutes good and bad writing and speaking. They conclude that knowledge must precede eloquence. Knowing and composing, then, are inextricably bound together, and Plato hides the ends of the knot. The *Laws* declares that writing is not essential to man, particularly since there are so many dangerous writings handed down to the present generation (*VII* 810).

[5] See Émile Bréhier, *The Hellenic Age,* trans. Joseph Thomas, pp. 92–99.

power, contains at least as rigid an attitude toward poetry as the *Laws*.

In addition, we see the tacit sanction of the imagination in Socrates' writing verses.[6] Evenus, a poet, has inquired why Socrates, who never before created any poetry, should turn Aesop's fables into verse while in prison, and also compose a hymn in honor of Apollo. Socrates answers the question as posed by Cebes: "Tell him, Cebes, he said, the truth — that I had no idea of rivaling him or his poems; for I knew, the task would not be easy. But I wanted to see whether I could satisfy my conscience on a scruple which I felt about the meaning of certain dreams. In the course of my life I have often had intimations in dreams that I should make music. That same dream came to me sometimes in one form, and sometimes in another, but always saying the same thing: 'Set to work and make music'" (*Phaedo* 60de). No selfish dream of fame prompts Socrates. He approaches poetry with his usual religious seriousness. As necessary for true poetic inspiration, the impulse comes from outside the man.

The highest form of music resembles the noble product of arts in the *Symposium* and *Phaedrus*. All the arts find their highest expression in the pursuit of wisdom.[7] Socrates had thought that this

---

[6] Sir Philip Sidney states that "even the Greeke *Socrates*, whome *Appollo* confirmed to bee the onely wise man, is said to have spent part of his olde time in putting *Esopes* Fables into verses. And therefore full evill should it become his scholler *Plato*, to put such words in his maisters mouth against *Poets*" (*Defence of Poesie, Prose Works* III, pp. 34–35).

[7] The *Gorgias* 503d–04a banishes poetry generally and tragedy specifically, but then recognizes a higher form of composition:

Will not the good man, who says whatever he says with a view to the best, speak with a reference to some standard and not at random; just as all other artists, whether the painter, the builder, the shipwright, or any other look all of them to their own work, and do not select and apply at random what they apply, but strive to give a definite form to it? The artist disposes all things in order, and compels the one part to harmonize and accord with the other part, until he has constructed a regular and systematic whole; and this is true of all artists, and in the same way the trainers and physicians, of whom we spoke before, give order and regularity to the body: do you deny this?

And Callicles is ready to admit Socrates' point.

exhortation was only urging him to continue what he was already doing, just as spectators encourage a competitor in a race to run when he is already running. "The dream, then, was encouraging me to make music (μουσικὴν ποιεῖν) since philosophy is the greatest music, and I was already practicing this" (*Phaedo* 60e–61a). But he was not certain. "The dream might have meant music in the ordinary sense of the word, and being under sentence of death, and the festival giving me a respite, I thought that it would be safer for me to be sure I had done what I ought, and in obedience to the dream, to compose some verses before I departed" (*Phaedo* 61a). The outward voices do not speak with the clarity desired by philosophy, yet they must be followed as best as possible in this life.

Some types of poetry are worthy of the philosopher.[8] One may either invent praises of gods or virtuous men or render other men's stories more metrical. Socrates says, "First I made a hymn in honor of the god of the festival, and then considering that a poet, if he is really to be a poet, should not only make speeches, but should invent myths, and that I am not a myth-maker, I took some fables of Aesop, which I had at hand and which I knew by heart — they were the first I came upon — and turned them into verse" (*Phaedo* 61b). Plato recognizes no clear distinction between the arts; Socrates makes verses to fulfill the requirement of composing music (μουσική). But Plato consistently insists on one step more — that the creation and production of art, like the presentation of philosophy, come as a result of ultimate concerns. The poet must be a creator or an inventor; he must interpret rather than imitate the observable world. Socrates, lacking such invention, modestly turns to versifying Aesop. Nor does Plato claim an invention superior to that of his teacher: even when he has created a tale, he attributes the myth to some previous source. The arbitrariness of normal poetical invention is to be eschewed. The fables of Aesop have straightforward morals, and the hymn in honor of Apollo is obviously a moral teaching.

---

[8] *Republic X* 607 admits the same sorts of praises of gods and noble men.

1

POETRY AND THE MORAL EDUCATION

Thus, throughout the discussion of inspiration, beauty, effectiveness, Plato levels no attack against poetry. He attributes to Socrates the same sense of wonder about poetry that he himself possesses. But so far, Plato's comments on poetry have been incidental to the purpose of the dialogues. And indeed, Plato never does separate art from human existence enough to pay undivided attention to poetry.[9] Yet in the *Republic* he gives us a picture of the proper role for poetry in the state. He describes the education of the young Guardians. Poetry is judged not for the pleasure it gives the masses, but in terms of its living effect on the best humans in the state. Inspiration is no longer a topic, and Plato speaks seriously and directly to the needs of the state. He emphasizes the necessity for the minds of the Guardians to be aware, correctly formed. Education consists not of strengthening man's response to his fellows and to the world around him, but of molding the individual's mind. "Know thyself" must precede a response to lesser concerns.

The context of Plato's comments on poetry in *Republic II* points out his immediate moral concern.[10] Glaucon presents the case for injustice. He cites Hesiod and Homer for examples of tolerance for the corruption of the gods. The passages cited are clearly taken out of context, but Plato still insists on a literal interpretation. Youth is particularly susceptible to the suggestions of poetry. Glaucon asks, "When all this stuff is talked about the estimation in which virtue and vice are held by gods and by mankind, what effect can we suppose it has upon the mind of a young man quick-witted enough to gather honey from all these flowers of popular wisdom and to draw his own conclusions as to the sort of person he should be and the way he should go in order to lead the best possible life?"

---

[9] Frederick A. G. Beck, in *Greek Education: 450–350 B.C.*, pp. 199–243, speaks of the role Plato gives poetry in the education of those of all ages.

[10] Paul Shorey states, "This is the challenge. The remainder of the *Republic* is the answer to it" (*What Plato Said*, p. 216).

(*II* 365a). He will probably agree with a passage of Pindar which suggests choosing the appearance of virtue. Only trouble results from being honest except when reputation follows. Everyone says the wicked may be happy; success is more important than virtue. Poetry therefore contains as many evil sententiae as good.

Still, if morality is unclear in this world, certainty on ethical issues may exist in a higher realm. But poetry simply echoes current tradition in encouraging these relative morals. Popular morality would say that the gods themselves are inconsistent, and money can win them over to the side of men. Glaucon states that apparently the penalty for our misdeeds on earth will fall neither upon us nor upon our children's children. The idea of future retribution can be countered "by reckoning on the great efficacy of mystic rites and divinities of absolution, vouched for by the most advanced societies and by the descendants of the gods who have appeared as poets and spokesmen of heavenly inspiration" (*II* 366a). Even poetic inspiration falls under attack. Immoral poetry, no matter how beautifully phrased, is still immoral. Poetry, therefore, the great authority on ultimate issues, is no fit guide to one earnestly seeking virtue.

Glaucon has called on the authority of poets to present his case for injustice. Poetry and tradition must be purged, for a study of man as he is and was can never point to man as he ought to be. Now Plato must create an environment which will reinforce man's better qualities at every point. Thus he sets the discussion of poetry within a larger consideration of the type of education fit for the Guardians.

Book *II* of the *Republic*, then, grows out of Plato's pervasive tendency to analyze poetry as integral to the state. Imaginative art — fiction of all sorts — exerts a powerful influence over the young, confirming them in good or bad habits.[11] Mature audiences

---

[11] Katherine Gilbert and Helmut Kuhn comment on Plato's concept of education by indirect means: "Plato conceived of the learning-process in children as involving a larger measure of immediate and unconscious absorption of form and habit, and less of the conscious acquisition of ideas and facts than we do today. In the program of education he recommended in the *Republic* and in the *Laws* he leaned heavily on this possibility of the uncon-

can likewise be instructed and corrupted, depending upon whether the production is temperate or violent. Plato calls only for a purification of art, but unfortunately this reform precludes the possibility of great literature. Subtle art does not present a clear moral; only a philosophical understanding can properly interpret a great or profound work. Since the masses are likely to lack such understanding, censorship should be a matter of course. But even the elite do not have poetry as part of their discipline. The rulers of the state must know good and evil, but poetry gives a kind of experience, not a course of instruction.

Throughout the *Republic*, the effect of poetry lies uppermost in Plato's mind. He refuses to divorce poetry from the urgent needs of the state. Indeed, Plato may be incapable of discussing art impersonally; the fabric of his mind is poetic. Feeling the effect of poetry himself, he cannot accept such an impersonal response as art for art's sake. Instilling wisdom in the young is one of the state's chief duties, and Plato goes straight to the heart of the problem.[12] Obviously, some sort of censorship will be necessary, through either an ignoring of the trivial or banishment of the immoral. Accordingly, stories — food for the mind — are the first part of the Guard-

---

scious assimilation of manners and taste, on the impressibility of a young spirit in the presence of a general spiritual quality" (*A History of Esthetics*, p. 41). One would think that of all human creations, poetry is most capable of suggesting a more nearly perfect world. But Plato rejects suggestiveness in language; all poets make brief explicit statements.

[12] The *Protagoras* contains the well-known description of Athenian education. All society joins in teaching the youth: After the first disciplines,

they send him to teachers, and enjoin them to see to his manners even more than to his reading and music; and the teachers do as they are desired. And when the boy has learned his letters and is beginning to understand what is written, as before he understood only what was spoken, they put into his hands the works of great poets, which he reads sitting on a bench at school; in these are contained many admonitions, and many tales, and praises, and encomia of ancient famous men, which he is required to learn by heart, in order that he may imitate or emulate them and desire to become like them. [325d–26a]

The entire description given in the *Protagoras* sounds much like that which Plato advocates in *Republic II* and *III*. But here Plato rejects this scheme, for virtue cannot be taught.

ians' education to be considered. Some of these stories — tales, legends, myths, narratives in poetry or in prose — are true, others are fictitious. Since the fictitious stories may have some elements of truth in them, they can be used in elementary education: "The beginning, as you know, is always the most important part of every work, especially so with anything young and tender. That is the time when the character can be molded and easily takes any impress one may wish to stamp on it" (377ab). The abuses of society are the chief corrupters of human nature. Should all evil stories be destroyed, man would be freed from temptation and further evil creations. Random stories from uninstructed teachers can thwart the values set by the intelligent society. Nurses in any state exercise the limbs of children to strengthen them. An enlightened state will insist that these teachers give attention to molding the souls of the children as well.

Any response may become habitual. "The opinions a child takes in at that age are likely to become indelibly fixed. Therefore we should take great pains that the first stories which they hear should be so composed as to bear the fairest lessons of virtue to their ears" (*II* 378de). Mothers shall not tell of the gods' misdoings. Such stories not only would be blasphemy, but would at the same time make cowards of the children. On the other hand, proper stories about the gods influence the youth "to revere the heaven and their parents and to value good relations with each other" (*III* 386a). Since the children also should be brave, the stories they hear should be of the sort that will help make them unafraid of death.

For effective teaching, characters in drama or epic must be simple and unchanging. The ascent from depravity to nobility may indeed glorify the heights which man can reach, but any admission of corruption in a hero encourages the innocent to be content with their inadequacies. Poetry should encourage self-control and obedience exclusively. Degrading stories about Achilles or Priam lessen their value as moral examples,

> For if our young men take such unworthy descriptions seriously instead of laughing scornfully at them, they will hardly feel themselves, who are but men, above behaving in that way or

repress any temptation to do so. Instead they would not be ashamed of giving way with complaints and outcries at the slightest suffering; and that would be contrary to the principle we have deduced and shall adhere to, until someone can show us a better. [*III* 388de]

But the Guardians must not indulge in excessive mirth. "Violent laughter tends to provoke an equally violent reaction" (*III* 388). When noble men or gods are meanly described, they make poor models for virtuous action. The youth must learn temperance in all things rather than any emotional extreme.[13]

2

THE ANALYSIS OF POETRY

The preceding discussion of the effect of poetry accords with Plato's general concern that every part of the state contribute directly to the moral life. There should be no fat on the lean and hard body of the state. This section will show that like every other form of education or entertainment, poetry must serve a specific, well-defined function. Although Plato does not consider the possibility that poetry can present examples of evil to warn people, he does suggest that examples of good rewarded can encourage. Indeed, by banishing the portrayal of evil, Plato may banish knowledge of evil — or at least any encouragement to put such evil into practice. The rulers of the just state must have a sort of knowledge about evil, if only to defend against outside imperfect states. Such knowledge should be rationally presented and objectively accepted; the imaginative arts allow no certainty of the proper interpretation. One must understand life before he can understand representations of life. Since Plato does not distinguish the faculty of reason from that of will, the worth of moral instruction depends on clarity of meaning. Thus, Plato mistrusts allegory as much as ambiguous or symbolic stories: "Stories like those of Hera being bound by her

[13] The *Laws* does not permit comic poets to ridicule any citizen for any reason, either by word or by mime (*XI* 935–36).

son, or of Hephaestus flung from heaven by his father for taking his mother's part when she was beaten, and the battles of the gods in Homer, must not be admitted into our state, whether they be allegorical or not. A child cannot distinguish the allegorical sense from the literal" (*Republic II* 378d). Youth are impressionable and may lack the objectivity to analyze the deeper meaning of poetry. Allegory, as Plato observes, does not present its meaning unequivocally; some preexisting understanding is necessary. Thus, poetry can reinforce some values, but art cannot create virtue.

The response to poetry must never be passive receptivity. Over and over, Plato stresses that poetry has meaning and that the listener must wrestle with the language. Poets are always deliberately obscuring their arguments. In the *Republic I*, Socrates again refers to the ambiguous pronouncements of the poets: "Simonides (after the manner of poets) would seem to have spoken darkly of the nature of justice; for he really meant to say that justice is the rendering to each man what is proper to him, and this he termed a debt" (*I* 332bc).[14]

A brief examination of the *Protagoras* will show that Plato's skepticism toward the interpretation of poetry is not confined to the *Republic*. Throughout, he stands directly opposed to the attitudes of his time. Criticism of poetry in Athens was a practical matter, and Plato brings his great common sense to bear on the issue.[15] Clearly the age looked to poetry for education. All common people and some teachers seemed to assume a natural link between utterance and practical action. Plato simply makes the all-important distinction. He gives a model of literary criticism, illustrating the difficulty and the techniques of textual analysis. The sophist Protagoras regards poetry as a ready encyclopedia of knowledge:

> I am of the opinion, Socrates, that skill in poetry is the principal part of education; and this I conceive to be the power of knowing what compositions of the poets are good poetry, and what are not, and how they are to be distinguished, and of explaining when asked the reason for the difference. And I propose to

[14] Also *Phaedo* 61 and *Alcibiades II* 147.

[15] See Eric A. Havelock, *Preface to Plato*, pp. 36–86.

transfer the question which you and I have been discussing to the domain of poetry; we will speak as before of virtue, but in reference to a passage of a poet. [*Protagoras* 338e–39a]

Socrates feels that Protagoras falls into an obvious error in making poetry integral to education. Both agree that the proper analysis of poetry follows from an understanding of its rational content. One must first know the poetry, then be able to reason about its truth or falsity, thus Protagoras' proposal to speak of virtue by reference to the poem. The passages cited merely illustrate a seeming contradiction. Protagoras has not only falsely elevated poetry, but also lacks a technique for even partial justification of his claims.

Meeting Protagoras on his own terms, Socrates will correct his misreading of the literal meaning of one of Simonides' poems. Socrates knows the poem in question and declares the work to be a good and true composition. His familiarity and approval stem from his having made a careful study of the ode. He later dismisses, however, the poetic qualities of the passage: "A great deal might be said in praise of the details of the poem, which is a charming piece of workmanship, and very finished, but such minutiae would be tedious" (344ab). Both men argue that if there is a contradiction, the composition cannot be good or true. Protagoras' concept of criticism follows that of Plato: excerpts from poetry are weighed for relevance beyond the language.[16] Protagoras claims that Simonides condemns and accepts the same thought in a single poem.

Socrates' first explanation shows the dangers inherent in the spell of language. Any clever man can twist the meanings of words. Characteristically, Socrates begins by seeking some other authority. He turns to Prodicus and, says, flatteringly: "how fortunate are we in having Prodicus among us, at the right moment; for he has a wisdom, Protagoras, which, as I imagine, is more than human and of very ancient date, and may be as old as Simonides or even older. Learned as you are in many things, you appear to know nothing of this; but I know, for I am a disciple of his" (340e–341a). Socrates

---

[16] *Phaedrus* 234–35 also makes a sharp distinction between the sentiments of the author and the clarity and grace of his language.

sophistically praises Prodicus for his "philosophy of synonyms," which enables him to distinguish "will" and "wish" and make other charming distinctions (340b). The argument then hinges on 'being' versus 'becoming.' When he twists the word "hard" ($\chi\alpha\lambda\epsilon\pi\acute{o}\nu$) to mean evil, Prodicus falls completely into the trap.

Protagoras, however, correctly rejects both of Socrates' suggestions. The sophist continues to judge the poem again in the untenable arena of general relevance: "The poet could never have been so ignorant as to say that virtue, which in the opinion of all men is the hardest of all things, can be easily retained" (340e). Socrates then proposes his analysis of the poem. He attempts to explain that the poem is not inconsistent, but rather that the entire work should be viewed as a terse refutation of Pittacus. Both excerpts under consideration reflect the commendable brevity of the pithy sayings which make up Lacedaemonian philosophy. The error of the first two interpretations has been explicitly pointed out; the reader must now trace the error of this very complex analysis for himself. Like Prodicus, the modern reader is greatly impressed. Both the length of Socrates' analysis, betraying as it does his pleas for brevity, suggests virtuosity rather than sincerity. He proceeds by analogy and paradox, always with reference to the poem's relevance to external fact (345).

Socrates concludes his minute analysis by interpreting the poem to fit his own philosophy of the involuntary nature of evil. Simonides is interpreted as arguing an intellectual point with his fellow poet Pittacus, and oddly enough Simonides reflects Plato's general attitude toward poetry: "And you, Pittacus, I would never have blamed, if you had spoken what was moderately good and true; but I do blame you because, putting on the appearance of truth, you are speaking gross falsehoods about the highest matters (346e–47a). And to illustrate the variability of interpretation, Hippias says, "I think, Socrates, that you have given a very good explanation of the poem; but I have also an excellent interpretation of my own which I will propound to you, if you will allow me" (347ab).

Such discourse about poetry does not further the discussion at hand, however. Socrates sees that the response to poetry is negative acceptance rather than the construction of useful arguments. The poets, being absent, cannot explain or defend their teachings.[17] Most significantly, Plato attacks those who bring poetry or sayings into the context of discussion as if past authority were essential to present reasoning. Ordered discourse or conversation certainly is more productive than the vulgar entertainment which poetry often affords. Such amusements — flute-girls, dancing-girls, or harp-girls — only mask man's basic stupidity. Educated men

> are contented with one another's conversation, of which their own voices are the medium — each speaking and listening decently in his turn — even though they are very liberal in their potations. And a company like this of ours, and men such as we profess to be, do not require the help of another's voice, or of the poets whom you cannot interrogate about the meaning of what they are saying; people who cite them declaring, some that the poet has one meaning, and others that he has another, and the point which is in dispute can never be decided. This sort of entertainment they decline, and in social intercourse prefer to rely on their own resources, and put one another to the proof in conversation. And these are the models which I desire that you and I should imitate. Leaving the poets, let us discourse with one another from our own resources and make proof of the truth and of ourselves in conversation. [*Protagoras* 347e–48a]

Each man must speak with his own voice. The proper interpretation of poetry involves cutting through the haze of conflicting statements to the clear meaning lying behind the words.

Thus, the greatest sophist of the times, Protagoras, has allowed — or encouraged — Socrates to study poetry on the level of its educational merit. But the analysis has not proven fruitful, for an adequate instrument does not exist even for Socrates. Moreover, the

---

[17] Carleton Brownson observes that "the poet can charm his audience or his readers, but he cannot withstand the cross-examination of the philosopher or give a logical explanation of his own verses. It is the reason which Plato seeks to exalt and glorify, and this belongs to the philosopher, not to the poet" (*Plato's Studies and Criticisms of the Poets*, pp. 14–15).

interpretation of poetry is largely subjective and variable — as Hippias suggests and Socrates asserts. If the literal meaning of Simonides is open to such questioning, the allegorical approach poses even more danger for ordinary men.

3

POETRY AND TRUTH

If Socrates himself can find so little certainty in analyzing poetry, children are even more likely to be baffled. "Since they cannot understand poetic subtleties, art may permanently corrupt some children (*Republic II* 378de). Allegory (ὑπόνοια) demands a foreknowledge that might not exist. Plato's attack is entirely negative; he refuses to say which compositions may suit the ideal state. He clearly states his primary concern to be education, not poetics. "You and I, Adeimantus, are not, for the moment, poets, but founders of a commonwealth. And as founders, we must know the patterns to be followed by the poets in making their stories and the limits beyond which they must not be allowed to go" (*II* 379a). Guidelines may exist for the creation of good poetry, but Plato feels no obligation to describe the artistic process.

Throughout this part of the *Republic* Plato deals with gods and heroes. As entities larger than life, such examples naturally tend to be models. And Plato wants poetry to be relevant to nature. He does prescribe for the poet, but his proposals are eminently fair. Poetry should follow the patterns set by those who are privy to the secrets of the universe.[18] Evil larger than life cannot instruct without involving an allegorical interpretation. "A poet, whether he is writing epic, lyric, or drama, surely ought always to represent the divine nature as it really is. And the truth is that that nature is good

---

[18] The *Laws* confirms the *Republic*'s concern for fidelity of poetry to truth: "Our poets, understanding prayers to be requests which we make to the gods, will take especial heed that they do not by mistake ask for evil instead of good. To make such a prayer would surely be too ridiculous" (*VII* 801ab). Lacking knowledge of good or evil, the poet will teach incorrectly in the very important area of piety (see ch. III, sec. 3).

and must be described as such" (*II* 379ab). He at least tentatively accepts dramatic or imitative poetry here. There is little prescription in Plato's censorship of poetry. He will not discuss the divine nature himself, but simply demands that the poet must, when dealing with divinity, treat it realistically. Likewise, the nature in which these gods reside is basically good and purposeful; any poetry to the contrary is a trivial waste of time. Good poetry cannot contain logical errors: "a god, then, is not responsible for everything, but only for what is as it should be. It is not responsible for evil" (*II* 379b). Fundamentally, poetry must make sense — its primary meaning should be readily intelligible.

Plato's discussion of poetry's treatment of the gods follows from his analysis of the ultimate sources of good and evil. The gods are merely representations of the realities of man's relation to the Good. Human misconduct should not be applied to the divine. Since the divine is good, evil must not be attributed to the gods. Homer's description of Zeus as the "dispenser of both good and ill" will be termed a foolish error:

> We shall disapprove when Pandarus' violation of oaths and treaties is said to be the work of Athena and Zeus, or when Themis and Zeus are said to have caused strife among the gods. Nor must we allow our young people to be told by Aeschylus that "Heaven implants guilt in man, when his will is to destroy a house utterly." If a poet tells of the sorrows of Niobe or the calamities of the house of Pelops or of the Trojan war, either he must not speak of them as the work of a god, or if he does so, he must devise some such explanation as we are now requiring: he must say that what the god did was just and good, and the sufferers were the better for being chastised. One who pays a just penalty must not be called miserable, and his misery then laid at heaven's door. The poet will only be allowed to say that the wicked were miserable because they needed chastisement, and the punishment of heaven did them good. [*II* 379e–80b]

The strongest measures should be taken to prevent anyone from confusing other citizens by having the divine responsible for evil. "Neither young nor old must listen to such tales, in prose or verse.

Such doctrine would be impious, self-contradictory, and disastrous to our commonwealth" (*II* 380bc). Plato denies representations of evil and of undeserved punishment even to the mature audience. Sensational stories which corrupt the young can hardly serve those older. Thus poetry must not hold the heavens responsible for everything — only for the good.

Plato next turns to sensationalism in art. We who look back through 2000 years of monotheism see little danger in presenting descriptions of Grecian anthropomorphic gods in all sorts of indecorous actions. Plato, on the other hand, faces an immediate challenge not only in careless tales, but in firmly entrenched ignorance as well. He would keep the religious figures but strip them of all recognizable traditions. Here Plato does not directly attack the traditional stories, yet he demands a more sophisticated interpretation. He is not so much concerned with censorship as with clear thinking about the gods. Certainly no respectable theology would describe a god as a magician appearing in various shapes and undergoing transformations. Since things in the most perfect condition are those least affected by external change, the god will probably maintain his proper shape: "The state of the divine nature must be perfect in every way, and would therefore be the last thing to suffer transformations from any outside cause" (*II* 381b). A god cannot become better: "Any change could only be for the worse; for we cannot admit any imperfection in divine goodness or beauty" (*II* 381c). Every god, being perfect, remains simply and eternally in his own form. Plato applies this principle to poetry:

> The poets must not tell us that "the gods go to and fro among the cities of men, disguised as strangers of all sorts from far countries." Nor must they tell any of these false tales of Proteus and Thetis transforming themselves, or bring Hera on the stage in the guise of a priestess collecting alms for "the life-giving children of Inachus, the river of Argos." Mothers, again, are not to follow these suggestions and scare young children with harmful stories of spirits that go about by night in all sorts of outlandish shapes. They would only be blaspheming the gods and at the same time making cowards of their children.
>
> [*II* 381de]

Mothers in Athens had no more right to frighten their impression-able children with evil and powerful divinities than have present mothers to tell that an all-powerful Satan might defeat God.[19]

Again, Plato feels that poetry must be true to human and divine nature. Poetry that violates moral and rational sense cannot be justified on purely aesthetic grounds. Stories about the gods have a direct bearing on human conduct. No true god would willfully indulge in metamorphosis, nor will the intelligent man. Alteration in one's essential self shows an unhealthy ignorance, a kind of living lie (ἀληθῶς ψεῦδος). Both men and gods hate lies; the worst thing of all is to harbor untruth in the soul. And "the spoken falsehood is only the embodiment or image of a previous condition of the soul, not pure unadulterated falsity (*II* 382b). The true or real false-hood, then, consists of ignorance. The spoken falsehood reflects an ignorance on the part of the man. Man's utterances issue from his own soul. Soul precedes language. Falsehood in words merely imitates or copies the corruption in the soul.

Some utterances not entirely true may have a therapeutic value. They must be employed, however, by men who know exactly why the false statement is applicable. The real falsehood, ignorance, is hated both by gods and by men. "But is the falsehood in words always a hateful thing? Is it not sometimes helpful — in war, for instance, or as a sort of medicine to avert some fit of folly or mad-ness that might make a friend attempt some mischief? And in those legends we were discussing just now, we can turn fiction to account;

---

[19] Cf. *Laws XII* 941bc:

Theft is a mean, and robbery a shameless thing; and none of the sons of Zeus delight in fraud and violence, or ever practiced either. Wherefore let no one be deluded by poets or mythologers into a mistaken belief of such things, nor let him suppose, when he thieves or is guilty of violence, that he is doing nothing base, but only what the gods themselves do. For such tales are untrue and improbable; and he who steals or robs con-trary to the law, is never either a god or a child of gods; of this the legis-lator ought to be better informed than all the poets put together.

Plato more explicitly asserts the identity of the legislator and the true poet here than in earlier dialogues, but this theme is suggested in the *Phaedrus* as well as the *Republic*. Ordinary poets are always accused of usurping the function of the moral educator.

not knowing the facts about the distant past, we can make our fiction as good an embodiment of truth as possible" (*II* 382cd). In the world of man, practicality deems that some utterances need not conform absolutely to truth. Yet truth must be the ultimate end of all speech, particularly within the commonwealth itself. Paralleling to some extent the argument of *Republic X*, false language here can be used to deceive men in war or to affect the emotions of citizens while the fictions can pacify frenzy in the demented. Plato shows no inclination to allow falsehoods to instruct normal humans. Besides these persuasive purposes, the fabrications of myth may embody partial truths to flesh out knowledge which is certain and absolute. But fiction teaches by truth, not by pleasure, to edify the hearers.

But Plato's argument has been pointing out bungling, earthbound descriptions of heavenly matters. And the Athenians were confusing fiction and truth, men and gods. The gods, having a divine nature, do not act as men would — there is no need. Faults can hardly be accepted in men; they are intolerable in gods, who are greater than men. "A god is a being of entire simplicity and truthfulness in word and in deed. In himself he does not change, nor does he delude others, either in dreams or in waking moments, by apparitions or oracles or signs" (*II* 382e–83a). Therefore the second principle in writing about the gods is that they neither change by magic nor do they lie. Plays alleging that they do must not be produced: "We shall not allow the teachers to use such poetry in educating the young, if we mean our Guardians to be godfearing and to be godlike themselves so far as man may (*II* 383c). In the *Laws* Plato recognizes that poets have said many things well. But their bad sayings are enough to make him "affirm that much learning is dangerous to youth" (*VII* 811b).

Up to this point, Plato has not so much considered poetry as he has attacked stories which complacently attribute man's vices to the gods. He cannot openly deny the conventional polytheism; this charge had been falsely laid against Socrates.[20] A certain amount of lip service to tradition must be observed. Today we can accept

[20] *Apology* 26.

the legends of the anthropomorphic gods as tales, but the majority of Greeks absorbed their religion and morals from performances such as Ion gave. Plato insists that serious religious attitudes cannot come from blind acceptance of stories emerging from racial traditions. He has been talking about "what sorts of stories about the gods may, or may not, be told to children who are to hold heaven and their parents in reverence and to value good relations with one another (*Republic III* 386a). Plato is indeed concerned only with elementary education here, but there is little suggestion that the older citizens can profit from blasphemy and sensationalism in poetry.

4

THE INCULCATION OF VIRTUE

This discussion of the gods and heroes as models for conduct leads Plato to consider the moral impact of art on the souls of children. The stories they hear should make them unafraid of death. A man with that fear in his heart cannot be brave. Tales of the terrors of the underworld are particularly troublesome. "The poets must be told to speak well of that other world. The gloomy descriptions they now give must be forbidden, not only as untrue, but as injurious to our future warriors" (*III* 386bc). Thus, Homer's account of the despair of Achilles in Hell must be omitted. "If most people enjoy them as good poetry, that is all the more reason for keeping them from children or grown men who are to be free, fearing slavery more than death" (*III* 387b). The extent to which the words are pleasing determines the effect the poetry has on the hearers. Men cannot withstand the ravishments of poetry and are likely to lose the fine tempering of their souls. Each of the above criticisms of poetry comes from its violation of some ethical precept. He does not so much condemn poetry as stress the necessity for all utterance to serve the needs of the state. Brief poetic excerpts can convince the individual who lacks the rational faculty which can see the context of the passages.[21]

---

[21] The young readily believe fantastic tales such as the improbable story of the Sidonian Cadmus rather than the truth; the poets therefore have a

Not only descriptions of the sufferings of the dead, but the words themselves tend to weaken the warriors. Plato's own eschatological myths inspire enjoyment of beauty rather than terror. But the poets can thwart the intellect by aiming their words toward the spirited and appetitive elements: "We must also get rid of all those terrifying and fearsome names, the very sound of which is enough to make one shiver: 'loathsome Styx,' 'the River of Wailing,' 'infernal spirits,' 'anatomies,' and so on. For other purposes such language may be well enough; but we are afraid that the habit of such thrills may melt down the fine-tempered spirit of our Guardians. So we will have none of it; and we shall require speech and verses in the opposite strain" (*III* 387bc). Strength of will, restraint, self-control, all are preferable to wallowing in strong emotions. From the earliest dialogues Plato has maintained that inward harmony finds a parallel in the outward, physical appearance.[22] Even momentary laments can weaken the soul's harmony.

Poetry tends to cause man to seek truth in society before he has established his inner self-control. Since physical death holds no terrors for the wise, only the weak and the ignorant will mourn a friend's death. "We also believe that a noble man, above all, possesses within himself all that is necessary for a good life and is distinguished from other men by being least dependent on anyone else, so that he has less to fear from the loss of a son or brother or of his wealth or anything else of the sort. When such misfortune comes, he will bear it patiently without lamenting" (*III* 387de). Man must be calmly autonomous of the affairs of this world before he can respond fully to higher influences. The poetic words of other

---

disproportionate influence on education. The story of Cadmus is a tale of "armed men springing up after the sowing of teeth, which the legislator may take as a proof that he can persuade the minds of the young of anything; so that he has only to reflect and find out what belief will be of the greatest public advantage, and then use all his efforts to make the whole community utter one and the same word in their songs and tales and discourses all their life long" (*Laws II* 663e–64a). The legislator must take over the function of the poet; the *Laws IX* 858 echoes this point.

[22] For Plato, the soul of man always finds expression in the outward appearance; see *Republic III* 402, *V* 462, *Timaeus* 87–88.

men call attention to social problems. The true poets and the philosophers of the *Phaedrus* lose themselves in beauty beyond the human rather than reveling in their own emotional response to human predicaments.

Plato would encourage the young rulers to stand apart from all trivial shows of passion. Response of any sort to an appearance leads to involvement. Thus that appearance becomes a model for conduct in one way or another. "For if our young men take such unworthy descriptions of the gods seriously instead of laughing at them, they will hardly feel themselves, who are but men, above behaving in that way or repress any temptation to do so. They would not be ashamed of giving way with complaints and outcries on every trifling occasion; and that would be contrary to the principle we have deduced and shall adhere to, until someone can show us a better" (*III* 388de). And violent laughter, as well as terror, tends to provoke an equally violent reaction. And again, the gods in particular must not be described in terms of ordinary human laughter.

As in the *Ion*, poetry gives instruction directly. Poetry must be true before we dare allow it to be beautiful. The arts have a real and direct power for good or evil; falsehoods are medicine for the soul: "The gods do not need falsehood and it is useful to mankind only in the way of a medicine; obviously a medicine should be handled by no one but a physician" (*III* 389b). The intent lies immediately behind the utterance. A thorough knowledge of the truth should precede any use of feigned sentences, for truth lies in the soul before being verbally embodied. All statements are assertions to be judged in terms of truth or falsity.

Just as the virtuous alone should make poetry in the *Laws*, only the rulers of the Republic can practice the art of deception.[23] Hav-

---

[23] The *Laws* affirms the possibility of useful lies. The Athenian reasons that the unjust life is not only base and depraved, but more unpleasant than the just life. "And even supposing this were otherwise, and not as the argument has proved, still the lawgiver, who is worth anything, if he ever ventures to tell a lie to the young for their good, could not invent a more useful lie than this, or one which will have a better effect in making them do what is

ing eliminated all lies from their essential beings, the rulers can dispassionately and correctly minister to their subjects:

> If anyone is to practice deception, either on the country's
> enemies or on its citizens, it must be the Rulers of the common-
> wealth, acting for its benefit; no one else may meddle with
> this privilege. For a private person to mislead such Rulers we
> shall declare to be a worse offense than for a patient to mislead
> his doctor or an athlete his trainer about his bodily condition,
> or for a seaman to misinform his captain about the state of the
> ship or of the crew. So, if anyone else in our commonwealth "of
> all that practice crafts, physician, seer, or carpenter," is caught
> not telling the truth, the Rulers will punish him for introducing
> a practice as fatal and subversive in a state as it would be in
> a ship. [*III* 389bc]

So only the rulers can write poetry or anything less than explicit and
unambiguous truth. The later discussion suggests that the Rulers
must avoid falsity as a habit; even therapeutic deception is
dangerous.

Poetry is admissible, and even praiseworthy, to the extent that
self-control follows. The citizens must have self-control. This virtue
consists of both respectful attention to one's political superiors and
personal discipline and order. Politically, man must obey his rulers.
Personally, he must heed his rational part. While many passages
of Homer must therefore be omitted, some poetry can be valuable.
"We shall allow the poets to represent any examples of self-control
and fortitude on the part of famous men, and admit such lines as
these: 'Odysseus smote his breast, chiding his heart: Endure, my
heart; thou has borne worse things than these'" (*III* 390d). Poetry
does not have to deny the existence of all powerful emotions even
though weakness and confusion are prohibited. Strongly willed control — the disciplined intellect — may be necessary to thwart the
baser demands of the appetite. In any event, poetry must be clear

---

right, not on compulsion but voluntarily" (*II* 663de). Cleinias accepts this
compromise, for "truth, Stranger, is a noble and lasting thing, but a thing of
which men are hard to be persuaded" (*II* 663e).

and simple to have the power to guide man away from his confused animal perception into the purity of intellectual beauty.

Whatever Plato's subject may be throughout the dialogues, his critical method remains fairly constant to this pattern. He cites a number of brief and unconnected passages which show some undignified situation or immoral exhortation. Each excerpt provides a focus for thought. Single statements or phrases predominate, and each idea expressed exists autonomously of other sections of this or other poems. One cannot have recourse to another part of the poem, for the context of the excerpt is life, not art.

Poets are forbidden traditional tales of the gods, for Plato has already proved that the gods cannot create or indulge in evil. The young and uneducated are likely to interpret all parts of a poem literally, missing sense and context entirely. But so far Plato has dealt only with literature of elevated subject matter; these tales purport to portray those better than man. He has legislated for heroic poetry — the gods, demons, heroes, and tales of the underworld. He objects to the high mimetic representation of evil, for a larger-than-life portrayal of evil might be an incentive to evil deeds. Evil must be weak; the forces for good must be overwhelmingly strong. The artist cannot clearly condemn the actions of an impressive scoundrel. A life of mixed good and evil cannot serve as a pure model for virtue; Plato refuses to let merely human characteristics influence absolute criteria.

To conclude, Plato has examined the great poetry of the Greek tradition and attempted to set this poetry into the best possible educational system. He has proposed radical surgery to excise immorality and triviality from the lovely body of poetry. Although he does praise certain sententiae, he vigorously forbids descriptions of strong emotions by gods or men as well as any language which fills the soul with terror. And in the process of this cleansing of language, Plato has thrown out baby, bath water, and nearly the bathtub as well. What remains after Plato's study is not poetry but brief didactic verses. There is no way that meditating on poetry — the shadow of enlightened humanity — can lift and sustain man in his quest for truth. What we would call richly complex poetry glorifies confusion. No language can teach, even though brief passages may be an aid for those who need this temporal support.

Still, Plato's negative argument has not really touched the essence of poetry. Plato himself suggests a limit to his attack on language. He has been discussing, first, the effects on the young and impressionable. And, second, he has been discussing only a use of poetry in education. He has demanded that poetry used as a model must indeed be more nearly perfect than imitations of human actions are likely to be. He has spoken about gods, demons, heroes, and the underworld. He has not spoken of any poetry he thought likely to be heard just as poetry. A knowledgeable response of the individual listener is an undiscussed possibility so far. All communication of poetry comes directly to the individual from the poet-rhapsode, always in the public performance.[24] But, unwilling to

---

[24] Throughout the dialogues, the public performance dominates both the creation and the judgment of poetry. Plato observed humanity teaching itself, falling into the same mistakes over and over again. Only the knowledgeable judge can resist the still, sad music of humanity:

> Thus far I too should agree with the many, that the excellence of music is to be measured by pleasure. But the pleasure must not be that of chance persons; the fairest music is that which delights the best and best educated, and especially that which delights the one man who is pre-eminent in goodness and education. And therefore the judges must be men of character, for they will require both wisdom and courage. The true judge must not draw his verdict from the audience, nor ought he to be unnerved by the clamor of the many and his own incapacity; nor again, knowing the truth, ought he through cowardice and unmanliness carelessly to deliver a lying judgment, with the very same lips which have just appealed to the gods before he judged. He is sitting not as the disciple of the theater, but in his proper place, as their instructor, and he ought to be the enemy of all pandering to the pleasure of the spectators. The ancient and common custom of Hellas, which still prevails in Italy and Sicily, did certainly leave the judgment to the body of spectators, who determined the victor by show of hands. But this custom has been the destruction of the poets; for they are now in the habit of composing with a view to pleasing the bad taste of their judges, and the result is that the spectators instruct themselves. Also it has been the ruin of the theater; they ought to be having characters put before them better than their own, and so receiving a higher pleasure. But now by their own act the opposite result follows. [*Laws II* 658e–59c]

One reason (to be discussed in the next chapter) for poetry's exile from the *Republic* is that there is no way characters better than the Guardians can be presented.

prescribe for poetry about men at this point, Plato leaves the subject until human beings are better understood. Too many people glorify poetry's effect on man before they understand what man really is or needs. Plato observes that most poets and speechmakers (ποιηταὶ καὶ λογοποιοί) are guilty of "serious misstatements about human life." They portray wrongdoers as happy and just men as miserable. For Plato, these lies are an ugly impossibility, and poetry dealing with the impossible must be of the most trivial nature. The lawgiver will therefore demand that the poets compose tales which do not offend the intellect with such blatant absurdities. Speech about men still remains: "We must postpone any decision as to how the truth is to be told about human beings, until we have discovered the real nature of justice and proven that it is intrinsically profitable to its possessor, no matter what reputation he may have in the eyes of the world" (*III* 392c). Man must know himself before claiming to understand any lesser topics like poetry and the arts.

Plato will wait until the *Republic X* before considering again the content of poetry. So far he has shown the inadequacy of complex and ambiguous poetry for elementary education. Heroic poetry offers itself as a model for heroic conduct — for good or for evil. As Plato moves to more advanced education, he shifts his attention to the form and the method of presenting poetry. He has argued that we cannot indiscriminately trust poetry to educate the young properly. Now he turns to the consideration of whether poetry can confirm the mature in their virtuous life.

IV

Poetry
and the Autonomy
of the Soul

And ever against eating cares,
Lap me in soft Lydian airs,
Married to immortal verse
Such as the meeting soul may pierce
In notes with many a winding bout
Of linkéd sweetness long drawn out
With wanton heed and giddy cunning,
The melting voice through mazes running,
Untwisting all the chains that tie
The hidden soul of harmony.

John Milton, "L'Allegro," 135–44

Plato has ended his consideration of poetry for instruction of the young. The literal statements of poetry, the most immediately perceived part, may indeed amuse fledgling minds.[1] But the first — and perhaps the only — response of the young to poetry is neither interpretation nor criticism, but acceptance.[2] Despite his insistence

[1] See Paul Shorey, *What Plato Said*, pp. 219–20.

[2] J. Tate distinguishes between the narrative (λόγος) and the principle (νόμος, τύπος, δόξα) expressed. He states that Plato does not attack myth for not having allegorical meanings, but just for propounding wrong principles. To defend poetry by citing a possible allegory is irrelevant, for understanding an allegory would not help a young mind already deeply mired in the influ-

that the wise man can generally see an object in its entirety, Plato makes an exception of poetry. Poetic discourse inevitably breaks into brief and separate *sententiae*. Plato never recognizes any relationship between the excerpt and other sections of the same work; these bits comment directly on life. And only the forearmed intellect can place the saying within the human context. While he does not allow the analysis of poetry to proceed deeper than its surface, he does approve certain noble exhortations. Thus, Plato's argument so far does not necessarily damn all poetry. He has discussed only elementary education, making the unobjectionable point that tender minds can be damaged by indiscriminate exposure to sensational materials.

But as Plato turns to consider the manner of poetry's presentation, he is concerned with the effect of habitual use of poetry. This chapter's epigraph from Milton shows how far apart the minds of the great philosophical poet and the great poetic philosopher really are. For the most part, Plato feels that poetry is dangerous to the stability of the soul. He does recognize that theoretically poetry can, like all skillful human creations, stimulate harmony in the soul; but any other artifact may serve equally well. Plato does not discuss here any period of transition from childhood to maturity, the time that poetry might be expected to reinforce the partly-aware intellect.[3] Instead, he shifts from the inculcation of excellence to the reinforcement of traits already established. He has considered the content (λόγων); now he will discuss the diction or manner (λέξεως). Any human action which violates decorum, the proper functioning

---

ence of the bad fictions. Although Plato does not condemn allegory, his allusions to the ignorance of poets suggest a skepticism concerning the existence of allegory ("Plato and Allegorical Interpretation," p. 146).

[3] The *Republic VII* 537 speaks of the transition from youth to maturity, but does not recognize any gradual acquisition of knowledge. R. Hackforth notices in this connection two tendencies in Greek thought. Virtue can consist either in manliness or in thought. "Now it is plain that the first of these two methods or attitudes is uppermost in *Rep.* ii–iv, the second in vi–vii. But where exactly is it that Plato passes from the one to the other, and why does he not indicate the transition explicitly?" ("The Modification of Plan in Plato's *Republic*," p. 267).

of man in society, stands condemned. Since the best of men, the Guardians, are simple and unchanging, the multiplicity and variation of poetry are condemned.

1

RESTRICTIONS ON THE PERFORMANCE OF POETRY

The beginning of Plato's discussion of the form of poetry could easily have led to a favorable statement. He approaches his subject by asking, "Any story in prose or verse is always a narrative of events, past, present, or future, isn't it?" (*Republic III* 392d). Although the event would take precedence over the narrative, Plato has opened the possibility of a temporal distance from the event. Presumably, the event could be represented as taking place in the remote past or future without commanding total absorption of the auditor's soul. But Plato treats all imaginative verbal discourse as occurring in the present.

Plato would have a work of the artistic imagination reproduce a concrete situation rather than a universal truth. The speaker sets forth and recreates the event; the interpretation of reality is beyond his powers. His presentation may be a dramatic representation (imitation) or simple narrative, or both together. The *Iliad* and *Odyssey* provide examples of all of these forms of storytelling. Where the poet is delivering a speech in character, he tries to make his manner resemble that of the person he has introduced as speaker. Any poet who does this by means of voice and gesture is telling his story by way of dramatic representation. On the other hand, if he makes no such attempt to suppress his own personality, the events are set forth in simple narrative. Plato shows no hesitation toward considering epic and drama together. Epic is the inclusive form; drama simply omits the intervening narrative and leaves only the dialogue. He feels that the drama endangers the soul especially, for the words of the speaker do not issue immediately from his own character.

At this point, Plato hints at the ultimate rejection of poetry in

Republic X.[4] Glaucon wonders whether we should admit the drama, tragedy and comedy, into our commonwealth. Socrates, however, wishes the option of extending the discussion: "the question may be wider still. I do not know yet; but we must go wherever the wind of the argument carries us" (*III* 394d). Here Plato is concerned with reinforcing the harmony and discipline of the soul. The *Laws* also states that the masses seldom make proper distinctions between serious and frivolous poets. People declare that "the youth who are rightly educated should be brought up in them and saturated with them; some insist that they should be constantly hearing them read aloud, and always learning them, so as to get by heart entire poets; while others select choice passages and long speeches, and make compendiums of them, saying that these ought to be committed to memory, if a man is to be made good and wise by experience and learning of many things" (*VII* 810e–11a).[5] *Republic III* shows the Guardians participating actively in rendering poetry for their own amusement and edification. *Republic X* discusses the passive response of society at large. Neither section considers the possibility of a personal, intelligent hearing of poetry. The Guardians become rhapsodes and assume the character of their portrayal; lesser men are either deceived or maddened.[6]

---

[4] F. M. Cornford feels that the *Republic* has sufficient unity to support his thesis that Plato adapted his psychology of the tripartite soul to his predetermined concept of society ("Psychology and Social Structure in the *Republic* of Plato, pp. 246–65). Hackforth answers his argument by analyzing some disparities in Plato's psychology: "When the psychological scheme comes to be formulated [in iv], what we get is the original scheme [in ii] accommodated to the new outlook, and so Plato is unconsciously involved in a *cross-classification* of temperamental tendencies and psychological faculties ("Modification of Plan," p. 271).

[5] Seconding Plato, Xenophon in his *Symposium III* 5 and *IV* 6 speaks of Niceratus, who was forced to learn the complete works of Homer in order that he might become a good man. In the earlier part of the *Republic*, Plato is still unsure of the extent to which he would modify traditional attitudes toward art.

[6] J. Tate, in "Plato and Allegorical Interpretation," suggests that Plato's theory of poetic criticism parallels his doctrine of inspiration: "How can we become certain that we have the correct interpretation of such passages?

A consideration of dramatic representation calls immediately to Plato's mind his principle of division of labor. The attack on poetry's usefulness in the *Ion* depends on this argument. Each man, being restricted by his finite amount of knowledge, must work in the particular role he best fits. The effectiveness of these rational patterns of work leads to Plato's deep concern with habit, the effects of accustomed action. As in the *Ion*, no ordinary man has a faculty for the disinterested interpretation of poetry. Either one calmly analyzes the words philosophically, or one frantically responds by complete participation in the action. Plato's earlier discussion had the nurses handing moral tags to children. He now shows responsible men and their performance of poetry. The Guardians themselves will recite the words of whatever poetry is allowed. Complex and profound poetry has already been found inadequate to teach morality to the young; rigorous censorship, however, may unearth some useful exempla. But the influence of poetry on mature men deserves far greater attention. Plato puts the question to Adeimantus: "Do we want our Guardians to be capable of playing many parts? Perhaps the answer follows from our earlier principle that a man can only do one thing well. If he tries his hand at several, he will fail to make his mark in any of them. Does not that principle apply to acting? The same man cannot act many parts so well as he can act one" (*III* 394e). Each of the rulers of the state, then, must play one role well; he becomes identified wholly with that part. Skill in other roles would detract from ability in the one designated for him.

The *Republic* suggests that any action not directly bearing upon one's political function makes the person less valuable to the state.[7]

According to Plato we cannot attain much certainty; for just as the poets followed no rational process in composing, so the interpreters also must work by inspiration, not by reasoning from general principle" (p. 150).

[7] Plato's rejection of the morality traditionally ascribed to the gods influences his attitude toward arts and pleasure. T. B. L. Webster, in "Greek Theories of Art and Literature Down to 400 B.C.," observes "To those later writers art and poetry, if they are meant to please, are only a luxury. Earlier, however, when it was assumed that the pleasures of the gods were the same

Since the welfare of the individual and that of the state are identical, a man has no need to assert his individuality.[8] There are no moments of self-exaltation; the just man at all times completely fulfills his social responsibility. Creating poetry and playing a role have nonrationality in common. Just as the actual creation of poetry involves a loss of identity, playing a role calls into question the integrity of the actor's soul. Moreover, the presentation of a variety of persons intensifies the confusion. This total commitment to one's occupation leaves neither time nor place for the vulgar projection of multiplicity: "The just man will hardly be able to pursue some worthy occupation and at the same time represent a variety of different characters. Even in the case of two forms of representation so closely allied as tragedy and comedy, the same poet cannot do both with equal success. Again, the recitation of epic poetry and acting on the stage are distinct professions; and even on the stage different actors perform in tragedy and comedy" (*III* 395a). In the *Symposium* Socrates argues that theoretically poets should be able to write both tragedy and comedy.[9] However, he gives no examples of a poet doing both. And here in the *Republic*, Plato states that virtually no poet seems able to do so. He does admit that there are distinctions between epic and drama as well as between tragedy and comedy, but the differences are apparently so slight that later he disregards them.

Damning with exaggerated praise, Plato states that the arts call for an almost superhuman range of talent. The world of art and the world of man impose identical standards on success: the limits of one's ability must be unambiguously established. The categories of poet, rhapsode, comic and tragic actors are far too formless for

---

as the pleasures of men, these luxuries were of extreme importance, since the goodwill of the gods must be secured" (p. 172). Beauty, then, pleased the gods as much as it pleased man. The early Greeks managed a perfect union of *dolce* and *utile*.

[8] An excellent statement of the relationship between individual and society in the dialogues may be found in John Wild's *Plato's Theory of Man*, pp. 132–73.

[9] See John Warry, *Greek Aesthetic Theory*, pp. 59–60.

Plato's taste. The *Ion* has already shown that Plato can ascertain no clear distinction between poet and rhapsode. And since human talent possesses less range of versatility than does artistic talent, knowledge of one's limitations is even more important. "No man can successfully represent many different characters in the field of art or pursue a corresponding variety of occupations in real life" (*III* 395b). The worlds of life and art are thus parallel and separate. Dramatic presentation reproduces life on a higher, but non-human, plane.

Only the Guardians — those citizens eminent in knowledge — are not completely bounded by their craft. The lives of these people take definition from their total commitment to the needs of the state. Plato separates the lesser crafts from the real creation — the establishment and maintenance of the state. "If we are to hold fast to our original principle that our Guardians shall be set free from all manual crafts to be the artificers of their country's freedom, with the perfect mastery which comes of working only at what conduces to that end, they ought not to play any other part in dramatic representation any more than in real life" (*III* 395bc). Any representations by the people would hardly be acting, for they should play only characters like themselves.

> But if they act, they should, from childhood upward, impersonate only the appropriate types of character, men who are brave, religious, self-controlled, generous. They are not to do anything mean or dishonorable; no more should they be practiced in representing such behavior, for fear of becoming infected with the reality. You must have noticed how the reproduction of another person's gestures or tones of voice or states of mind, if persisted in from youth up, grows into a habit which becomes second nature. [*III* 395cd]

The Guardians work solely for the good of the state; actions not directly related to this end can only detract from the ruler's purpose. The portrayal of various characters has a powerful and direct influence on the actor, setting up a dangerous osmosis between the feigned and the real. Even momentary deviations from the lofty principles of the state may become habitual.

Throughout the dialogues, attention to poetry inescapably involves the individual's participation in recreating actions. The typical response is a total commitment at that moment. Again in the *Republic* Plato attempts to circumscribe the province of poetry, for an unlimited range of subjects and treatments would render poetry useless for education. Since the Guardians must not deviate from their attention to state affairs, poetry can, at best, merely reinforce their determination. Although he allows the Guardians to portray only characters as noble as themselves, Plato does not show how even this limited representation could be useful. Here he reverses his usual sharp distinction between art and nature; the art of the Guardians comes as close as possible to their true nature. They reinforce their own understanding rather than seek further experience. But certainly these good actions should persist from youth onward, thus presumably progressing from external copying to internal nature. While Plato seems to admit that theoretically drama might be useful in the discipline of the Guardians, he later explicitly states that practically the drama does not lend itself to portraying the temperate man.

Plato is more clear about what the Guardians should not imitate than he is about what they should. He lists base human actions as unfit for the dignified rulers. While his prescriptions eliminate a good deal of what we would call great art, his rules would prohibit much vulgarity and sensationalism. Transvestism is certainly prohibited. The Guardians will not be allowed to play either violent or peaceful roles of women. Petty railing against one's husband, or impious boasting to the gods would provide poor models for both sexes. Representation of women's misfortunes are now forbidden as were those of gods and heroes earlier. Mundane feminine experiences such as those of love, sickness, or labor offer no direct edification for noble and austere men. Likewise, slaves of either sex going about their menial work are unfit matter for portrayal. Also forbidden are "men of a low type, behaving with cowardice and all the qualities contrary to those we mentioned, deriding one another and exchanging coarse abuse, whether drunk or sober, and otherwise using language and behavior that are an offense against themselves as well as their neighbors; nor must they copy the words and actions of madmen" (*III* 395e–96a). We would hate to lose Othello overwhelmed with passion and Lear mad, but few of us would object to being spared the sight of the austere Guardians playing as women in love. Thus, Plato's list includes mostly trivial or vulgar actions.

Knowledge or understanding lies outside the action, never within. The Guardians must be aware of all evils. "Knowledge they must have of baseness and insanity both in men and women, but not reproduce such behavior in life or in art" (*III* 396a). Awareness of evil helps a person to avoid it. The *Laws* states, "It is necessary also to consider and know uncomely persons and thoughts, and those which are intended to produce laughter in comedy, and have a comic character in respect of style, song, and dance, and of the imitations which these afford. For serious things cannot be understood without laughable things, nor opposites at all without opposites, if a man is really to have intelligence of either" (*VII* 816d). Participation endangers the focus of the soul. To copy baseness either seriously or in jest requires undue attention to dangerous matters. Some areas of human experience are closed to the rulers, for they must have vision beyond the particular human condition. Inferior imitation always causes Plato to refer to men working at specific tasks as poor examples for imitation. Art can present only the externals of behavior and work. The Guardians should not impersonate craftsmen such as smiths or rowers at work. Glaucon suggests that perhaps "they are not even to take any notice of such occupations" (*III* 396b).

The *Laws* suggests that the rulers might have some casual knowledge of inferior matters in order to avoid falling inadvertently into some ridiculous or out-of-place action. The leader "should command slaves and hired strangers to imitate such things, but he should never take any serious interest in them himself, nor should any freeman or freewoman be discovered taking pains to learn them; and there should always be some element of novelty in the imitation (*VII* 816e). Innovation in grotesque or low representations presumably helps insure some small advance beyond rote

memorization. Effective rhetoric does depend on understanding of
all sorts of people: "Unless the aspirant to oratory can on the one
hand list the various natures amongst his prospective audiences, and
on the other divide things into their kinds and embrace each individual thing under a single form, he will never attain such success
as is within the grasp of mankind" (*Phaedrus* 273de). Only hard
work can give the speaker this ability. The wise man makes such
an effort to please the gods, not his fellow man.

Some men will say anything or make inhuman noises without
discretion; others show more respect for decorum. Dramatic rendering should interrupt narrative only when the speech will produce
little discord with the innate character of the man speaking.

> When the sensible man comes in his narrative to some speech
> or deed of a good man, he will be willing to report it as though
> he himself were that man, not being ashamed of such an imita-
> tion. He will imitate the good man most when he acts steadily
> and sensibly; less, and less willingly, when he is upset by diseases,
> love, drink, or some other misfortune. But when he comes to
> someone unworthy of himself, he will not be willing seriously to
> represent himself as an inferior, except on the few occasions
> when the man does something good. Instead, he will be em-
> barrassed both because he is unpracticed at imitating such men
> and because he is repelled by molding himself and fitting himself
> into the models of worse men. In his mind he despises them,
> unless it is done in play. [*III* 396cde]

A noble man can consciously assume a protective restraint when
presenting low characters; this understanding will prevent his form-
ing dangerous habits. The more vulgar the man, the more likely he
is to say anything or to make any physical sounds. This latter sort
of man's "whole style will be based on imitation of voice and
appearance or else includes only a bit of narrative" (*III* 397b).
The *Republic X* will later emphasize that dramatic presentation
always copies the external and the physical.

According to Plato, the amount of variation determines the
effect on character. A simple presentation reinforces the unity of
one's soul. The good dramatic role would involve little change and

variety. Only the slightest modulation is necessary when the words have been fitted to a suitable musical mode and rhythm. The recitation can keep almost to the same mode and rhythm throughout. The other form of presentation has no harmony or order, and thus introduces confusion and triviality. All sorts of variation mindlessly involve diverse modes and rhythms. This formless complexity has no value at all, and noble men should avoid it altogether. Between the simple and the complex lies a middle style which common people, children, and nurses will probably like best. But men of distinction prefer the simple mode which represents a fine character.

By reflecting a manifold humanity, poetry encourages disharmony in the new state. No man in the commonwealth can have more than one identity or perform many trades well. Each man should fulfill his specific function in the state, for from this duty come order and individual accomplishment. Poetry encourages looking at other people, other professions, and to have one's attention so divided — even in play — simply dissipates one's energies. Poets are not so much idle entertainers as outright frauds:

> Suppose that an individual clever enough to assume any character and give imitations of anything and everything should visit our country and offer to perform his compositions, we shall bow down before a being with such miraculous powers of giving pleasure. But we shall tell him that we are not allowed to have any such person in our commonwealth; we shall crown him with fillets of wool, anoint his head with myrrh, and conduct him to the borders of some other country. For our own benefit, we shall employ the poets and story-tellers of the more austere and less attractive type, who will reproduce only the manner of a person of high character and, in the substance of their discourse, conform to those rules we laid down when we began the education of our warriors. [*III* 398ab]

Poetry of course gives pleasure, but Plato says here, as in *Republic X*, that we must not on that account admit all poets into our state.

Plato envisages a similar discourse between philosophers and poets in the *Laws*. He scorns the pretensions of tragedians who present inferior options to the laws established by reason. Even the serious poets must ask permission to enter the city. The rulers' answer should be, "Best of strangers, . . . we also according to our ability are tragic poets, and our tragedy is the best and noblest; for our whole state is an imitation of the best and noblest life, which we affirm to be indeed the very truth of tragedy. You are poets and we are poets, both makers of the same strains, rivals and antagonists in the noblest of dramas, which true law can alone perfect, as our hope is" (*VII* 817b). Life itself has all the excitement of drama; the rulers' disciplined imaginations alone can penetrate to the high seriousness of human intercourse.

Songs of the softer poets must conform to the noble standards of the city. Purely poetic language may improperly compete with the dicta of the rulers, who must therefore tell the poets:

> Do not then suppose that we shall all in a moment allow you to erect your stage in the agora, or introduce the fair voices of your actors, speaking above our own, and permit you to harangue our women, children, and common people, about our institutions in language other than our own, and very often the opposite of our own. For a state would be mad which gave you this license, until the magistrates had determined whether your poetry might be recited, and was fit for publication or not. Wherefore, O ye sons and scions of the softer Muses, first of all show your songs to the magistrates, and let them compare them with our own, and if they are the same or better we will give you a chorus; but if not, then, my friends, we cannot. [*VII* 817abcd]

Plato feels that inferior poets are especially likely to exaggerate their own worth (cf. *Phaedrus* 268–69).

The dramatic presentation of poetry sets up models for conduct. For Plato, poetry exists only within a social framework, asserting itself in a public function.

Whether acting or dramatically reciting, the performer must imitate good examples, saying things the Guardians themselves might speak in ordinary discourse. And, indeed, Plato makes no distinction between good poets and Guardians. Both artist and ruler should be engaged in the creation/representation of the just and self-contained man. Since the Guardians are the pinnacle of humanity, art and nature combine to make them the true poets of the state.[10] Plato knows the serious portrayal of virtuous men to be more austere and less interesting to the masses than current art, but then philosophy has never seemed attractive to the uninitiated. Since order and harmony in life are the avowed goals, Plato banishes dramatic confrontation or conflict in art. Drama consists of separate presentations by individuals. The audience receives no consideration at this point, but Plato has discussed the educational value of poetry earlier. The ruler's proper involvement in the drama is limited to calm portrayals of nobility. The *Republic* will admit austere poets who are superficially indistinguishable in function from the Guardians.

2

THE EFFECT OF MUSIC

Plato's comments on music follow logically from his discussion of poetry. All lyric poetry should be set to music, and all song should have a verbal component. The *Timaeus* agrees with the *Republic* that music may stimulate harmony in the soul:

So much of music as is adapted to the sound of the voice and to the sense of hearing is granted to us for the sake of harmony; and harmony, which has motions akin to the revolutions of our souls, is not regarded by the intelligent votary of the Muses as given by them with a view to irrational pleasure, which is deemed to be the purpose of it in our day, but as meant to correct any discord which may have arisen in the courses of the soul, and to be our ally in bringing her into harmony and agreement with herself; and rhythm too was given by them for the same reason, on account of the irregular and graceless ways which prevail among mankind generally, and to help us against them. [47cde]

[10] The rulers of all good states must have a more precise knowledge of excellence in both speech and action. The city will take its character from the abilities of the leaders (*Laws XII* 964d).

Song consists of three elements: words, musical or harmonious mode, and rhythm. The words must conform to the rules already made for the content and form of poetry. Since the other two components depend on language, Plato can judge music for its rational content likewise. Dirges and laments have already been considered unfit subjects for poetry. Now the musical counterparts, sorrowful modes like the Mixed Lydian and Hyperlydian, are similarly deemed unsuitable.[11] Soft, slack modes such as the Ionian and some of the Lydian flourish at drinking parties. These decadent forms give amusement rather than encourage discipline.

On the other hand, two modes, the Dorian and the Phrygian, can inculcate the virtues Plato admires. While claiming no great authority concerning any of these modes, he suggests that the Phrygian can fittingly represent the tones and accents of a brave man either in war or in hard and dangerous tasks.[12] This mode can profitably show the courageous man about to be defeated or facing wounds and death, for he will endure all the blows of fortune. The accents of courage in adversity would doubtless instruct the young. So, impassioned scenes can be suggested where the immediate didacticism precludes any misinterpretation. But although Plato seems to admit didactic musical modes, he places almost impossible conditions on the art. Since dramatic conflict has been ruled out, the Guardians must speak or sing in their own persons. So while Plato accepts the representations of noble men facing peril and

[11] J. F. Mountford, in "The Musical Scales of Plato's *Republic*," states that "There is reliable evidence for the actual musical scales to which Plato makes reference. They were of a semi-primitive nature, and lacked that homogeneity which a fully developed musical system would show. They differed from each other by the varying sequence of the larger and smaller intervals of which they were composed. The extant list of scales shows them in the enharmonic form, but parallel chromatic and diatonic forms may be conjectured, and in one instance demonstrated. Finally, the precise intonation of the scales can be reconstructed with the aid of the musical rations of Archytas" (p. 136). See also Richard L. Crocker, "Pythagorean Mathematics and Music," pp. 189–98, 325–35, and Warren D. Anderson, *Ethos and Education in Greek Music*, pp. 64–110.

[12] Satirists must not write in anger against their fellow citizens, but some innocent humor may be beneficial (*Laws XI* 935–36).

death, he rejects the accompanying agony which would make the portrayal convincing. Thus, paradoxically, a good man can portray gods and men suffering nobly, but he must not show any undeserved suffering. He must clearly and unambiguously present a real conflict, yet show complete mastery on the part of the noble protagonist.

While one can hardly imitate the sounds and accents of a courageous man in battle within the bounds of restrained narration, Plato is correct in thinking that the Dorian mode could successfully imitate the temperate man. This mode will "express peaceful action under no stress of hard necessity; as when a man is using persuasion or entreaty, praying to the gods or instructing and admonishing his neighbor, or again submitting himself to the instruction and persuasion of others; a man who is not overbearing when any such action has proved successful, but behaves always with wise restraint and is content with the outcome" (*III* 399b). Restraint and submission could be presented without introducing the violent antagonism which would make warfare unacceptable on the stage. Here, as in *Republic X* Plato knows that moderate actions do not make exciting drama, but he is willing to make this sacrifice.

Plato has been purging the commonwealth of the luxurious excess described earlier in the dialogue. Craftsmen who cater to the undisciplined whims of the masses will be eliminated from the orderly state. Even musical instruments will be simplified; the range of the flute makes it particularly dangerous. Such instruments of large compass can modulate into unauthorized modes. Townspeople can use the lyre and the cithara; the herdsmen may have some sort of pipe. Plato implies that music is engrained in the habits of men. These simple pleasures all presumably promote order rather than encourage the decadent innovations Plato feels prevalent in contemporary art.

The rules of rhythm, like those of harmony, follow from Plato's antipathy toward artistic subtleties and variety. Just as the modes should be simple and the instruments have limited range, the rhythms should suggest order and regularity. Subtlety and variety of meter will be unnecessary, for the rhythms need only evoke a life of courage and self-control. Once these rhythms have been deter-

mined, meter and melody will follow from the words expressing a
life of that sort. Plato feels that the word is primary in the performance, so that speech must not be adapted to the meter and
melody. Glaucon must explain which rhythms are useful just as
earlier he had to establish the modes. Plato is concerned with principles, not with actual designation of the preferred forms. Certainly,
rhythms which express meanness, insolence, frenzy, must be omitted, and their opposites retained. But Plato admits that he has not
thought the subject through, and he disclaims any interest in pursuing the matter. Instead, he will leave the technical matters to
Damon, a famous musician, a friend of Pericles.[13]

3

Harmony and the Crafts

Plato has dealt so far with the art of poetry and its musical
accompaniment. Now he will expand his argument to include all
beautiful and useful works of man. Skillful craftsmanship can be
harmonious in the same sense as any formal art. Grace and decorum
in form and movement naturally accompany good rhythm; ugliness
and unseemliness go with bad. The rhythm and tunefulness can
suit the quality of the speech. But as before, the Logos is primary;
meter and music must be adapted to the sense of the words. Beauty
in art comes from its depiction of noble character. From the
Charmides on, Plato has argued that the soul finds expression in
outward appearance.[14] Socrates suggests in *Republic III* 403d that
"a sound and healthy body is enough to produce a sound mind;
while, on the contrary, the sound mind has power in itself to make
the bodily condition as perfect as it can be." Similarly, the content
of the poetry and the manner of its presentation follow from a

---

[13] Other references to Damon may be found in *Laches* 200 and *Alcibiades I* 118.

[14] See *Republic V* 462–64 and *Timaeus* 87. G. M. A. Grube, in "Plato's
Theory of Beauty," speaks of this sympathy between body and soul (pp.
274–75).

quality of the soul. "Excellence of form and content in discourse [ἐυλογία] and of musical expression and rhythm, all depend on goodness of nature, by which I mean, not the foolish simplicity sometimes called by courtesy 'good nature,' but a nature in which goodness of character has been well and truly established" (*III* 400de). The character of the poet, then, precedes both form and content of poetry.

The words and rhythms of art cannot be separated from the man who uses them. Knowledge invariably leads to skill in the arts, especially rhetoric. The *Phaedrus* states:

> All the great arts need supplementing by a study of Nature: your artist must cultivate garrulity and high-flown speculation; from that source alone can come the mental elevation and thoroughly finished execution of which you are thinking; and that is what Pericles acquired to supplement his inborn capacity. He came across the right sort of man, I fancy, in Anaxagoras, and by enriching himself with high speculation and coming to recognize the nature of wisdom and folly — on which topics of course Anaxagoras was always discoursing — he drew from that source and applied to the art of rhetoric what was suitable thereto. [269e–70a]

Artistic language does not exist in isolation, for poetry lives only in the concrete performance created and delivered simultaneously by the poet-actor. In refusing to grant poetry any existence apart from immediate human uses, Plato must be particularly rigorous in legislating its specific ethical role. Every poem directly addresses human knowledge or human desires. The effect, then, is both immediate and particular. Since the poem exists only in the performance, one must respond immediately or not at all.

Plato applies the same rules to art that he does to any human making. Art can include all that man does. Beauty is to be found in all crafts such as painting, weaving, embroidering, building, and the making of furniture. The human frame and all the works of nature likewise may have this grace and decorum. The usual artistic criteria of grace, rhythm, and harmony apply to thought and expression as well as to human character. Man responds so immediately to his surroundings that disharmony in nature encourages ugliness in speech and disposition. Good art, on the other hand, depends on goodness of character, a quality which may exist in man or in nature anywhere. The purification of poetry is the natural outcome of improving man and the state. The Guardians must constantly seek this goodness (*III* 400), yet earlier Plato has specifically forbidden them to "impersonate men working at some trade, such as a smith's, or rowing a galley or giving the time to the oarsmen" (*III* 395). The Guardians will profit from observing the goodness in the workmanship, but they would violate their proper role if they were to indulge in the idle pretense of reproducing the craft.

Plato would allow intelligent supervision to encourage the creation of good poetry as well as good craftsmanship in any art. The ignorant self-indulgence of artists makes such direction necessary. Images of both human vice and natural disharmony are undesirable. Since the commonwealth is to be free of imperfections, crafts reflecting the old corrupt order will be forbidden. Plato associates poetry with the myriad forms of unimproved humanity; poetry about recognizable human subjects hardly fits into a simplified and purified state. Because even the rulers can feel improper temptations, the environment should be as safe as possible. "We must not only compel our poets, on pain of expulsion, to make their poetry the express image of noble character; we must also supervise craftsmen of every kind and forbid them to leave the stamp of baseness, license, meanness, unseemliness, on painting and sculpture, or buildings, or any other work of their hands; and anyone who cannot obey shall not practice his art in our commonwealth" (*III* 401b). The *Laws* affirms that poetry cannot legitimately circulate among individuals. The Athenian asks, "Shall we make a law that the poet shall compose nothing contrary to the ideas of the lawful, or just, or beautiful, or good, which are allowed in the state? nor shall he be permitted to communicate his compositions to any private individuals, until he shall have shown them to the appointed judges and the guardians of the law, and they are satisfied with them" (*VII* 801cd). All craftsmen have the ability to create moral art. Ugly sculptures and buildings represent moral deformity rather than aesthetic disharmony. Thus the products of all these craftsmen must serve the citizens as moral examples.

For Plato a great deal of the long-term influence of art is unconscious. Everywhere he speaks of the power of habit; apparently the Guardians have no more mechanism for rejecting the accumulation of disharmonious sensations than any other citizens. "We would not have our Guardians grow up among representations of moral deformity, as in some foul pasture where, day after day, feeding on every poisonous weed they would, little by little, gather insensibly a mass of corruption in their very souls" (*III* 401bc). The will of the rulers grows out of traits begun in youth and continued into their maturity. This faculty should be strengthened only in moderate exercises, for health depends on the clear supremacy of the reason. Sensations gradually gather in the soul, bypassing the rational part. Internal harmony can be maintained only with great difficulty when the environment presents ugly discords.

The healthy state will employ noble craftsmen whose natural instinct leads them to make graceful objects. Plato admits in the *Phaedrus* a variation in artists' skills. A tragedian must have the knowledge to make a harmonious whole from the individual parts of his craft. "Now suppose someone went up to Sophocles or Euripides and said he knew how to compose lengthy dramatic speeches about a trifling matter, and quite short ones about a matter of moment; that he could write pathetic passages when he chose, or again passages of intimidation and menace, and so forth; and that he considered that by teaching these accomplishments he could turn a pupil into a tragic poet" (268cd). The real dramatists would laugh at a man who took such a simple view.

In both the *Laws* and the *Republic*, these creators are primarily men of good natural endowments and only secondarily artists. Stressing the character of the poet, the *Laws* holds that noble men alone should make poems even though others may have more musical talent.

> The magistrates should distribute prizes of victory and valor to the competitors, passing censures and encomiums on one another according to the characters which they bear in the contests and

in their whole life, honoring him who seems to be the best, and blaming him who is the opposite. And let poets celebrate the victors, — not however every poet, but only one who in the first place is not less than fifty years of age; nor should he be one who, although he may have musical and poetical gifts, has never in his life done any noble or illustrious action; but those who are themselves good and also honorable in the state, creators of noble actions — let their poems be sung, even though they be not very musical. And let the judgment of them rest with the instructor of youth and the other guardians of the laws, who shall give them this privilege, and they alone shall be free to sing; but the rest of the world shall not have this liberty.

[*VIII* 829cd]

The guardians of the laws should prohibit even songs sweeter than those of Thamyras and Orpheus unless two conditions have been met. First, the poems must have been judged sacred and dedicated to the gods, and second, the works must proceed from good men according to the appropriate design.

If the intention of the artist is formed by harmony and knowledge, the created work will inevitably be good. Unfortunately, most poets lack sufficient knowledge. The Athenian asks, "And what has it been the object of our argument to show? Did we not imply that the poets are not always quite capable of knowing what is good or evil? And if one of them utters a mistaken prayer in song or word, he will make our citizens pray for the opposite of what is good in matters of the highest import; than which, as I was saying, there can be fewer greater mistakes" (*Laws VII* 801bc). The commonwealth strives to perpetuate the harmony which permeates all areas of men's endeavor. Representations of evil are unnecessary to appreciation of the good. If all the workmen have done their job properly, "our young men, dwelling in a wholesome climate, may drink in good from every quarter, whence like a breeze bearing health from happy regions, some influence from noble works constantly falls upon eye and ear from childhood upward, and imperceptibly draws them into sympathy and harmony with the beauty of reason, whose impress they take" (*III* 401cd). Both directly and indirectly, the entire state constantly encourages harmony in the soul.

Plato asserts that viewing harmonious physical objects will have an enduring beneficial effect on the citizens. By inference, the artistic moment is too brief and fleeting to do more than agitate the soul. Plato goes from intention to effect without really looking at the intermediary; the products of either artist or craftsman are subordinate to the larger concerns. The didactic effects are imperceptible and not susceptible to conscious control. Plato here speaks in terms of the continuing influence of beauty in general; in *Republic X* he will consider the immediate influence of poetry and painting in particular. In education the response to art is passive and irrational; Plato does not mention a specific point at which a man can move from accepting as instruction to criticizing as object. The performing arts stimulate the senses of vision and hearing rather than the mind.

Because of their immediate and powerful effect, noble rhythms and harmony in general are integral to education.[15] Well-educated men will recognize ugliness only as the negative of what they have been taught. Musical training with its combining of word and song has a decisive importance because:

> rhythm and harmony sink deep into the recesses of the soul and take the strongest hold there, bringing that grace of body and mind which is only to be found in one who is brought up in the right way. Moreover, a proper training of this kind makes a man quick to perceive any defect or ugliness in art or in nature. Such deformity will rightly disgust him. Approving all that is lovely, he will welcome it home with joy into his soul and, nourished thereby, grow into a man of noble spirit. All that is ugly and disgraceful he will rightly condemn and abhor while he is still too young to understand reasonable speech; and when reasonable speech comes, he will greet her as a friend with whom his education has made him long familiar. [*III* 401d–2a]

---

[15] The *Laws* goes so far as to suggest that the festivals of the Muses and of their leader, Apollo, were created by the gods to aid in man's education (*II* 653). Indeed, the first education known came from the Muses (*II* 654). But poetry can by no means be the sole instrument in education (*Laws VII* 810–11).

A man need not respond actively to the influences about him, for rhythm and harmony can grasp the soul without its cooperation. The rational part develops later in the process of education, so at first, harmony goes immediately into the innermost part of the soul.

Lacking exposure to ugliness at any time, the child will be led to perceive goodness without any hindrance. The youth should be kept from those who advocate relativism in law and authority. The Athenian cites some false materialistic arguments which are "the sayings of wise men, poets and prose writers, which find a way into the minds of youth. They are told by them that the highest right is might, and in this way the young fall into impieties, under the idea that the gods are not such as the law bids them imagine; and hence arise factions, these philosophers inviting them to lead a true life according to nature, that is, to live in real dominion over others, and not in legal subjection to them" (*Laws X* 890a). The reasonable order of the environment, on the other hand, encourages the natural advent of reason within the man.

The true appreciation of beauty requires a discipline akin to the intellectual acquisition of reading. The *Republic*, like the *Statesman* 278, would have a child first recognize the essential similarities of letters in all words — simplicity among seeming multiplicity. Even the most insignificant letter needs to be carefully distinguished. Knowledge of the reality of the letters precedes the recognition of their images. The same study in learning the letters applies to perceiving any truly beautiful object. As in learning to read, "we and these Guardians we are to bring up will never be fully cultivated until we can recognize the essential Forms of temperance, courage, liberality, high-mindedness, and all other kindred qualities, and also their opposites, wherever they occur. We must be able to discern the presence of these Forms themselves and also of their images in anything that contains them, realizing that, to recognize either, the same skill and practice are required, and that the most insignificant instance is not beneath our notice" (*III* 402bc). This attention to detail provides a solid basis for more general understanding.

But Plato does not explain how a man can notice all these insignificant instances while maintaining his ability to generalize.

All good and true forms belong to one art and discipline.[16] The educated man must have a wide perception of both the reality and its temporary embodiment.[17] Nevertheless, Plato does not describe a faculty of discretion for knowing yet rejecting evil. The Guardians may encompass isolated examples of evil in their broad awareness, but their perceptions automatically maintain a rational distancing. Since evil and ignorance are intimately linked in Plato's mind, he might argue that *knowledge* of evil is impossible. But certainly, intimate knowledge of such evil would make the individuals worse than the state around them.

Plato associates this sensitivity to environmental beauty with openness to human love. The inward beauty of the soul can find its suitable counterpart in both artifacts and other humans.[18] Human relationships find a solid foundation in perception of a more universal harmony. Once a good disposition has been established in the soul, the individual can find the highest pleasure in contemplating other noble characters of the same sort. Because beauty springs from internal harmony, the fairest is also the most worthy of being loved. "So the man who has been educated in poetry and music [μουσικός] will be in love with such a person, but never with one

---

[16] Monroe Beardsley, in *Aesthetics from Classical Greece to the Present*, discusses Plato's theory of one beauty in all concrete beautiful things. He cites the *Symposium* 210, *Republic* 476, 479, *Phaedo* 65, 75, 78, and the *Phaedrus* 250 in this connection (p. 39).

[17] A more comprehensive discussion of the Forms may be found in *Republic V* 474–80. This doctrine forms a major part of the attack on poetry in *Republic X*. Among the many commentaries on the Forms, one might examine J. A. Stewart, *Plato's Doctrine of Ideas*, pp. 1–197; G. M. A. Grube, *Plato's Thought*, pp. 1–50; Robert S. Brumbaugh, *Plato for the Modern Age*, pp. 92–112, 142–50; Paul Friedländer, *Plato: An Introduction*, pp. 13–31, 59–84; and Arthur L. Peck, "Plato Versus Parmenides," pp. 159–84.

[18] John Warry cogently observes, "Both Plato and ancient Greek thought in general closely associated Beauty, in its objective as in its subjective aspect, with a sense of harmony which pervaded Nature, provided the basis of all art and skill, was requisite in all happy human and social relationships, and, as Socrates pointed out, was the sole principle by which man might hope to bridge the gap between the human and the divine" (*Greek Aesthetic Theory*, p. 46). See also G. M. A. Grube, "Plato's Theory of Beauty," pp. 269–88.

who lacks this harmony" (*III* 402d). Only careful education can train the individual to look past outward deformity to see another's admirable inner harmony. Human beings, then, may possess the sort of physical ugliness not permitted elsewhere in the commonwealth. Rigorous instruction in poetry and music will prepare the individual to resist superficial and dangerously undisciplined physical love.

One's enjoyment of art cannot be differentiated from his response to *any* physical situation. The harmony of sound and sense provides an essential discipline in all areas for both unformed and mature minds. The instruction inevitably contained in poetry and music especially promotes order in the soul concerning matters of love. But the individual must not over-respond to any manifestations of harmony outside himself. Excessive pleasure is incompatible with temperance, for pleasure unsettles the mind as much as does pain. Rather than encouraging virtue, pleasure leads to insolence and licentiousness. In particular, the pleasure in sex is akin to frenzy; this pleasure is the greatest and keenest of all, "Whereas love rightfully is such a passion as beauty combined with a noble and harmonious character may inspire in a temperate and cultivated mind. It must therefore be kept from all contact with licentiousness and frenzy; and where a passion of this rightful sort exists, the lover and his beloved must have nothing to do with the pleasure in question" (*III* 403b). True and moderate love does not tax the order and purpose of the intelligent individual. There is a creative interplay of the passion and the individual soul. This love can be as real and almost as noble as the divine madness of the *Phaedrus* and the *Symposium*. On the other hand, frenzied passion, or human madness, conflicts with the ennobling passion which arises when a harmonious mind sees and responds to beauty in another.

A final requirement for a true relationship demands that the passion benefit both parties. A lover must act at all times in a manner which will instruct his beloved. Seeking pleasure for its own sake testifies to disharmony in the lover: "It appears that in this commonwealth we are founding you will have a law to the effect that a lover may seek the company of his beloved and, with his consent, may kiss and embrace him like a son, with honorable intent, but must never be suspected of any further familiarity, on pain of being thought ill-bred and without any delicacy of feeling" (*III* 403). Thus, Plato's analysis of the role of poetry and music in the state concludes with a discussion of love. He asserts the relevance of these comments on human relations to art. The account of education in poetry and music "has ended where it ought to end, in the love of beauty" (*III* 403). Thus the beauty of art finds its direct counterpart in the beauty of personal relationships. Both forms of beauty exert such an immediate and powerful attraction that only an extended, unambiguous grounding in harmony can keep the soul from being overwhelmed. Having broken down the traditional distinction between the fine arts and the useful arts, Plato has suggested a legitimate, if limited, role for poetry and music in the state. Noble art may, under the proper conditions, teach discrimination and knowledge of excellence.[19]

The next chapter, however, will show that Plato ultimately denies poetry the ability to instruct or to amuse men properly. These earlier books have admitted the use of certain purified sayings, excerpts of immediate didactic value. The young may profitably hear accounts of virtue, and the Guardians are permitted to narrate the deeds of noble men like themselves. Plato encourages harmony in all crafts, including those of poetry and music. So far he has examined the value of selections of noble and divine poetry as models for instruction. But when in *Republic X* he examines the causes and effects of poetry, such as that of Homer, Plato states that he has previously banished all mimetic poetry. Moreover, he extends his definition of the mimetic to include all poetry. He then justifies his condemnation of art by challenging the intellectual and emotional value of poetry. His analogies may not represent his most logical thought, but his vigor and sincerity cannot be legitimately doubted.

---

[19] Plato speaks of higher education in *Republic VI* 509–*VII* 541.

V

Republic X

on

Artistic Imitation

> Do not all charms fly
> At the mere touch of cold philosophy?
> There was an awful rainbow once in heaven:
> We know her woof, her texture; she is given
> In the dull catalogue of common things.
> Philosophy will clip an Angel's wings.
>
> John Keats, *Lamia*, 29–34

> There is a long-standing quarrel between poetry and philosophy.
>
> Plato, *Republic X* 607b

> But now indeede my burthen is great, that *Plato* his name
> is laide uppon mee, whom I must confesse of all *Philosophers*,
> I have ever esteemed most worthie of reverence; and with
> good reason, since of all *Philosophers* hee is the most
> *Poeticall*: yet if hee will defile the fountaine out of which
> his flowing streams have proceeded, let us boldly examine
> with what reasons hee did it.
>
> Sir Philip Sidney, *Defence of Poesie*

Republic II and *III* show Plato restricting, but not condemning, poetry. Unquestionably, his love of poetry causes him to pay frequent tribute to its beauty and charm. He himself sometimes forgets his subtle distinctions between poetic inspiration and philosophical rapture. And his great pleas for morality in poetry will offend only those effete souls who remove poetry from the arena of human needs and desires. Yet Plato's ambiguous pronouncements allow — indeed insist upon — a vigorous and sophisticated response to his thought. Within his generous and humane philosophy, men of radically differing persuasions find assurance as well as challenge. If poets and critics wish to make Plato the enthusiastic patron of the arts, they need only to ignore the qualifications he places on poetic inspiration. Or one might stress Plato's respect for ethical verse by citing his pervasive commendation of noble examples of poetry. But to speak intelligently or completely on Plato's poetics, we must face (as the Neoplatonist Sidney did) the argument in *Republic X*. This book is baffling, unpopular, and, on the surface, almost absurd in its exaggeration. But Plato is seldom muddled in thought or gauche in presentation. Therefore, since the last book of his greatest philosophical discussion contains Plato's most explicit statement on the nature of poetry, the censures in *Republic X* must take precedence over scattered comments elsewhere.

The Republic cannot be dismissed as an "ideal," nor do Plato's dialogues make an unqualified endorsement anywhere of poetic inspiration or of ethical poetry.[1] His mistrust of poetry obviously exists side by side with his love of poetry. In this chapter our task is to consider whether Plato's reasons for banishing poetry are consistent and well thought out. If the same attitude toward art underlies both the *Laws* and the *Republic*, the more extended discussion of poetry in *Republic X* should carry more weight.[2] The *Repub-*

---

[1] D. R. Grey, in "Art in the *Republic*," pp. 291–310, feels that Plato, full of aesthetic appreciation, identifies the true poet with the philosopher. He reasons that "Plato in discussing art is not talking about what we are talking about when *we* discuss art" (p. 292). Katherine Gilbert in "The Relation of the Moral to the Aesthetic Standard in Plato," pp. 279–94, proposes the same sort of facile solution: "All of Plato's strictures on poetry are relative to a proposed state-policy, not absolute expressions of taste or definitions of fine art" (p. 279).

[2] The essential similarity of the stances taken in the *Republic* and the *Laws* toward poetry has been often recognized. J. Tate, in "On Plato:

lic X, the source of a good deal of the controversy over Plato's aesthetics, alone contains his explicit expulsion of poetry. In this book, he first considers poetry's misleading of the intellect, then its catering to the emotions. Poetry is guilty of both offenses. In 595a–600e Plato argues that a carpenter follows a divine form in making a bed, and an artist copies that imitation. He proceeds from the analogy between the painter and the poet. At this point he seems to leave room for poetry which encourages virtue and restraint, as he has suggested in *Republic II* and *III*. But Plato then extends his attack to all art in *Republic X* 601a–8b. By stimulating the emotions, poetry confuses the intellect. Although he does not advance new arguments concerning poetry's effect on the emotions, the four previous books have introduced a theory of the soul which renders poetry largely unnecessary. Indeed, poetry's appeal to the soul directly through beauty introduces a dangerous disharmony. The soul's perception of beauty must be mediated through knowledge, not immediately grasped through the emotions. When he banishes Homer, he also excludes the ethical poetry he has praised in earlier books. Nevertheless, Plato then seems to permit poetry to reenter the state precisely under the same conditions as in *Republic II* and *III*. Since Plato feels that he has banished lyric, epic, and drama, his admission of didactic verse must have little resemblance to what he deems to be poetry.[3] The combination of his

---

Laws X 889cd," pp. 48–54, points out their agreement and then shows that *Laws X* 889 attributes to materialists the same arguments Socrates uses in *Republic X*. Tate concludes that *Republic X* attacks only realistic art whereas *Laws X* 889 attacks those who attack all art. R. G. Collingwood, in "Plato's Philosophy of Art," pp. 154–72, also feels the *Laws* and *Republic* to express similar views. Songs and dances are termed mimetic in *Republic X*. In the *Laws*, "the doctrine of two removes is not explicitly stated, but appears to be presupposed rather than abandoned" (p. 168).

[3] N. R. Murphy points up Plato's seriousness in his condemnation of art in *Republic X* in *The Interpretation of Plato's Republic*, pp. 224–37. Bernard Bosanquet, in *A History of Aesthetic*, observes of Plato that "Images and imagination, for him, rank below nature and science. What he cares about, as every sympathetic student must feel, is reality at first-hand; and the generalization that representative art is reality at second-hand is still fresh and serious in his mind" (p. 48). Thus despite his image of the sun, Plato's

censure of poetry with his "poetic" style creates a problem of interpretation, but the confusion is ours, not Plato's.

1

THE IMPORTANCE OF *REPUBLIC X*

The *Republic X* is central to any discussion of Plato's aesthetics,
both for its inherent philosophy and for its historical importance.
Without this book, most critics would accept, albeit unwillingly,
Plato's right to link poetry with morality as in the earlier parts of
the *Republic* and in the *Laws*. His epistemological attacks on
poetry and his *ad hominem* attack on Homer in Book *X*, however,
have seldom appealed to readers. Critics are at loggerheads over
the significance of this book in the dialogue as well as its explicit
content. Cornford states in his translation of the *Republic* that "the
attack on poetry in this Part has the air of an appendix, only superficially linked with the preceding and following context. Possibly
the strictures on dramatic poetry in Chapter IX had become known
and provoked criticism to which Plato wished to reply." [4] Havelock, on the other hand, holds that "an author possessing Plato's
skill in composition is not likely to blunt the edge of what he is
saying by allowing his thoughts to stray away from it at the end." [5]
They agree that the discussion of poetry is a break in the argument
of *Republic IX* and the Myth of Er.

The first books of the *Republic* are tentative positions in Plato's
study of man and the state. His comments on poetry are not
extreme here; his ideals obviously resemble those in the *Laws*. One
argument maintains that Plato was serious in the first part; in the
last book he is stretching the point. Plato's argument may carry

---

explicit theory of representative art does not recognize the embodiment of
invisible realities in sensuous form.

[4] Cornford, *Republic*, p. 321. Nettleship earlier had said much the same
thing in his chapter "Digression on Poetry," in *Lectures on the Republic of
Plato*, pp. 340–54.

[5] *Preface to Plato*, p. 3.

him further than he would willingly go: "In X. there is an unmistakable trace of sophistry, a use of arguments which cannot have appealed to the better judgment of the writer; the reasoning in II. and III. is direct, serious, and convincing . . . . In the latter book he seems to be seeking strictly philosophical considerations to support the verdict of the earlier passage, to be trying to show that this almost *a priori* conclusion is in harmony with the great principles upon which the Republic rests." [6] Superficially, Plato does seem to change his position.[7] In *Republic II* he attacks the content of contemporary poetry, in *III* the form. Some useful and purified poetry would then be a possibility.

But Plato progressively develops the description of the best state and the ruler of that state. The fourth book discusses the nature of the soul, and as early as *Republic VIII*, the tragic poets are excluded: Plato ironically terms poets such as Euripides wise.

> That being so, the tragedians will give further proof of their wisdom if they will excuse us and all states whose constitution resembles ours, when we deny them admittance on the ground that they sing and praise despotism. At the same time, I expect they will go the round of other states, where they will hire actors with fine sonorous voices to sway the inclination of the assembled crowd towards a despotic or a democratic constitution. Naturally they are honored and well paid for these services, by despots chiefly, and in a less degree by democracies. But the higher they mount up the scale of commonwealths, the more their reputation flags, like a climber who gives in for lack of breath. [*VIII* 568abcd]

The tenth book, then, treats the effects of the lesser beauty of poetry on the soul. The enlightened soul should contemplate the beauty of virtue directly. Knowledge, not the impure mixture of emotion and thought found in poetry, should guide man. Since the last part of the *Republic* was probably written much later than the earlier

---

[6] C. L. Brownson, *Plato's Studies and Criticisms of the Poets*, p. 97.

[7] See J. Tate, " 'Imitation' in Plato's *Republic*," pp. 16–23, and "Plato and 'Imitation,' " pp. 161–69.

parts, we may conjecture that the tenth book answers or at least responds to some contemporary objections to his previous discussion of poetry.[8] Plato states that "our commonwealth has many features which make me think it was based on very sound principles, especially our rule not on any account to admit the poetry of dramatic representation. Now that we have distinguished the several parts of the soul, it seems to me clearer than ever that such poetry must be firmly excluded" (*X* 595ab). The reason for the exclusion is that poetry may injure minds which do not understand its true nature.

Critics not only disagree on the relationship of the tenth book to the rest of the dialogue, but they question the relevance of Plato's comments to any useful study of poetry. Havelock argues that the *Republic* does not launch a philosophical attack on the poets, but rather proposes a social criticism. He states that the political framework of the dialogue may be utopian, but Plato is serious about the role of poetry in education. "It is obvious that the poetry he is talking about is not the kind of thing we identify today as poetry. Or more properly that his poetry and our poetry may have a great deal in common, but that what must have changed is the environment in which poetry is practiced. Somehow, Plato is talking about an overall cultural condition which no longer exists." [9] A. E. Taylor, however, would extend Plato's attack to poetry for all times. "It is not the floridity of Timotheus or Agathon which is the object of attack, but the art of the Periclean age. We are only throwing dust in our own eyes if we suppose that Socrates wants merely to repress the cheap music-hall and the garish melodrama, or the equivalents of freak movements like *Dada*. He is seriously proposing to censure just what we consider the imperishable contributions of Athens to the art and literature of the world, because he holds that they have tendencies which are unfavourable to the highest development of moral personality." [10] Plato saw too clearly to confuse the degenerate art of his own time with all possible art. If Plato's aesthetics

[8] See Paul Shorey, *What Plato Said*, p. 248.

[9] Havelock, *Preface to Plato*, p. 10.

[10] A. E. Taylor, *Plato: The Man and His Work*, pp. 279–80.

comments only on a vanished social situation, his thought has value only for the antiquarian.

The *Republic* does not attack simply a way of interpreting poetry. Plato argues as if Homer himself were claiming authority, not just the ignorant rhapsode. Cornford, however, would make Plato's criticism mainly of the sophists and their brand of criticism: "The main object of attack . . . is the claim, currently made by sophists and professional reciters of the Homeric poems, that Homer in particular, and in a less degree the tragedians, were masters of all technical knowledge, from wagon-building or chariot-driving to strategy, and also moral and religious guides to the conduct of life." [11] While the *Ion* does not sanction any use of contemporary poetry, the dialogue does not explicitly condemn all possible uses of art. In the *Ion* Plato suggests that not just the professionals but everyone interprets poetry incorrectly. So Plato attacks false literary criticism in the *Ion*, but he extends his reasoning in the *Republic*. Here Plato does not accuse the sophists of using poetry to bolster their effectiveness. In fact, he even cites them as his allies against the poets; Homer's authority challenges that of Protagoras of Abdera and Prodicus of Ceos (*Republic X* 600c).

2

IMITATION AND THE FORMS

The *Republic X* opens with a clear and sweeping attack on poetry.[12] Earlier in the dialogue Plato has abolished only trivial and immoral poetry about gods and heroes while at the same time praising all general representations of harmony and beauty. He has limited his consideration of poetry itself to the educational effects of

---

[11] Cornford, *Republic*, p. 322.

[12] Brownson, in *Plato's Studies*, states that "Art which before has received at best less than its due is now still further degraded. Poetry is no longer even the lowly friend of philosophy but its enemy. Poetry appeals to the soul through concrete representations; philosophy would direct its gaze toward the abstract ideal" (p. 148).

brief poetical selections. Now he turns to entire works of poetry and finds them pitifully lacking in value for the intelligent man.[13] He has gradually been purging the just state of its luxurious excess by developing sound principles. At this point he must lance one major pocket of corruption. One of these effective instruments of purification is the rule which excludes the poetry of dramatic representation. This sort of poetry can poison the mind. The antidote, a knowledge of its real nature, suggests an objectivity which renders the poetry trivial and useless. Plato now expands the definition of mimesis to include poetry of all sorts. Any representation of ordinary men in action is vulgar and misleading; portrayals of virtuous men are boring and ineffectual. He groups drama and epic together at this point. The conditions placed on poetry earlier he now feels impossible of fulfillment by any actual poet. Plato's love of Homer in childhood makes him reluctant to condemn the poet. But at last, the mature and responsible Plato must speak the truth.

The first attack on poetry follows from the theory of Forms, a doctrine not necessarily antithetical to poetry.[14] But Plato slants his argument so that poetry consists of a superficial correspondence to the physical world. He first assumes that every set of things called by the same name has a single essential nature or Form. "We are

---

[13] Brownson argues that Plato here exaggerates the extent of the earlier restrictions on poetry (*Plato's Studies*, p. 90).

[14] Collingwood, in "Plato's Philosophy of Art," gives an interpretation of the imitation of an imitation which makes *Republic X* more favorable to poetry:

> The world of perception is wholly distinct from the world of thought, but not merely distinct. It has a positive relation to it, which is expressed by saying that it copies it. Similarly, the work of art, though wholly distinct from the world of perception, has a positive relation of the same kind to it. This cannot mean that Socrates is expounding a crudely naturalistic view of art as a quasi-photographic reproduction of nature; anyone who makes that suggestion need only be invited to explain how nature can be a quasi-photographic reproduction of a world of concepts; and this, if anything can, will convince him that it is dangerous to jump at what may seem the most obvious interpretation of the term μίμεσις. [p. 159]

I argue that while man's imitation is indeed quasi-photographic, the god's creation is on a different level altogether. Man imitates in shadows what the god imitates in reality.

in the habit of saying that the craftsman, when he makes the beds
or tables we use or whatever it may be, is looking to the Form of
one or other of these pieces of furniture. The Form itself is, of
course, not the work of any craftsman" (*X* 596b). The artisan's
work of embodying the Forms lies in the physical realm. By insist-
ing that the craftsman produce practical objects, Plato has denied
lasting value even to this imitator.[15] Technical knowledge has
inherent limitations. Despite the craftsman's vision of the Forms,
his handiwork is one removed from reality. As in the *Sophist* 265–
67, human activity follows from divine creation. The physical faithfulness of the imitation provides the only criterion for judgment.

Both artisan and artist make particular products which have no
apparent significance beyond the immediate function. But the work
of the manual craftsman at least has the virtue of usefulness. Plato
chooses to attack dramatic representation by two questionable visual
analogies — the mirror and the painting. Both the *Sophist* 233–35
and the *Republic X* have the artist shadow forth a variety of objects
through a passive response to the physical world. "Besides producing any kind of artificial thing, this same craftsman can create all
plants and animals, himself included, and earth and sky and gods
and heavenly bodies and all the things under the earth in Hades"
(*X* 596c).[16] Moreover, any untrained lout could easily duplicate
this miraculous feat of virtuosity without discipline or difficulty.
"The quickest perhaps would be to take a mirror and turn it around
in all directions. In a very short time you could produce sun and
stars and earth and yourself and all these other animals and plants
and lifeless objects (*X* 596de). Of course, only the appearances are

---

[15] The *Timaeus* states to the contrary that "everything that becomes or is
created must of necessity be created by some cause, for without a cause
nothing can be created. The work of the creator, whenever he looks to the
unchangeable and fashions the form and nature of his work after an unchangeable pattern, must necessarily be made fair and perfect; but when he
looks to the created only, and uses a created pattern, it is not fair or perfect"
(28ab).

[16] If Plato seems to exaggerate his position, cf. Giovanni Pico della
Mirandola's "Oration on the Dignity of Man."

reproduced, not the actual things. The artisan holds a mirror up to physical nature. Such a glass is carelessly held and unfocused. Moreover, he constantly shifts the mirror to take in as much as possible. These changing reflections certainly cannot fix one's attention on some single part of nature. There is neither harmony nor unity in this dizzying kaleidoscopic effect; art is inherently a process rather than a series of fixed objects.

Plato then applies the analogy of mirror reproduction to the craft of the painter. The dynamic but structureless rotation of the mirror gives a two-dimensional image of a bed, a representation which a painting makes static. The painter, as mindless a craftsman as the holder of the mirror, seeks only to portray a particular object. "You may say that the things he produces are not real; but there is a sense in which he too does produce a bed" (*X* 596e). But physically he makes only the appearance of a bed. Using paints and materials of the physical world, he can only copy what is set immediately before him. Like the poetry discussed in the *Republic II* and *III*, painting here consists solely of the surface texture. The proper interpretation of both arts calls for a faculty to universalize or to fix the diverse and shifting sense impressions. But these shallow, particular representations neither contain permanence within themselves nor encourage the observer to make the leap of interpretation.

The physical product of imitation is always a particular artifact. The human maker, in this case a carpenter, stands as an intermediary between the Form and the painter. The carpenter makes a particular bed rather than the Form, the essential nature of Bed. And no work of a carpenter or any other artisan can be a perfectly real thing. Even an actual bed is somewhat shadowy compared with reality. "We have here three sorts of bed: one which exists in the nature of things and which, I imagine, we could only describe as a product of divine workmanship; another made by the carpenter; and a third by the painter. So the three kinds of bed belong respectively to the domains of these three: painter, carpenter, and god" (*X* 597b). Clearly, Plato stresses the unfavorable meaning of mimesis.[17] Throughout, of course, imitation must instruct and strengthen, not merely entertain.[18]

Neither god nor man has the freedom to create as he chooses. Human ignorance restricts the man; the eternal nature of the Forms limits the god.[19] Plato stresses the integrity, the fixed quality, of the divine creator's work. The god made only one essential Bed. Two or more can neither be created nor possibly come into being. "If the divine maker engendered even so many as two, then once more a single ideal Bed would make its appearance, whose character those two would share; and that one, not the two, would be the essential Bed. Knowing this, the god, wishing to be the real maker of a real Bed, not a particular manufacturer of one particular bed, created one which is essentially unique" (*X* 597c). The god is the real artist, for like the inspired philosopher of the *Symposium*, he brings forth realities. The carpenter, the manufacturer of a bed, transforms the true bed into a physically useful article. The god makes one product, the craftsman many.

The Form is one, and the particular embodiment is one. Yet the painting is neither one nor the other. Plato refuses to give the particular work of the artist an autonomous existence; the painting is too intimately bound to the physical world. Whether the work is good or bad as art is irrelevant. Plato argues that the quality of a work of art depends on its subject matter, not its static form. The painter does not create a painting; he is rather the "imitator of that which others make." The painter has no special art. Like the philosopher, a true artist must present or embody ultimate reality. But the physical tools of the artist — paint and surface — make his job almost impossible.

---

[17] J. Tate points out that Plato uses the word in a more favorable sense in *Republic* 500–1 ("Plato and 'Imitation,'" pp. 161–69).

[18] See *Sophist* 236 and 265–68 and *Laws II* 667–68.

[19] John Warry, in *Greek Aesthetic Theory*, comments about the *Sophist* 264: "Reflection and shadow bear the same relation to material (divinely created) nature as artistic portrayal (imitation) does to practical crafts and their products. The neatness of the classification is to some extent marred by the recollection that the divine creations may also be objects of artistic portrayal, but the point of the observation need not be lost" (p. 53).

Republic III has suggested that beautiful physical objects may contain the harmony necessary to lift the soul above its natural, shadowy environment. But *Republic X* indicates that a separate "fine" art upsets the balance between the two worlds. Only the vital individual soul, not beautiful physical objects, can grasp or embody the Forms. Yet painting and poetry, having no continuing contact with their originators, smugly fix one's attention on the physical and the particular. The artist represents in the physical world the things which the other two creators make, so that his work is twice removed from the essential nature of the object. The painter and the tragic poet have a similar function: "The tragic poet, too, is an artist who represents things; so this will apply to him: he and all other artists are, as it were, third in succession from the throne of truth" (*X* 597e). The analogy seems absurd to us, but the exaggeration is revealing. Plato insists that the meaning of poetry and painting only exists on the surface level. Even a heightened reality on the human level begins with man as he is, whereas Plato wishes a direct statement on man as he should be. And art, immediately felt, does not lend itself to this hypothetical presentation. Plato does not distinguish between "realistic" and "intellectual" poetry or painting. Instead, here he speaks simply of the fabric or the tools of the artist.

3

The Poets' Knowledge

Plato extends his analysis of the physical and nonintellectual basis of art to the purposes of the artist. The artist's intent is flawed. He tries to represent, not the reality that exists within the nature of things, but merely the products of the craftsman. Moreover, the artist copies the appearance alone. One can look at a bed from any angle, but the only difference lies in its appearance. A painting, on the other hand, does not attempt to reproduce the actual object, but merely the visual surface. Rather than being a harmonious embodiment of an object, the painting gives only a semblance of reality.

Painters had indeed achieved great technical competence by Plato's time. Zeuxis supposedly had drawn a bunch of grapes so realistically that birds pecked at them, and Apollodorus had devised paintings with shadows (σκιαγραφία). T. B. L. Webster describes how Plato responded to the realism of Zeuxis and Euripides: "The Homeric poet and artist is a *poietes*, creating something which must be both complete and essential because it is to live and exercise an influence of its own. At the end of the fifth century poet and artist are more restricted and specialized, holding a mirror to the flux of appearance. Many stages separate the *poietes* from the *mimetes*. The turning-point is somewhere in the third quarter of the sixth century." [20] R. G. Steven feels that Plato's views as a philosopher and as an educator kept him from accepting art: "His philosophy compelled him to condemn it utterly, his educational ideals led him to disapprove of most types. He was thus precluded at the outset from appreciating the revolution achieved by Agatharchus and Apollodorus and its results.[21]

Plato intends to banish all such "realistic" poetry from the well-run state. Realism may in fact provide a momentary amusement at the artist's skill. Plato, however, goes further by asserting that a static painting can continue to bewilder an untrained observer. This art is banished, not for its illegitimate and momentary appeal to the emotions, but for its extended confusion of the intellect.

> The art of representation is a long way from reality; and apparently the reason why there is nothing it cannot reproduce is that it grasps only a small part of any object, and that only an image. Your painter, for example, will paint us a shoemaker, a carpenter, or other workman, without understanding any one of their crafts; and yet if he were a good painter, he might deceive a child or a simple-minded person into thinking his picture was a real carpenter, if he showed it them at some distance. [X 598bc]

[20] T. B. L. Webster, "Greek Theories of Art and Literature Down to 400 B.C.," p. 179.

[21] R. G. Steven, "Plato and the Art of His Time," p. 155.

Thus, anyone who claimed to be a practitioner of every trade must not be allowed in the state. Plato, of course, is thinking here of poetry and its claims to knowledge it does not possess. It has been argued, reasonably enough, that a painter could not put knowledge of cobbling into a picture even if he were also an expert cobbler. To this Plato might reply that according to his theory of the division of labor found in the *Ion* and the *Republic III*, no man can be a good painter and a good cobbler at the same time. The painter, like the poet, has no specific trade: all humanity is the province of the artist. But only the possessor of wisdom, the philosopher, can understand what is right for man. Just as Sir Philip Sidney closely identifies artist with philosopher, Plato makes the philosopher the supreme craftsman. Sidney stresses the virtue of beauty, Plato the beauty of virtue.

Whereas an apologist such as Sidney will stress poetry's effectiveness, its ability to move man's hardened heart, Plato seeks philosophical clarity. Since the poets lack knowledge, they agitate rather than guide the emotions. The effectiveness of specific presentations will follow from this prior vision of absolute truth and beauty, a perception open to the disciplined philosopher. Art is inherently amoral, and thus is a poor guide to virtue. Poetry is liable to the same misinterpretation that Jonathan Swift sees for satire. In the preface to *Battle of the Books*, the reverend Dean states, "Satire is a sort of glass, wherein beholders do generally discover everybody's face but their own; which is the chief reason for that kind of reception it meets in the world, and that so very few are offended with it." Poetry may confirm, but it seldom converts. Plato could argue that the rational part of the soul receives little instruction from its contemplation of the static picture of a cobbler at his trade. The painting might incidentally be beautiful. But a man must have virtue and knowledge first; otherwise he receives not happiness, but merely pleasure from beauty.

Nevertheless, Plato's condemnation of realistic art need not apply to all art. As Havelock notes, *mimesis* is truly a protean word.[22] Elsewhere in the dialogues, the good man "imitates" the

---

[22] *Preface to Plato*, p. 30.

Form of virtue. And as Sir Philip Sidney says in his *Defence of Poesie*, the poet "painteth not *Lucretia* whom he never saw, but painteth the outward bewty of such a vertue." [23] The artist need not be limited to literal copying, to "creating" the world with a mirror (596e). If a man can imitate the Form of virtue, the poet who copies his actions will be imitating that virtue.

Plato himself seems to admit a second kind of imitation in the *Republic*: "Then suppose a painter had drawn an ideally beautiful figure complete to the last touch, would you think any the worse of him, if he could not show that a person as beautiful as that could exist?" (*V* 472d). Plato admits that art may be true and poetry may contain great truths, but only as possibilities. Nevertheless, he does not explicitly allow the artist this ability, and the *Republic X* seems to deny even the possibility. Plato does not reconcile ignorant imitation in art with true copying of the eternal Forms: "Why should not works of art be imitations in the same sense, expressing the Ideas in the physical world, without the intermediate model of that physical world itself? There is nothing in Plato's conception of the relationship between the two worlds which precludes such an escape out of the difficulty. There is, however, a very definite objection, namely that he himself never says a word to indicate anything of the kind." [24] Similarly, a critic cannot argue for Plato's acceptance of good and ethical poetry on the basis of his admitting the divine origin of poetry. Plato never makes this connection. His thought on the nature of poetry does not directly relate to his discussion of the use of poetry in the education of the young. Critics may emphasize Plato's sanction of harmony in all creations, but they are liable to gloss over his real objections to poetry itself.

4

THE REPUTATION OF THE POETS

Certainly a major part of Plato's attack goes only against interpreting poetry as a repository of knowledge. Just as poet and

[23] *The Prose Works of Sir Philip Sidney*, ed. Albert Feuillerat, 3:10.
[24] G. M. A. Grube, *Plato's Thought*, p. 202.

rhapsode are considered together in the *Ion*, Plato makes no distinction here between a poet's claim and the claim made on his behalf. Both poet and interpreter perform a general public function and shall be judged according to their social effects. But in true philosophical discussions, a man must be present to advance his cause. The absent poet has received vulgar acclaim; he must now accept the penalty for the ignorance of his followers. Thus the poets themselves are illusionists who claim omniscience. Plato says we should consider the knowledge of the tragic poets and their master, Homer, because current theory holds that "they understand not only all technical matters but also all about human conduct, good or bad, and about religion; for, to write well, a good poet, so they say, must know his subject; otherwise he could not write about it. We must ask whether these people have not been deluded by meeting with artists who can represent appearances, and in contemplating the poets' work have failed to see that it is at the third remove from reality, nothing more than semblances, easy to produce with no knowledge of the truth" (*X* 598e–99a). The public seems to think that the poet has real mastery of the content of his discourse. The poet casts such a spell with his flow of words that an innocent human will assign him authority far beyond his real knowledge.

Manufacturing only the external images of virtuous men, the poet celebrates great exploits. Plato shifts the discussion from poetry as illusion to the incapacity of the poet to perform heroic deeds. He asserts that knowledge inevitably results in action. No distinction exists here between the performance and the article or deed produced. Who indeed can tell the dancer from the dance?

> If a man were able actually to do the things he represents as well as to produce images of them, do you believe he would seriously give himself up to making these images and take that as a completely satisfying object in life? I should imagine that, if he had a real understanding of the actions he represents, he would far sooner devote himself to performing them in fact. The memorials he would try to leave after him would be noble deeds, and he would be more eager to be the hero whose praises are sung than the poet who sings them. [*X* 599ab]

The poet, then, cannot create a new world; he commemorates the deeds of actual people. Whereas the poet in the *Symposium* creates "children of the soul," here the poet feebly memorializes the original deed. Since the poem has only an immediate effect, the verbal recording of the event can have little significance. The poet would be more useful in doing a heroic deed, thus making a second noble example instead of an echo of the original. This passage would almost deny Plato's later acceptance of praises of gods and famous men. All praises are inferior to the actual deed. If, as Plato suggests, the makers of praises are incompetent and ignorant workmen, the state possesses no respectable citizens who can make the encomia.

Plato becomes more explicit in his *ad hominem* attack on the poets.[25] Practitioners in any field have their followers just as do the poets. But this intimate relationship cannot legitimately exist on any level but the practical. The *Ion* has exposed the uselessness of poetry to instruct man directly in affairs of this world. Even while performing poetic exhortations, the rhapsode does not apply his words to the situation immediately before him.[26] The *Republic* amplifies this reasoning:

> Here is a question that we may fairly put to Homer or to any other poet. We will leave out of account all mere matters of technical skill: we will not ask them to explain, for instance, why it is that, if they have a knowledge of medicine and not merely the art of reproducing the way physicians talk, there is no record of any poet, ancient or modern, curing patients and bequeathing his knowledge to a school of medicine, as Asclepius did. But when Homer undertakes to tell us about matters of the highest importance, such as the conduct of war, statesmanship, or education, we have a right to inquire into his competence. "Dear

[25] The *Phaedrus* contains a slighting reference to Homer's knowledge: "Now for such as offend in speaking of gods and heroes there is an ancient mode of purification which was known to Stesichorus, though not to Homer. When Stesichorus lost the sight of his eyes because of his defamation of Helen, he was not, like Homer, at a loss to know why: as a true artist he understood the reason" (243a).

[26] Socrates shows that the rhapsode Ion cannot exhort troops as a real general might (540–41).

Homer," we shall say, "we have defined the artist as one who produces images at the third remove from reality. If your knowledge of all that concerns human excellence was really such as to raise you above him to the second rank, and you could tell what courses of conduct will make men better or worse as individuals or as citizens, can you name any country which was better governed thanks to your efforts? Many states, great and small, have owed much to a good lawgiver, such as Lycurgus at Sparta, Charondas in Italy and Sicily, and our own Solon. Can you tell us of any that acknowledges a like debt to you?"

[*X* 599 bcde]

No war was won in Homer's day under his command or through his advice. The poet can claim no practical inventions or devices.

The ability of the poet comes from his knowledge, his ability to recognize virtue. The *Phaedrus* (278bcd) states that a poet must have knowledge and be willing to submit to immediate questioning:

Do you now go and tell Lysias that we two went down to the stream where is the holy place of the Nymphs, and there listened to the words which charged us to deliver a message, first to Lysias and all other composers of discourses, secondly to Homer and all others who have written poetry whether to be read or sung, and thirdly to Solon and all such as are authors of political compositions under the name of laws: to wit, that if any of them has done his work with a knowledge of the truth, can defend his statements when challenged, and can demonstrate the inferiority of his writings out of his own mouth, he ought not to be designated by a name drawn from those writings, but by one that indicates his serious pursuit.

The proper name for such a man would be "lover of wisdom." The composer's ability, then, does not rest with the work, but with his intention or knowledge. Poetry does not have a definite role in the Greek state, even in education. Many Greeks praise Homer and his knowledge, but few are willing to trust him. Thus Plato insists, and legitimately so, on a precise definition of poetry's role for the individual and for the state. He may realize that he overstates the popular acclaim for Homer, for he has Glaucon say that even the most devout admirers of Homer make no claim to his being a teacher.

Plato moves from his rather dubious insistence that the poet must have a practical role to a discussion of the poet's function as an educator. A man cannot depend on the vindication of posterity. Homer could not boast of a band of disciples like Pythagoras could, no intimates "who loved him for the inspiration of his society and handed down a Homeric way of life" (*X* 600b). Homer's words, the illusory public utterances, can possess a rhapsode, but his personal example commands little respect. If Homer had possessed the knowledge to enable him to improve the minds and morals of others, he would have attracted legions of devoted followers. The sophists are rivals of the poets, not their supporters. Protagoras of Abdera and Prodicus of Ceos have convinced their contemporaries that they cannot competently manage affairs of state or even their own households unless these masters superintend their education. "For this wisdom they are so passionately admired that their pupils are all but ready to carry them about on their shoulders" (*X* 600d). On the other hand, the contemporaries of Homer and Hesiod have let them wander about reciting their poems, for the poets are really incapable of helping their hearers to be better men. Little is known about the life of Homer, but Plato goes against the weight of tradition. Several cities vied for the services of the poet, and certainly after his death his poems were universally admired. But Plato sees that as a public figure, Homer as well as Hesiod resembles a vulgar rhapsode. The great sophists such as Protagoras and Prodicus impress men by their private intercourse, whereas the poets appeal to society at large. Even false instruction such as the sophists give is preferable to the emotional orgy encouraged by the poets.

Plato further clarifies the relationship between painter and poet. The poet cloaks the emptiness of his words in a thin layer of verse. Plato has just argued that shape and colors can make a shoemaker's likeness which will deceive an ignorant spectator. We might argue that the illusion of a painting's being a real cobbler can exist only for a moment; the lack of movement would soon betray the imposture to the simplest viewer. But Plato thinks that even this momentary deception is harmful. Both painter and spectator, joining in a conspiracy of ignorance, observe only the superficial characteristics of a profession:

> In the same way the poet, knowing nothing more than how to represent appearances, can paint in words his picture of any craftsman so as to impress an audience which is equally ignorant and judges only by the form of expression. The inherent charm of meter, rhythm, and musical setting is enough to make them think he has discoursed admirably about generalship or shoe-making or any other technical subject. When the things of the poet are stripped of the colors of music and are said by themselves, you know how they look. It is like a face which was never really handsome, when it has lost the fresh bloom of youth. [*X* 601ab]

The beauty of language enables the poet to show the artisan at work. Certainly he can give a convincing representation of the workers speaking on various subjects. Plain, prosaic discourse can easily be examined for its truth, whereas the music of poetry encourages a facile and unjustifiable acceptance of suspect material.

Not only is the poet ignorant of the artisan's craft, but he lacks understanding of the function of the articles produced. In his attempt to define the categories of human activity, Plato often makes a sharp distinction between maker and user. Thus he does not make clear their interaction. The artist, a maker of images, knows only appearances. "An artist can paint a bit and bridle while the smith and the leather-worker can make them. Does the painter understand the proper form which bit and bridle ought to have? Is it not rather true that not even the craftsmen who make them know that, but only the horseman who understands their use?" (*X* 601c). There are two worthwhile skills concerned with any object — the art of making and the art of using. While inextricably linked with these two, the third art, that of representation, is far inferior. Plato has already said that the maker refers to the Form of his product as he works. But the user possesses more knowledge than the maker; he must correct the maker's flawed vision of the Form.[27]

The mere existence of an object or the performance of some deed does not insure its excellence. The true worth of anything can be tested by its functioning properly in the just state. The virtue or beauty or rightness of any implement or living creature or action comes from the use for which each is made or adapted naturally. Using the example of the often-reviled flute, Plato states that the user, the best authority on his instrument, must report to the maker on its good or bad points. The instrument maker should submit to the performer's judgment. "So the man who uses any implement will speak of its merits and defects with knowledge, whereas the maker will take his word and possess no more than a correct belief, which he is obliged to obtain by listening to the man who knows" (X 601e). Plato would make an exception for poetry; the rhapsode is no closer to truth than the poet. The good educator, however, may have the knowledge to instruct the poets. Although the maker can partly embody a Form, only contact with those wiser will enable him to improve his next representations. Being compelled to heed the user, the maker somehow learns of the worth of his skill. But the artist's work does not allow this creative interplay, so the artist neither knows nor has right opinion about the function of his representation. Direct experience with the things he paints or writes could lead to knowledge, or association with one who does know could produce correct belief. But the artist has never submitted to the necessary discipline.

The *Critias* states that knowledge leads to a more critical response to imitations. Our ignorance of the natural world allows us a vague appreciation and an easy tolerance of artistic ineptitude:

All that is said by any of us can only be imitation and representation. For if we consider the likenesses which painters make

---

[27] This argument parallels his discussion of language in the *Cratylus*, which argues that the maker of words must rely on the dialectician or user to determine the correctness of language. See *Cratylus* 390, *Euthydemus* 289, and *Phaedrus* 274.

of bodies divine and heavenly, and the different degrees of gratification with which the eye of the spectator receives them, we shall see that we are satisfied with the artist who is able in any degree to imitate the earth and its mountains, and the rivers, and the woods, and the universe, and the things that are and move therein, and further, that knowing nothing precise about such matters, we do not examine or analyze the painting; all that is required is a sort of indistinct and deceptive mode of shadowing them forth. [107bcd]

Nevertheless, representation of the human form arouses our critical instincts; intimate knowledge makes us carefully examine points of similarity. And Plato again makes an analogy of words and painting: "We may observe the same thing to happen in discourse; we are satisfied with a picture of divine and heavenly things which has very little likeness to them, but we are more precise in our criticism of mortal and human things" (107d).

By making the use of an article superior to the production of that device, Plato has further lowered the value of poetry. A cobbler can learn about the limitations of a shoe from a runner, but a poet cannot respond to and improve the education which his work affords. The poet's absence when his works are discussed prevents both his defending his work and also his learning where he is wrong. Despite his lack of knowledge or right opinion, the artist shamelessly works without knowing in what way any of his representatives can be used. He reproduces only what pleases the taste and wins the approval of the ignorant multitude. The users of poetry probably lack understanding enough to direct the poet in his work even if he were present. This contemptuous discussion applies especially to tragic poetry, whether cast in heroic verse or iambics, epic or dramatic form. With this sarcastic thrust, Plato ends his consideration of the artist's ignorance and the superficiality inherent in painting and poetry.

But Plato has not finished with his charges against the arts. He must still show that beautiful language invariably has a detrimental effect on all but those who possess an antidote of knowledge. He has shown that poetry offends the intellect by thrusting sensory data before the vision. Next he will show that mimetic art appeals directly to the lower senses. As he has argued in the *Republic II and III*, Plato again maintains that poetry arouses man's instinct for self-indulgence. Although he mockingly recognizes the possibility of a defense of poetry, he holds little hope for its success.

5
POETRY AND THE SOUL

To complete his charges against poetry, Plato turns his attention to the effect of imitative art on the lower and susceptible part of the soul.[28] Not only does the subject of art tend to deceive the reason, but the beauty of art arouses and inflames the emotions. Physical art or language leads the mind away from the eternal Forms. Art in all its forms is seductive. Only the forearmed intellect can distinguish true beauty from the idle pleasure which art can powerfully suggest. After banishing imitative poetry for its liability of being misinterpreted, Plato discusses poetry which portrays men in action. He wishes to extend his argument that poetry is an imitation of an imitation. The conclusion toward which his discussion of realistic poetry has been leading is "that paintings and works of art in general are far removed from reality and that the element in our nature which is accessible to art and responds to its advances is equally far from wisdom" (*X* 602). Both visual art and poetry are condemned as mere representations.[29] Since the appreciation of art is not exclusively a rational process, Plato will seriously question the value of any artistic beauty.[30]

[28] Music in its broadest sense counterbalances gymnastics. But excessive indulgence in music leads to feebleness (*III* 410–12). A public performance, which Plato sees evoking total involvement, would not lend itself to the desired interaction of physical and spiritual exercise.

[29] Rupert C. Lodge finds *Republic X* atypical of Plato's aesthetics. He states that only imitative art comes under fire here, and elsewhere Plato has no objection even to the mimetic. After all, man's life is basically imitative (see *Plato's Theory of Art*, "Mimesis," pp. 167–91).

[30] The *Laws* continues Plato's attack on the degeneration of contemporary poetry. He does recognize the possibility of a noble and simplified art: "As

Plato's discussion of poetry's effect on man derives from his earlier analysis of the soul (*Republic IV* 434–41). The inferior part of a soul passively receives confusing sensory impressions; the higher, rational element sifts the data and corrects the distortions.[31] The formlessness of nature and the ugliness created by ignorant craftsmen cause the physical world to offer a constant source of confusion to the eye of the mind. Imitations present a particularly acute visual problem. "An object seen at a distance does not, of course, look the same size as when close at hand; a straight stick looks bent when part of it is under water. And the same thing appears concave or convex to an eye misled by colors" (*X* 602c). These physical aberrations find a corresponding faculty in our minds. Artists can exploit the weakness in our nature by many tricks of illusion such as scene-painting and conjuring. Although Plato ironically admires the magical effect, he clearly believes that the calculating or reasoning element alone keeps these illusions from overcoming the soul. This noble faculty counts, measures, or weighs, so that the entire soul is not baffled by apparent differences. Without the steady functioning of the reason, a man would be at the mercy of every random sense impression.[32]

The tension between the faculty for perceiving and the faculty for knowing provides proof that the soul is complex.[33] The soul is divided into two parts here, the inferior element being the one capable of immediate response to the physical world. The higher

---

time went on, the poets themselves introduced the reign of vulgar and lawless innovation. They were men of genius, but they had no perception of what is just and lawful in music" (*Laws III* 700).

[31] Elsewhere Plato stresses the soul's passive reception of external influences (see *Philebus* 39). Since the soul retains all of these impressions, every part of one's environment may have a profound and lasting effect.

[32] See also *Republic IV* 431, *VII* 523–24, *Laws IX* 863.

[33] H. J. Paton, in "Plato's Theory of ΕΙΚΑΣΙΑ," pp. 69–104, reasons that the line and cave images are central to Plato's philosophy. Knowledge and opinion have different "faculties" (δύναμεις), and therefore respond to different objects.

part of the soul, disciplined by mathematics (*Republic VII* 521–31), correctly measures and calculates:

> When the reasoning element has done its measuring and announced that one quantity is greater than, or equal to, another, we often find that there is an appearance which contradicts it. Now, as we have said, it is impossible for the same part of the soul to believe [δοξάζειν] contraries at the same time. Hence the part which agrees with the measurements must be a different part from the one which goes against them; and its confidence in measurement and calculation is a proof of its being the highest part; the other which contradicts it must be an inferior one. [*X* 602e]

The higher and lower parts of the soul do not profitably interact and reinforce the man in good actions. Instead, the ordinary element of the soul willingly endorses an illusion despite the correct measure ascertained by the calculating element.[34] Presumably the faculty of understanding could organize the illusions presented to the senses, but Plato does not recognize here a profitable relationship between the individual sense impression and the higher part of the soul.[35]

Art, like any illusion presented to the senses, appeals only to the lower part of the soul.[36] The reason itself is inaccessible to the

---

[34] The *Phaedrus* also points out the two antagonistic principles in the soul: "We must go on to observe that within each one of us there are two sorts of ruling or guiding principle that we follow: one is an innate desire for pleasure, the other an acquired judgment that aims at what is best" (237).

[35] D. R. Grey, in "Art in the *Republic*," points out that Plato adopts both traditional Greek theories of poetry as education and as imitation, yet he need not have taken both positions in order to refute contemporary claims for poetry (p. 300).

[36] Katherine Gilbert, in "The Relation of the Moral to the Aesthetic Standard in Plato," sums up her argument by saying that,

> the concept of measure rationalizes the connection between "beauty absolute" and aesthetic excellence in specific examples of beauty in the arts. The effulgence of beauty absolute is due to measure. Measure as principle may become a function in the empirical world and ground the delightfulness of a statue or a poem. There is Form-in-itself for the

blandishments of charming illusions. Imitation of all sorts, especially painting, keeps company with the imprudent element, the part which responds immediately to the advances of art. "The offspring of a connexion thus formed on no true or sound basis must be as inferior as the parents. This will be true not only of visual art, but of art addressed to the ear, poetry as we call it" (*X* 603b). Painting addresses the eye, poetry the ear; neither speaks directly to the rational part of the soul. The higher part of the mind cannot properly respond to the intelligible part of verbal imitation, for the tempting musical effects keep words impaled in the ordinary part of the mind. Visual and verbal art confirms the instincts of the inferior element rather than working for the reformation of the entire soul.[37]

The human conflict in art shows the essential confusion and immoral degradation of such representations.[38] Both painting and poetry have for their subject man's action and his earthbound fortunes. Drama focuses on human beings rather than on the Forms, or indeed on anything beyond the particular. Thus, the glorification of humanity leads only indirectly, if at all, to a higher under-

---

speculative intelligence, but this intelligible form embodies itself in the shadow-world of sense and then feeds the imagination with satisfaction and appeals to the lover of fine tones and colors as the magic of words or the plastic beauty of a picture. [p. 294]

Her argument would be more acceptable if Plato were explicit about the artistic embodiment of Forms in the physical world.

[37] Not only the inferior skills — cooking, flauting, harping — but also tragedy has only pleasure for an end. Socrates asks, "And as for the Muse of Tragedy, that solemn and august personage — what are her aspirations? Is all her aim and desire only to give pleasure to the spectators, or does she fight against them and refuse to speak of their pleasant vices, and willingly proclaim in word and song truths welcome and unwelcome? — which in your judgment is her character?" (*Gorgias* 502b). Callicles admits that tragedy seeks only the gratification of the audience.

[38] Bernard Bosanquet correctly states that "Plato has a clear view of aesthetic as distinct from real interest only in so far as he recognises a peculiar satisfaction attending the very abstract manifestations of purely formal beauty. In those concrete forms of representation which we think the higher arts, he was unable to distinguish the pleasure of expressiveness from the practical interest of morality, which he desired to see predominant, and from the pleasure of realistic suggestion which he utterly condemned" (*A History of Aesthetic*, p. 53).

standing. Instead of trusting merely to the analogy from painting, Plato directly discusses that part of the mind to which mimetic poetry appeals, an inquiry that will enable him to evaluate its moral worth. "Drama, we say, represents the acts and fortunes of human beings. It is wholly concerned with what they do, voluntarily or against their will, and how they fare, with the consequences which they regard as happy or otherwise, and with their feelings of joy and sorrow in all these experiences" (*X* 603c). These emotions are unsuitable for the state since displays of passion reveal a divided soul. Plato has previously argued that whereas reason springs from within, "the impulses driving and dragging the soul are engendered by external influences and abnormal conditions" (*Republic IV* 439d). Dramatic poetry appeals only to the lower part of the mind, and there is no productive transference from one part to another. Since the drama copies the actions and emotions of fallible human beings, all such representations are suspect.[39]

Because of its explicit presentation of conflict, Plato finds the drama fundamentally vicious.[40] Representations of internal conflict or tension — the subtle interplay of the parts of the soul — reflect the opposition and confusion commonly found in man's soul. Ineffective and purposeless deeds portrayed on the stage suggest discord in the soul of the actor. "And in all these experiences has a man an undivided mind [ὁμονοητικῶς ἄνθρωπος διάκειται]? Is there not an internal conflict which sets him at odds with himself in his conduct, much as we were saying that the conflict of visual impressions leads him to make contradictory judgments?" (*X* 603cd). Plato has already shown that innumerable conflicts of this sort con-

[39] R. G. Collingwood, in "Plato's Philosophy of Art," presents a very convincing argument to the effect that Plato is seeking to vindicate poetry. In refuting Croce, Collingwood says that "no one has more emphatically than Plato, or at any rate the Platonic Socrates, maintained the existence of opinion and imagination side by side with intellect" (p. 162). I would argue that Plato's emphasis on the supremacy and autonomy of the rational element prevents him from recognizing the function of imagination in art.

[40] I. M. Crombie, in *An Examination of Plato's Doctrines*, attempts to soften Plato's blows in *Republic X* by arguing that he condemns only mistaken judgments of the artistic products (pp. 143–50).

stantly occur in the mind. Art simply exaggerates a natural confusion. Incomplete human actions create a visual confusion, a counterpart to the internal conflict of the soul. Plato asserts that the wise man will somehow be sensible despite the presence of pain (μετριάσει δέ πως πρὸς λύπην). The ambiguity of this "somehow" shows Plato's unresolved attitude toward conflict within the soul.

Viewing public performances of any sort discourages the individual's pursuit of knowledge and self-control. Plato legislates primarily for the reasonable members of the state, but the amusement allowed the ordinary workers can hardly deviate from that suggested for the best and wisest members of the state. Just as he argued in *Republic III* as if the Guardians were themselves actors, Plato now involves the spectator totally in the performance. No one can respond partially or passively to the drama. Earlier the Guardians had been allowed to copy the literal words and deeds of noble men; this sort of performance introduces no extraneous data into their souls. But Plato does not suggest any way for them to project this virtue outside themselves. Since public attention tends to encourage sensationalism, drama cannot effectively present a man of high character. In public, the noble man will subdue his grief in order to preserve his dignity. By himself, he may express his feelings more freely. Any true interaction of individual and society can come only after the individual has established his independence from social concerns. Privacy, not public action, encourages excellence. Exposure to others' gaze makes the individual responsible for his value as a model to others; deliberate seeking of such attention shows the individual's lack of self-respect.

Unfortunately, Plato's discussion of the interaction of art and soul does not follow from his earlier tripartite division of the soul.[41] He had previously allowed the spirited element, "the natural auxiliary of reason" (*Republic IV* 440e), to reinforce the judgments

---

[41] In his *The Greeks and the Irrational* E. R. Dodds has entitled a chapter, "Plato, the Irrational Soul, and the Inherited Conglomerate" (pp. 297–35). Although he is concerned primarily with Plato's religious thought, Dodds does provide an interesting discussion of "Plato's fission of the empirical man into daemon and beast" (p. 214).

of the rational element. But now, omitting any mediating principle, he simplifies his categories to the rational and the nonrational. And under the malevolent influence of art, the nonrational becomes anti-rational. The lower part of the soul responds to art without reservation. The emotional element, encouraged by external displays, finds ready and natural expression before the gaze of society.

Any arousal of the appetite disturbs the balance between the components of the soul. The interests of the reason and of the appetite have little or nothing in common. The strength to act intelligently comes from within; personal discipline and steady adherence to recollection enable the rational part to maintain its just supremacy. "What encourages him to resist his grief is the lawful authority of reason, while the impulse to give way comes from the feeling itself" (*X* 604ab). The suffering compounds itself, drawing the soul to its own pain. The presence of contradictory impulses proves that the soul possesses two distinct elements. The rational part responds to the higher principle, not to the immediate situation. This authority declares that one should bear misfortune as quietly as possible, without showing irritation. The moment of stress does not readily lend itself to objective appraisal. A misfortune may be a blessing in disguise; certainly an overreaction accomplishes little. Moreover, in the instance of a physical injury, acquiescence to pain may interfere with one's seeking urgently needed help.

The opportunity to deliberate ($\tau\tilde{\omega}$ $\beta o\upsilon\lambda\epsilon\acute{\upsilon}\epsilon\sigma\theta\alpha\iota$) on misfortune keeps the individual from responding directly to his own or to others' problems. The lower part clings to past and present griefs, whereas the reason should possess enough distance from the immediate to "decide on the best move in the game of life that the fall of the dice permits. Instead of behaving like a child who goes on shrieking after a fall and hugging the wounded part, we should accustom the mind to set itself at once to raise up the fallen and cure the hurt, banishing lamentation with a healing touch" (*X* 604cd). The correct discipline of the entire soul comes from constant training.[42] Since one does not learn by exposure to evils, habit

[42] Cf. *Republic VII* 518, *X* 619, *Laws II* 655, *VII* 792–94.

is particularly essential in times of stress. A soul divided against itself cannot cope adequately with the difficulty. Emotional involvement with a concrete situation is a childish response which prevents the reasonable objectivity necessary to act wisely.

The nobler element contains within itself the ability to reason as well as the faculty to act upon that calculation.[43] This reinforcement of the reason by the will strengthens the proper basis of the entire soul. The rational element alone helps men to respond constructively; only this faculty of deliberation encourages bravery and nobility in man. The lower element, responding primarily to the physical, does not engage in legitimate interplay with the higher part of the soul. Instead, this emotional part wishes to dwell upon the suffering, reveling insatiably in self-pity. Plato sees no good whatsoever in this unreasonable, idle, and cowardly part of man's soul. Lacking any access to discretion, this lower element tends to continue in its misdeeds. Self-indulgence perpetuates itself, leading to greater and greater outward displays.[44]

6

THE SENSATIONAL BASIS OF ART

Plato feels that his comments on the incompatibility of reason and outward displays of emotions apply directly to art. Only with great difficulty can one portray a man of wisdom and temperance on the stage. He observes that only ugly emotions make characters interesting for the masses: "This irritable disposition gives scope for a great diversity of dramatic representation; whereas the calm and

[43] The *Theaetetus*, agreeing with *Republic X*, says "the mind, by a power of her own, contemplates the universals in all things" (185e).

[44] Socrates' deliberately sophistic definition of love recognizes the detrimental effects of the combination of irrational desire and beauty: "When irrational desire, pursuing the enjoyment of beauty, has gained the mastery over judgment that prompts to right conduct, and has acquired from other desires, akin to it, fresh strength to strain towards bodily beauty, that very strength provides it with its name: it is the strong passion called Love" (*Phaedrus* 238bc).

wise character in its unvarying constancy is not easy to represent, nor when represented is it readily understood, especially by a promiscuous gathering in a theater, since it is foreign to their own habit of mind" (*X* 604e). The temperate character usually maintains his balance; his actions are more nearly unified and self-contained. This deep and secret harmony does not lend itself to variable external representation. Since the imitative poet has an innate bias toward strong and variable emotions, a steadfast disposition does not naturally attract this popular imitator.[45] Moreover, the poet lacks the skills to make the austere representations of virtue palatable to the masses, even if he had the correct instincts.[46] A good reputation among the many depends on the artist's mirroring their myriad dispositions.

The complex and contradictory emotions presented on the stage find their way into the souls of even the most noble men. Only a rare few are exempt from the dangers in poetry. Plato feels the awesome attraction of poetry to be the source of its destructive power. To hear and see a speech presented causes a complete relaxation of one's discretion. Having his emotional part drawn outward to the scene, the spectator follows and observes the imitation. Again, there is no distinct intermediary between poet and spectator; the rhapsode for all practical purposes becomes Homer:

> When even the best of us listen to Homer or some other tragic poet imitate a hero moaning over his sorrows in a long tirade, or to a chorus beating their breasts as they chant a lament, you know how the best of us enjoy giving ourselves up to follow the performance with eager sympathy. The more a poet can move our feelings in this way, the better we think him. And yet when

[45] Plato divides men into nine classes according to the amount of truth in their souls. Although the philosopher, the artist, and those with musical and loving natures are in the highest group, the poet and other imitative artists fall into the sixth level. See E. R. Dodds, *The Greeks and the Irrational*, p. 230, n. 56.

[46] Truth always must precede true rhetoric. Socrates asks, "In good speaking should not the mind of the speaker know the truth of the matter about which he is going to speak?" (*Phaedrus* 259e). See also *Phaedrus* 262, 269, 273, 277.

the sorrow is our own, we pride ourselves on being able to bear it quietly like a man, condemning the behavior we admired in the theater as womanish. Can it be right that the spectacle of a man behaving as one would scorn and blush to behave oneself should be admired and enjoyed, instead of filling us with disgust? [*X* 605cd]

The enjoyment of the presentation of poetry and the reflection upon its significance call for two states of mind. Plato himself enjoys giving himself up to the performance. But even he does not feel capable of controlling poetry's direct appeal to the lower element of his soul. When a man loses his rational authority in the performance, he has no assurance of finding his soul's equilibrium again.

Plato does not discuss a faculty with which man can profitably interact with other humans. Only the inferior element communes with a corresponding element in another man. In dealing with emotions and moments of stress, the poet puts on stage the very actions we in our own lives would try to keep backstage. Since poetry bypasses the calculating element, a performance may break down the control a noble man has established by long habit. Even momentary indulgence in a response to another's suffering gives rise to a useless and dangerous sentimentality. The noblest part of us cannot be too thoroughly schooled by reason or habit. There is no occasion for this element to relax its watch over these irritating feelings; an emotional sympathy is mere weakness. If a man has some pretensions to goodness, his grief — even if excessive — calls for some admiration and pity. But still, the extent to which one adopts another's grief as his own determines the degree of the intellect's suppression. Misplaced human sympathy, then, leads not to greater understanding or strength of character, but to self-indulgence.

Since only the intellect can see a work in its totality, the emotional element responds to particular segments of the performance. Enjoyment of these purple passages keeps the immature person from disdaining a work fundamentally vicious. The lower element usually seizes upon sensational passages; this part of the soul can neither understand the meaning of the entire work nor seek its context. Clearly not limiting his censure to realistic art, Plato states that any involvement with human emotions corrupts the nobler part of man. He makes no distinction between the enjoyment of an artistic presentation of suffering and the direct response toward another individual. Few men realize that to enter into another's feelings necessarily affects one's own soul. The individual tends to extend to his personal conduct the emotion of pity which sympathy for others has strengthened.

Enjoyment of any sort of performance encourages irresponsible actions. The individual makes a private quest to strengthen his reason, whereas the public presentation of emotions tempts him to forsake his carefully established habits. Vulgarity on the stage can insensibly destroy the decorum patiently set up by the intellect. As in *Republic III* 388–89, laughter holds the same danger as pathos:

> You are doing the same thing if, in listening at a comic performance or in ordinary life to buffooneries which you would be ashamed to indulge in yourself, you thoroughly enjoy them instead of being disgusted with their ribaldry. There is in you an impulse to play the clown, which you have held in restraint from a reasonable fear of being set down as a buffoon; but now you have given it rein, and by encouraging its impudence at the theater you may be unconsciously carried away into playing the comedian in your private life. [*X* 606c]

Plato the artist feels the temptation to challenge the poets directly. Men who lack his discretion become low comic poets through exposure to buffoonery.[47] Poetic representations of love and anger, as well as exhibitions of pleasure or pain, which accompany all human action, endanger the supremacy of the soul's calculating and reasonable element. "Poetry waters the ground of passions which should be allowed to wither away and sets them up in control, although the goodness and happiness of our lives depend on their being held in subjection" (*X* 606d). The audience, by participating during the performance, extend the public spectacle over into their private lives.

---

[47] Comic poets are the especial antagonists of Socrates. See *Apology* 18–19, *Phaedo* 70c.

7

THE BANISHMENT OF PLEASURE AND PAIN

Plato ends the discussion of poetry in what seems, at least to him, to be a complete rejection of all except explicitly didactic verse.[48] One may dispute whether he has proven his point, but he himself is satisfied with his reasoning: "You must be quite sure that we can admit into our commonwealth only the poetry which celebrates the praises of the gods and of good men. If you go further and admit the honeyed muse in epic or in lyric verse, then pleasure and pain will usurp the sovereignty of law and of the principles always recognized by common consent as the best" (*X* 607a). As in the earlier books of the *Republic* and in the *Laws*, Plato here admits the poetry which praises gods and virtuous men. Epic and drama are too directly anthropocentric. Plato's theory of knowledge does not allow him to develop a system of literary criticism which would honor the presentation of strong emotions. But one might ask why he does not group lyric poetry with encomia, for a well-wrought eulogy of virtue may give pleasure. Presumably these encomia need not resemble such lyric modes as the Mixed Lydian or Hyperlydian, which have already been censured.[49] Indeed, pleasure and pain would not necessarily corrupt the principles of his state, for an effective tribute to "gods and good men" may cause both delight and agony. But Plato here is not concerned with the effectiveness of poetry. Earlier he has discussed its usefulness in promoting harmony in the souls of its hearers; the last book of the

---

[48] Collingwood, in "Plato's Philosophy of Art," points out that in *Republic III* some art is mimetic, some is not. *Republic X*, he says, argues that all art is mimetic and this is the key to its nature: "Nor does Plato ever again in later works assert or imply the existence of non-mimetic art" (p. 166). But Collingwood seems to reverse his position in *The Principles of Art* when he states that "in the tenth book Plato's position has changed. But it has not changed in the direction of regarding all poetry as representative. The change is that whereas in Book III some representative poetry is banished because what it represents is trivial or evil, in Book X all representative poetry is banished because it is representative" (p. 263).

[49] *Republic III* 398.

Republic simply states that the only safe poetry for this purpose is the obviously didactic.

Plato's admission of any poetry at this point would seem to convict him of inconsistency either in his reasoning or in the example presented by his dialogues. The dialogues seldom confine themselves to straightforward praises of virtue; the description and dramatization of Socrates' encounters resembles the art Plato has condemned. The earlier dialogues — the *Charmides,* the *Lysis,* the *Laches* — show Socrates in deliberately inconclusive arguments. The *Phaedrus* contains a praise of selfish desire, the *Gorgias* a praise of injustice, and the *Symposium* offers conflicting speeches on love. Thus, his own dialogues, with all their artistic power, must prove themselves to be "praises of the gods and of good men." And conversely, these praises of virtue must prove themselves to be something other than poetry.[50]

Plato mockingly invites some defense of poetry, and critics throughout the ages have not been slow to take him up. But for Plato all poetry whose end is to give pain or pleasure must be justified in the terms he has set up generally for the ideal state. Only complete devotion to reason could make Plato reject the arts which afford him so much personal pleasure. The poets have traditionally been antagonistic to the philosophers:[51]

> Lest poetry should convict us of being harsh and unmannerly, let us tell her further that there is a long-standing quarrel between poetry and philosophy. There are countless tokens of this old antagonism, such as the lines which speak of "the cur which at his master yelps," or "one mighty in the vain talk of fools"

---

[50] A noble craftsman need pay little attention to his material: "One who has nothing to show of more value than the literary works on whose phrases he spends hours, twisting them this way and that, pasting them together and pulling them apart, will rightly, I suggest, be called a poet or speech-writer or law-writer" (*Phaedrus* 278de).

[51] The *Laws* states that earlier thinkers misunderstood the soul and the sources of causes. "Such studies gave rise to much atheism and perplexity, and the poets took occasion to be abusive, comparing philosophers to she-dogs uttering vain howlings, and talking other nonsense of the same sort" (*XII* 967c).

or "the throng of all-too-sapient heads," or "subtle thinkers all in rags." None the less, be it declared that, if the dramatic poetry whose end is to give pleasure can show good reason why it should exist in a well-governed society, we for our part should welcome it back, being ourselves conscious of its charm; only it would be a sin to betray what we believe to be the truth. You too, my friend, must have felt this charm, above all when poetry speaks through Homer's lips. [*X* 607bc]

This apparent love of Homer, coupled with the inflexible determination to expel poetry, shows the ambiguity of Plato's mistrust of poetry. No human poet is adequate: "Of that place beyond the heavens none of our earthly poets has yet sung, and none shall sing worthily. But this is the manner of it, for assuredly we must be bold to speak what is true, above all when our discourse is upon truth" (*Phaedrus* 247c). So in his rapture, Plato will from time to time attempt the task which he denies to any man of this world. Unquestionably, he has banished the epic and drama, indeed all poetry dealing with human actions and desires. Elsewhere he would use Homer to provide examples of good poetry, but here he has excluded all poets he knew. No one is left to write the didactic verse allowed in *Republic X*.

Before poetry can be readmitted from exile, her advocates will have to present a defense in lyric verse or some other meter. The unpoetic lovers of the arts may even use unmetrical language to prove that poetry is not merely a source of pleasure. Plato shall listen favorably; he would be happier on the whole if his beloved poetry could be proven beneficial:

But if it cannot, then we must take a lesson from the lover who renounces at any cost a passion which he finds is doing him no good. The love for poetry of this kind, bred in us by our own much admired institutions, will make us kindly disposed to believe in her genuine worth; but so long as she cannot make good her defence we shall, as we listen, rehearse to ourselves the reasons we have just given, as a countercharm to save us from relapsing into a passion which most people have never outgrown. We shall reiterate that such poetry has no serious claim to be valued as an apprehension of truth. One who lends an ear to it should rather beware of endangering the order established in his soul, and would do well to accept the view of poetry which we have expressed. [*X* 607e–8b]

The great danger in poetry comes from its seductive appeal to the lower part of the soul. Lacking a serious claim to the truth, poetry upsets the soul's proper order. One must decide for truth over pleasure, for "it is a choice between becoming a good man or a bad. And poetry, no more than wealth or power or honors, should tempt us to be careless of justice and virtue" (*X* 608b). Art and human excellence are natural antagonists.

While he does invite a defense, Plato clearly thinks a successful counterargument is unlikely. The attack on Homer and the poets is serious; Plato loves poetry too much to banish explicitly every example of poetry he knows without good reason. The next chapter will show that poetry embodies all the dangers of any verbal discourse. Language only imitates the real. "All that is said by any of us can only be imitation and representation" (*Critias* 107b). Words can suggest truth, but beautiful language has the dangerous property of entangling the mind in the words themselves. Just as the Forms precede their temporal embodiments, knowledge precedes language. Words arise from a knowledge of reality; man must look through, not into, language in order to grasp reality.

VI

Language
and the
Imitation of Reality

And who that hath nothing but language only may be no more praised than a popinjay, a pye, or a stare when they speak featly. There be many nowadays in famous schools and universities which be so much given to the study of tongues only, that when they write epistles, they seem to the reader that, like to a trumpet, they make a sound without any purpose, where unto men do harken more for the noise than for any delectation that thereby is moved.

Sir Thomas Elyot, *The Boke Named the Governour*

Clearly, an intense personal regret accompanies Plato's condemnation of poetry. A deep-seated frustration with poetry underlies his multifaceted consideration of art and beauty in the public realm. Tacitly, Plato has embraced the beauty and usefulness of art. His dialogues contain dramatic conflicts of ideas, fascinating myths, lyric descriptions of the joys of the philosopher. Moreover, he reveals a long and loving acquaintance with poetry. Quotations abound throughout the dialogues, and the poets are often named among the wise men worthy of veneration. His statements on poetic inspiration recognize the presence of beauty in this world; only a god could be capable of producing such beautiful language. While this inhuman art would be dangerously opaque to intellectual examination, Plato's admiration is by no means totally ironic. And even in *Republic X*, he explicitly declares his love for poetry.

But in the crucial *Republic X*, his dedication to philosophy demands the censure of poetry. The pleasure and pain of lyric poetry must be excluded from the good state; Homer's banishment shows that Plato would condemn epic as well as drama. The consideration of the nature and use of poetry throughout the *Republic* finds no worthwhile beauty or harmony in this art. *Republic II* deems that the value of myths and stories depends solely on their content as teachers and as models. Uninformed by criticism or restraint, children and uneducated men can see poetry only in terms of the mundane world. Complex or lengthy poems cannot be tolerated any more than can immoral verse, for only the prepared intellect can establish the proper context. Plato allows imaginative language for instructing children and subduing the insane, but not for the inspiring of reasonable and dignified men. *Republic III* further emphasizes poetry's involvement with life and ethics. Here Plato discusses the response to poetry of the most enlightened people in the state. Poetry always exists in the public performance, optimally both given and witnessed by the Guardian himself. This performance cannot properly be called a distinct art, an action separate from ordinary events, for the speaker is concerned only with reinforcing his own nature. Then in *Republic X* Plato considers poetry for people in general; here public performances lack even the virtue of reinforcing noble characters. This book of the dialogue whittles the province of poetry to the point of oblivion.

1

THE PROBLEM OF LANGUAGE

One underlying reason for Plato's implicit love and his explicit contempt for poetry can be seen in his ambivalent attitude toward language. Any worth of an artifact beside its immediate use lies in its ability to stimulate harmony in the observer.[1] Since words are

---

[1] F. Sontag, in "The Platonist's Conception of Language," reasons that language cannot be isolated as an end in itself: "Language, when it leads us

already a physical imitation of reality, both poetic manipulation and critical study of language can only fix man's attention on a level inferior to reality itself.[2] Other physical imitations, through their mathematical proportions, can express the necessary harmony. But language arises both from ordinary human convention and from correspondence to nature. This inherent human element precludes language from being completely faithful to reality. Language can express only a partial truth and therefore cannot in itself be recognized as beautiful.

The mingling of the divine with the human, the conventional with the absolute, keeps Plato from taking a systematic position toward language. His one dialogue devoted to the subject, the *Cratylus*, provokes rather than satisfies.[3] Based on the theory of Forms, this eristic dialogue probes, with caution, the origins, nature, and use of words.[4] Socrates himself recognizes the inaccuracies of

---

to a study of the natural structures themselves, can be a powerful ally. When it leads only to itself, language can be the worst of all deceivers, since it has enough similarity to the structure of the world to give a good imitation of real knowledge" (p. 826).

[2] The people in Plato's cave metaphor are incapable of real communication: "If they could talk to one another, would they not suppose that their words referred only to those passing shadows which they saw?" (*Republic VII* 514b). See also *Republic V* 476 and *Phaedrus* 259. A good speaker must know the truth before he can speak meaningfully.

[3] The uncertainty of the date for the *Cratylus* does not have a great importance for our present purposes. As Paul Shorey states in *What Plato Said*, "Whether early or late, it shows Plato 'already' in possession of many of the principles which he elaborates more fully in the *Theaetetus* and the *Sophist*" (p. 260). Gilbert Ryle, in *Plato's Progress*, agrees that the *Cratylus* "has close links with the *Theaetetus* and the *Sophist*, and, being philosophically more primitive than either, it must be earlier than the *Theaetetus*" (p. 273). Ryle then suggests that the *Cratylus* was at one time intended to be part of a trilogy with the *Theaetetus* and the *Sophist*. Most contemporary scholarship accepts the later date for the dialogue.

[4] In *Plato's Doctrine of Ideas* J. A. Stewart links the *Cratylus* with other dialogues that discuss the Forms. Only minor differences in formulation separate the theory here from that revealed in such dialogues as the *Phaedrus*, *Euthydemus*, *Gorgias*, and *Theaetetus*. "The chronological treatment of the Doctrine of Ideas has, in my opinion, diverted attention from what is constant in it to verbal alterations in the statement of it which are made to

some of his etymologies and phonetic analyses. His fanciful exaggerations apparently represent a satire of contemporary interpretations of words and stories.[5] Amid his deliberately specious arguments, Plato discusses the relationship of language to the true essences in nature. Despite the pervasive irony, we can be sure of his contempt for the close study of words; we should not rummage around in the foul rag and bone shop of language.[6] Socrates himself can speak of names only when possessed by spirits, a sure indication of Plato's reservations about the whole inquiry.

Plato thinks that language imitates reality in some way, either closely or loosely; knowledge lies outside the realm of language.[7] As an imitation, language can only reflect, imperfectly, a reality outside itself. The *Laws* makes a word even further from reality than the *Cratylus*: "We know the essence, the definition of the essence, and the name" (*Laws* X 895d).[8] The creation of language, like the

---

appear as essential modifications of its methodological character — modifications which, if they had existed, would, indeed, have left the Doctrine without any methodological character at all" (p. 35). While Stewart's argument seems as biased as that of Socrates against flux, the *Cratylus* does seem to accept the theory of Forms without further question.

[5] In "Plato and Allegorical Interpretation" J. Tate points out the use of etymologies by the sophist Prodicus and especially by the Heracliteans to explain poetry. Democritus of Abdera also appears "to have made occasional use of etymology — that pseudo-science which, assuming that the original form (τὸ ἔτυμον) of a word represented its true meaning, furnished many fanciful clues to the hidden significance of the myths" (p. 143).

[6] This dialogue also attacks the sophists' claim to the interpretation of language. Socrates says ironically to Hermogenes: "If I had not been poor, I might have heard the fifty-drachma course of the great Prodicus, which is a complete education in grammar and language — these are his own words — and then I should have been at once able to answer your questions about the correctness of names" (384b). His erstwhile allies of *Republic X* are again his enemies.

[7] Cf. *Theaetetus* on the primacy of knowledge: "And is it not shameless when we do not know what knowledge is, to be explaining the verb 'to know'? The truth is, Theaetetus, that we have long been infected with logical impurity" (196de).

[8] The *Sophist* 218 makes a similar distinction between name and definition.

creation of any physical artifact, is at a first remove from reality. Plato judges both poetry and language by their faithfulness to nature. As a tool, a name can teach and distinguish. But even so, words are treacherous guides to knowledge of real things. Since names can be applied ambiguously, the legislator of names must be some human agent, and therefore fallible. The gods would not thus contradict themselves. Both the original maker and the current user of a word apply language to an immediate practical use. Thus, human limitations and ignorance will flaw individual words as well as their arrangement in speech or poetry.

Plato's recognition of the complexity of his subject represents a commendable sophistication for this time. The two other persons of the dialogue, Cratylus and Hermogenes, propose radically differing errors.[9] Cratylus would deny any value whatsoever to convention; language takes its meaning through nature (φύσει).[10] Hermogenes, on the other hand, would make language meaningful by custom (νόμῳ). An individual decides arbitrarily what to call an object. Completely ignoring the social origins of language, Hermogenes feels one's personal choice is always correct. Socrates takes a much sounder position between these extremes. He particularly objects to Hermogenes' contention that language is completely arbitrary. But

---

[9] Traditionally, scholars have agreed that Hermogenes expresses an Eleatic position, Cratylus a Heraclitean. But G. S. Kirk, in "The Problem of Cratylus," proposes that Cratylus is not a convinced Heraclitean. Since Plato fails to condemn Cratylus as a wild Heraclitean, Aristotle is probably mistaken in his assertion about the man. Basing his interpretation heavily on *Cratylus* 440, Kirk states that Socrates introduces the concept of flux before Cratylus does; Cratylus mistakenly accepts the idea to support his thesis of the natural validity of names (pp. 225–53). For a discussion of the basic similarity in the apparently contradictory positions of Hermogenes and Cratylus, see Paul Friedländer, *Plato: The Dialogues, First Period*, p. 198, and A. E. Taylor, *Plato: The Man and His Work*, pp. 85–86.

[10] Cratylus' position is far too simple and mechanical. Friedländer, in *Plato: The Dialogues, First Period*, holds that "Kratylos, as we know, is a Herakleitean; but for him the secret harmony between words and things, which the great Herakleitos himself felt intuitively, has become a purely rational exercise by which the mind tries to gain easy access to the nature of things" (p. 197).

despite his dissatisfaction with his analysis of language as an imitation, he cannot bring himself to endorse social custom either.

Socrates repeatedly expresses his skepticism not only about the end of the inquiry, but also of the worth of the search. As the Stranger says to Socrates, "If you continue to be not too particular about names, you will be all the richer in wisdom when you are an old man" (*Statesman* 261e). Any study of the language of men provides at best an obscure way to the truth. All we can do is seek to discover something about words according to the measure of our abilities. Any higher truth about language, as with knowledge about the gods, does not come with any certainty to mere mortals; we can entertain only human notions of them. "In this present inquiry, let us say to ourselves, before we proceed, that the higher method is the one which we or others who would analyze language to any good purpose must follow; but under the circumstances, as men say, we must do as well as we can" (*Cratylus* 425c). While Socrates, a man himself, cannot describe this higher approach, he need not on this account compromise his standards.

Socrates refuses to ground the origin of basic words in man's uninformed society. He admits the ridiculousness of his theory that things can be imitated by letters and syllables (γράμμασι καὶ συλλαβαῖς) but he can think of no better principle. Thus, like painting (and by Plato's analogy, poetry), language is a physical imitation of physical objects. One questionable alternative to his theory involves "recourse to divine help, like the tragic poets, who in any perplexity have their gods waiting in the air; and must get out of our difficulty in like fashion, by saying that 'the gods gave the first names, and therefore they are right'" (*Cratylus* 425d). A second spurious approach would derive these first words from some ancient barbarous people. But to reason that antiquity has cast a veil over the source simply denies the possibility of any serious inquiry.

Current usage gives no clue to the all-important pristine meaning of words. Awareness of an entire language would not lead directly to knowledge, for language as commonly used has various degrees of purity. One must know the meaning and relevance of original words; any ignorance of the primitive names involves a corresponding ignorance of words derived from them. But knowledge of language resembles knowledge of any other physical imitation. The observer must dispassionately seek the relationship of the particular representation to the general reality. The application of words to things differs little from any other practical skill. The creation or use of a name requires one's conscious participation.

2
The Physical Basis of Language

Thus, Plato does not allow knowledge to reside statically in the language of man.[11] Existing independently of any verbal embodiment, knowledge precedes the correct application of language to a human situation. Words also must have an objective existence; otherwise the consistent study and use of language would be impossible. Plato is not sure, however, about the relationship between language and meaning. Socrates' opponents in the *Cratylus* simply do not realize the complexity of the problem. Hermogenes would maintain that the name of anything is that which anyone affirms to be the name. "I can conceive no correctness of names other than this; you give one name, and I another. And in different cities and countries there are different names for the same things; Hellenes differ from barbarians in their use of names and the several Hellenic tribes from one another" (385de). The name in his personal language (ἰδίᾳ) has no integral relationship with the word in the public language (δημοσίᾳ). But Socrates reasons (unconvincingly to a modern) that since true and false propositions exist, a proposition must be entirely true or false down to the smallest part, the name. Simply, Hermogenes, while agreeing with Socrates on absolute standards of truth and virtue, does not realize that a system of language relative to one individual would be trivial.

---

[11] For further comments on the identity of thought and felicity of expression, see *Phaedrus* 260, 269–70 and *Laws XII* 956–66.

Language for Plato can be relative neither to the individual nor to humanity. The existence of standards in ethics and metaphysics suggests that the same certainties must apply to language. Protagoras erroneously thinks that man is the measure of all things, thus making distinctions between wisdom and folly impossible. On the other hand, Euthydemus cannot correctly claim that all things equally belong to all men, for then vice and virtue would apply equally to all. "If neither man is right, and things are not relative to individuals, and all things do not equally belong to all at the same moment and always, they must be supposed to have their own proper and permanent essence: they are not in relation to us, or influenced by us, fluctuating according to our fancy, but they are independent, and maintain to their own essence the relation prescribed by nature" (*Cratylus* 386de). The options are either variation with the whim of the individual or stability by accordance to eternal truth. That language could be relative to a body of individuals and thus achieve some sort of standard does not occur to Plato.

Plato does not make a sharp distinction between speech and thought. The essentially human process of thought can find an immediate and direct presentation in speech.[12] "Are not thought and speech the same, with this exception, that what is called thought is the unuttered conversation of the soul with herself . . . . The stream of thought which flows through the lips and is audible is called speech" (*Sophist* 263e). Plato makes speech akin to the things of the senses, which trouble the soul, yet elsewhere he would also have speech and thought fairly closely identified. Utterance of

---

[12] Effective speeches often flow from the mind without any intervening faculty for verbal composition. Socrates knows that he has heard a better speech than that of Lysias, "because I perceive that my bosom is full, and that I could make another speech as good as that of Lysias, and different. Now I am certain that this is not an invention of my own, who am well aware that I know nothing, and therefore I can only infer that I have been filled through the ears like a pitcher from the waters of another, though I have actually forgotten in my stupidity who was my informant" (*Phaedrus* 235cd). This metaphor agrees with Plato's more direct statements in such dialogues as the *Sophist* and the *Theaetetus*.

any sort corrupts the pursuit of truth,[13] for "thought is best when
the mind is gathered into herself and no things of the senses trouble
her — neither sounds nor sights nor pain nor any pleasure, — when
she takes leave of the body, and has as little as possible to do with it,
when she has no bodily sense or desire, but is aspiring after true
being" (*Phaedo* 65c). The truly inspired man will be self-contained;
the aspiration toward true being admits no verbal discourse.

Thought arises from man's perception of the Forms, not from
his manipulating words and sentences.[14] Only observation of things
can lead to understanding words. Primary names, those created by
the first name-giver, must show the "nature of things" as far as
possible. If these words do not imitate their referent, they are not
real names in any sense. "Suppose that we had no voice or tongue,
and wanted to communicate with one another, should we not, like
the deaf and dumb, make signs with the hands and head and the
rest of the body?" (*Cratylus* 422e). Obviously thinking of the
physical world, Plato cites several human gestures which indicate
direction and movement. These motions are the limit of such conversation, for the body can express things only by direct physical
imitation. From this physical basis come Plato's reservations about
words: language is only an extension of physical gestures. Socrates
suggests tentatively that "when we want to express ourselves, either
with the voice, or tongue, or mouth, the expression is simply their
imitation of that which we want to express" (423b). But he rejects
a completely mechanistic language. People who imitate sheep,
cocks, or other animals do not name that which they imitate. Here,
as in the *Republic*, Plato scorns those who would mistake the sounds
of physical nature for acceptable human discourse.

[13] In particular, poetry, a loose combination of song, meter, and discourse, always has an unfortunate public dimension for Plato: "Suppose that
we strip all poetry of song and rhythm and meter, there will remain speech.
And this speech is addressed to a crowd of people. Then poetry is a sort of
rhetoric; the poets in the theaters are rhetoricians" (*Gorgias* 502cd). Address-
ing their rhetoric impartially to a crowd of men, women, and children, free-
men and slaves, these entertainers seek to give pleasure rather than to improve man.

[14] See *Parmenides* 132.

Plato wishes to distinguish only partially the nature of language from the natures of music and painting. On one hand, while the ingredients differ, all these arts lead to the same sort of imitation. On the other, language cannot be exclusively a vocal art, since words do not imitate the kinds of things which music imitates, and a name expresses a more fundamental relation to the underlying reality than do music or painting: "Is there not an essence of each thing, just as there is a color or sound? And is there not an essence of color and sound as well as of anything else which may be said to have an essence? And if any one could express the essence of each thing in letters and syllables, would he not express the nature of each thing?" (423e). The musician and the painter are two sorts of imitators; the name-giver is the third maker. But, unlike the musician, this giver of names expresses the essence, the nature of the thing, as he utters the physical sounds. Yet Plato will argue that any subsequent embodiment of the word represents the physical only.

Since sounds may indeed express immutable essences, nothing prevents Plato from allowing the study of language a legitimate role in education. But just as the painter deliberately chooses colors and shapes as a prerequisite to making a picture, the namer must first understand both his material and his subject. The analysis of language, like the study of music, proceeds from generalization. We begin with basic sounds (στοιχεῖα), first separating and classifying the vowels, then the consonants, mutes, and semivowels. "And when we have made these divisions properly, we shall give names to the appropriate things and see whether, like the basic sounds, there are any classes to which they may be all referred; and hence we shall see their natures, and see, too, whether they have in them classes as there are in the sounds" (424d). This study will suggest how to apply them to what they resemble — whether one letter is used to denote one thing, or whether there is to be an admixture of several. Thus, either single or multiple sounds can express objects. Out of the combination of sounds come syllables, which in turn make up nouns and verbs.[15] And, finally, from the combinations of nouns

[15] H. S. Thayer, in "Plato: The Theory and Language of Function," pp. 303–18, points out that Plato says each statement must have at least one

and verbs, one arrives at language, "large and fair and whole" (425a). In learning, one works toward this mighty synthesis.[16] But once one has come to this knowledge, no further arrangement can improve language. The painter's understanding of the smallest elements of color and shape enables him to make a figure. Similarly, every sound in a word, the word itself, and all possible combinations of the word with others express or should express an essence. Thus, no skillful arrangement of words is superior to another as all essences are equal; the end of the acquisition of language is unchanging understanding.

3

THE ORIGIN OF LANGUAGE

Although words imitate reality, they originate in a knowledgeable human response at a particular moment.[17] Any subsequent use of a word must be judged by the same standards as the first application. Actions ($\pi\rho\acute{\alpha}\xi\epsilon\iota\varsigma$) as well as objects or affairs ($\pi\rho\acute{\alpha}\gamma\mu\alpha\tau\alpha$) have a reality ($\phi\acute{\upsilon}\sigma\iota\nu$) of their own, and accordingly one may judge them for correctness.[18] In addition, words resemble other physical objects in that they have a maker and a proper use. The giving of names is an important part of the act of speaking. The act of naming should be done naturally and with a proper instrument. But the word itself is an instrument to convey information and to distinguish things according to their nature. Names are the tools of the teacher, and when the teacher uses a name, he uses the work

---

noun and one verb (see *Cratylus* 431, *Sophist* 261). Each sentence then has at least two names — one of an action, and one of an agent or object. Thayer argues that the action word is more basic to the meaning and has a more general application within the sentence.

[16] In the *Sophist* 261ff Plato reasons that words which have no meaning when in sequence cannot be connected. Man's first linguistic act is to name; thereafter he learns to connect nouns and verbs. Discourse consists of words fitting together.

[17] Cf. *Parmenides* 147–48.

[18] Cf. *Theaetetus* 155.

of the legislator. Only the skillful can have any success at the task:
"Not every man is able to give a name, but only a maker of names;
and this is the legislator, who of all skilled artisans in the world is
the rarest" (*Cratylus* 388e–89a). This maker is always one of the
revered men of the past: "As the ancients may be observed to have
given many names which are according to nature and deserving of
praise, so there is an excellent one which they have given to the
dances of men who in their times of prosperity are moderate in their
pleasures — the giver of names, whoever he was, assigned to them
a very true, and poetical, and rational name" (*Laws VII* 816ab).
Every present individual has the power to apply names to particular
things, but he can add nothing of value to the further application
or development of language.

The product of the word maker (νομοθέτης, ὀνοματουργός),
like those of all artisans, is at one remove from reality. The worth
of his artifacts depends on their conformity to the eternal Forms.
The good craftsman thinks about the purposes of his handiwork,
not about his personal reaction to his materials. "When a man has
discovered the instrument naturally adapted to each work, he must
express this natural form, and not others which he fancies, in the
material, whatever it may be" (*Cratylus* 389c). All names should
closely correspond with the ideal of that name. The legislator should
not only have knowledge of the prototype, but know how to embody
the true natural name of each thing in sounds and syllables as well.
To be a worthwhile namer, he must work with the Form of that
name always before him. By relegating the raw materials of language to the physical world, Plato can maintain that different legis-
lators need not use the same syllables. By analogy, although making
the same instrument for the same purposes, various smiths do not
have to use the same iron. "The form must be the same, but the
material may vary, and still the instrument may be equally good of
whatever iron made, whether in Hellas or in a foreign country; —
there is no difference" (389e–90a). Minor differences in sounds
and syllables count for little. The languages of different countries
point to a common truth. Since Plato refuses to invest any language
with knowledge itself, he is not committed to defend the supremacy

of his own language. For Plato, all existing languages are probably about equally removed from the ultimate reality.

Plato makes a sharp distinction between maker and user of words. Bound by the necessity of directly serving the user, the word-maker has little freedom of creation.[19] Plato uses the analogy of word to practical object: The weaver is a better judge of the proper form for a shuttle than its maker, the carpenter. Similarly, reflecting his concept of the division of labor, the user judges the workmanship of a lyre or a ship. The user of language is, in particular, the one who can respond actively to the appropriateness of the words. Just as the pilot directs the work of the carpenter in making a rudder, so the dialectician, the proper judge of discourse, must direct the legislator of words. The *Phaedrus* 266 likewise distinguishes mere speakers such as Lysias and Thrasymachus from the real authorities, the dialecticians. The dialectician judges the extent to which the name-giver has faithfully reproduced reality in words. The dialectician, not the poet, is the true user of words. He does not create the words or ideas. Just as the philosopher recollects the forms he formerly saw, the dialectician seizes upon the words previously made.

The dialogues maintain that all good things are made by the intelligent individual, not by the ignorant mob. Accordingly, a mass of people can neither generate nor use words correctly. Reflecting popular thought, Protagoras has stated that man "was not long in inventing articulate speech and names" (*Protagoras* 322a). Plato has no such faith in mankind's natural creative powers. The giving of names can be no such light matter as Hermogenes thinks, nor the work of any chance person. Cratylus more nearly states Plato's theses that things have true names and that not every man is an artificer of names. The maker of words must have three skills. First, he must understand the object to be named. Second, he must perceive the name which each thing by nature has. And, finally, he must be able to express the true forms of things in letters and sounds.

---

[19] His product passes from him to the user of language. Plato has argued a similar division of producer and user in his flute-playing analogy.

These three areas of knowledge are essential to the study of language; the superficial cleverness of the sophists will be of little help in determining the nature of words. But lacking other records from the past, Plato must fall back on the poets to suggest some etymologies. And, as always, the past must be honored but accepted no further than reason decrees.

4

THE DEGENERATION OF WORDS

With the passage of time, society's bumbling has introduced corruption into language. One can try etymological studies to penetrate the cloud of ignorance, or one can with more certainty seek truth directly. But word study itself is not totally vacuous.[20] Homer often cites different names used by gods and by men, thus implying different degrees of correctness. Wise men or the gods are more likely to give "correct names" (*Cratylus* 392c), just as they do everything more skillfully. If the meaning or essence remains the same, we can alter freely a few syllables or individual sounds. Many words may be applied with equal justification to a single object. These synonyms show that even great variations in the physical form of a word do not make a corresponding change in the underlying meaning of the object. Like drugs or other physical substances, the real nature of a word may not be plain to the ignorant.[21] But the wise man can see beyond these superficial physical changes.

Socrates has been enjoying rummaging through his vast treasury of traditional lore to find his etymologies. But his inquiry has been largely nonrational. Socrates' mistrust of this easy source of apparent

[20] A. Nehring, in "Plato and the Theory of Language," distinguishes between Plato's epistemological and linguistic interests. There is a serious purpose behind Plato's etymologies (p. 16). A pioneering linguistic, Plato's discussion on sound-symbolism has been supported, Nehring says, by the modern studies of Humboldt and Jespersen (pp. 18–19).

[21] Cf. *Laws II* 659–60. Robert S. Brumbaugh thinks that the position taken by Cratylus is not entirely naïve (*Plato for the Modern Age*, p. 71).

wisdom shows his awareness that this treacherous method of inquiry has definite limitations.[22] "If I could remember the genealogy of Hesiod, I would have gone on and tried more conclusions of the same sort on the remoter ancestors of the gods, — then I might have seen whether this wisdom, which has come to me all in an instant, I know not whence, will or will not hold good to the end" (*Cratylus* 396cd). The recipient lacking the discipline of reason, any inspiration of this sort may sour and turn inconsistent. With irony, Socrates admits to being like a prophet newly inspired to utter oracles:

> I believe that I caught the inspiration from the great Euthyphro of the Prospaltian deme, who gave me a long lecture which commenced at dawn: he talked and I listened, and his wisdom and enchanting ravishment has not only filled my ears but taken possession of my soul, and today I shall let his superhuman power work and finish the investigation of names — that will be the way; but tomorrow, if you are so disposed, we will conjure him away, and make a purgation of him, if we can only find some priest or sophist who is skilled in purifications of this sort. [396d–97a]

We dare not read Plato too seriously here.[23] Still, this same rapture seizes Socrates before the chariot myth of the *Phaedrus*. These

---

[22] Socrates says that Euthydemus and Dionysodorus, two noted sophists, "will plead themselves and teach others to speak and to compose speeches which will have an effect upon the courts. And this was only the beginning of their wisdom, but they have at last carried out the pancratiastic art to the very end. They have mastered the only mode of fighting which had been hitherto neglected by them; and now no one dares even to stand up against them: such is their skill in the war of words, that they can refute any proposition whether true or false" (*Euthydemus* 272ab). These men began this art of disputation late; just one or two years ago they had none of their so-called wisdom.

[23] A. E. Taylor says, in *Plato: The Man and His Work*,

It is plain that we are not to find the serious meaning in the dialogue here, especially as, after delighting Cratylus by a pretended demonstration that language supports the Heraclitean philosophy, since the names of all things good contain references to movement, and the names of all bad things to arrest of movement, he turns round and produces equally ingenious and far-fetched etymological grounds for supposing that the original "giver of names" must have held the Eleatic doctrine that motion

etymologies, like the myths, suggest an approach rather than a conclusion. Plato would not lock the door to any house where knowledge might reside.

Because society seldom looks to natural fitness, names given to ordinary men may not correspond with a truth. Socrates has begun with proper names engraved in tradition. Since convention or arbitrary decision may have obscured correct meanings in such names, we cannot achieve much certainty here. "There will be more chance of finding correctness in the names of immutable essences; — there ought to have been more care taken about them when they were named, and perhaps there may have been some more than human power at work occasionally in giving them names" (*Cratylus* 397bc). Since mankind has little to do with what is unchanging, here there has been less human distortion of the words. Just as poetic enthusiasm originates beyond man, the source of words might possibly be superhuman. But, as usual, the gods and their actions are not readily susceptible to rational examination. So tradition rather than empirical observation must provide clues to the meanings of words describing lofty beings such as gods and heavenly bodies, heroes and demons.

Even if mistaken, the first name-givers must have had some sort of special knowledge. Possibly they might have been worthy of the name "philosophers." Nevertheless, one cannot rely on these primeval givers of words: only present inquiry into truth can suffice. No clear principles exist for the study of etymologies. Certain words "may be variously interpreted; and yet more variously if a little permutation is allowed" (400b). Certainly, violent interpretation should be avoided (410a). Any original confusion about words may extend into the present; human ignorance is persistent:

> By the dog of Egypt I have not a bad notion which came into my head only this moment: I believe that the primeval givers of

---

is an illusion, since all the names of good things appear to denote rest or stoppage of motion. Obviously, we are to take all this as good-humoured satire on attempts to reach a metaphysic by way of "philology"; as far as etymologies go, a little ingenuity will enable us to get diametrically opposite results out of the same data. [pp. 77–78]

names were undoubtedly like too many of our modern thinkers, who, in their search after the nature of things, are always getting dizzy from constantly going round and round, and then they imagine that the world is going round and round and moving in all directions; and this appearance, which arises out of their own internal condition, they suppose to be a reality of nature; they think that there is nothing stable or permanent, but only flux and motion, and that the world is always full of every sort of motion and change. [411bc]

Since most of the names seem to suggest flux, even serious study of language may not result in philosophical certainty. And the demonstrably false etymologies offered by the sophists cast the whole method into disrepute.

Society as well as individuals may obscure original meanings. Certain words within a language do not clearly fit into any pattern. But words seemingly of a foreign origin may just be corrupted by the passage of time. By stripping away the irrelevancies added by society, one might trace words back to their original and true meanings. But in its entirety, present language seems to be a corruption of an original fidelity to nature. Names have been so twisted in all manner of ways, that if the original language were compared with that currently in use, pure language might appear to be a barbarous tongue.

Eventually, this inquiry into the constituents of names reaches the limits of its usefulness. A thinker must stop when he comes to the names which are the elements of all other names and sentences. These basic names cannot be supposed to be made up of other names. "The word ἀγαθόν [good], for example, is, as we were saying, a compound of ἀγαστός [admirable] and θοός [swift]. And probably θοός is made up of other elements, and those again of others. But if we take a word incapable of further resolution, then we shall be right in saying that we have at last reached a primary element, which need not be resolved any further" (422ab). Both primary and derived names are supposed to indicate the nature of things, but the derived take their significance from the primary. Since some names turn out to be irreducible elements, directly studying their correspondence to nature will be more profitable than haggling over mere verbal characteristics. The difficult and largely arbitrary examination of tradition to derive etymologies lacks whatever certainty comes from a philosophical inquiry into the physical correspondence of language to nature.

5

WORDS AND HUMAN USAGE

The preceding survey has shown that Plato sets almost impossibly high standards on the study of words. Derived words mingle with the primary, and no one can see much correspondence between word and physical nature. Human words are tools to attain truth. As such, they must not be bandied about: "If a person does not attend to the meaning of terms as they are commonly used in argument, he may become involved in great paradoxes" (*Theaetetus* 165a). A special beauty for language of course cannot be accepted, but a word's truth in expressing nature can point to a general beauty. *Cratylus* 385 has argued for a truth or falsity in language on the basis that a true proposition cannot have false parts. Naming must accord with reality just as actions are done "according to their proper nature, and not according to our opinion of them" (387d). While theoretically a word can express a nonphysical as well as a physical reality, only the dialectician is likely to see such relationships. As in Plato's specific comments on aesthetics, the poet has been supererogatory.

But in considering the human uses of language, Plato expresses a position more favorable to poetry. An image or word does not have to be absolute or perfect to be useful. Standards still exist, but practicality now has its day. Whatever its standing as an imitation of nature, a name is an invaluable human instrument of teaching and of distinguishing natures. Plato recognizes three legitimate authorities in this realm: the dialectician, the name-giver, and the teacher. First in point of time, the legislator of words creates the name; he is the rarest of all skilled artisans. But since he makes the name of something according to its natural form, the legislator is bound by nature.

The second authority, the dialectician, actually possesses knowledge superior to that of the name-giver. Whereas the legislator can only imitate what he sees in nature, the dialectician knows how to use the words to ask and answer questions (ἐρωτᾶν καὶ ἀποκρίνεσθαι ἐπιστάμενον). The greater knowledge of the dialectician enables him both to apply words effectively and to correct deficiencies in the word-artisan's creation. The dialectician alone can judge the effects of these created words. But as the *Theaetetus* 167–68 states, a serious dialectician will never argue from the customary use of names and words — unlike the vulgar, who pervert these terms in various ways, to the infinite perplexity of one another.

Third, later in time and far less significant, the teacher of the words simply tells how to use a particular word well. In giving a name, the instructor uses the work of the namer. While Plato states that a teacher can be effective in manipulating words, he makes little else of this figure. Perhaps his silence derives from his contempt throughout for men or institutions that claim undue authority. Even if Plato were to recognize a special agency for instruction, poetry could have no role. Words convey publicly information inferior in truth to one's private recollection of the Forms.

While Plato will not compromise the standards of truth in language, he also refuses to deny words an important practical use. On the other hand, Cratylus, holding an absolutist position toward words, thinks language to be the most important subject of all. Words apply entirely to the object or they do not apply in any way. Thus all words have been rightly imposed. Cratylus thus denies the existence of falsehood; a person who speaks nonsense "would be putting himself in motion to no purpose; a false word would be an unmeaning sound like the noise of hammering at a brazen pot" (*Cratylus* 430a). Language always expresses truth and meaning; sounds without sense are simply not words.

To the contrary, Plato feels that every word man uses can be judged in terms of its meaning. Ignoring the element of sound altogether, he thinks that the use of language depends on the degree of its reflection of truth. The familiar analogy of vision to language emphasizes the physical basis of words. But Socrates admits that a name differs from what is named, the name imitating the object. He asks whether "pictures are also imitations of things, but in another way?" (430b). Both forms — words and pictures — apply equally to what they imitate. Cratylus would still have names always correct, even if some pictures do not resemble what they purport. Socrates can show a picture to someone, "and may I not go to him again, and say, 'This is your name'? — for the name, like the picture, is an imitation. May I not say to him — 'This is your name'? And may I not then bring to his sense of hearing the imitation of himself, when I say, 'This is a man'; or of a female of the human species, when I say, 'This is a woman,' as the case may be?" (430e–31a). Thus a name is not identical with the thing named. If visual representations can suggest the entire man, there is no reason why sound cannot also imitate him. This doctrine of imitation, eminently favorable to poetry, does not occur to Plato in *Republic X*.

Even though a perfect image is impossible — and perhaps undesirable — we should strive to make language conform to the object as much as possible. Even if poetry itself has a fixed beauty, ordinary language can be improved. Properly used by men, words have a dynamic rather than a static relationship to nature. If primitive or first nouns represent things, we should assimilate the verbal representations to the objects. The untenable alternative — as held by Hermogenes — would make words simply the conventions of an ignorant society. If words have meaning through arbitrary human agreements, language will have no direct bearing on anything beyond human knowledge.

Plato suggests that man's limited knowledge does not prevent his using words intelligently. He must maintain a balance between the immediate and the ultimate: "The free use of words and phrases, rather than minute precision, is generally characteristic of a liberal education, and the opposite is pedantic; but sometimes precision is necessary" (*Theaetetus* 184c). Rather than manipulating chance signs, one can seek a representation by likeness. "If the name is to be like the thing, the letters out of which the first names are composed must also be like things. Returning to the image of the picture, I would ask, 'How could anyone ever compose a picture which would be like anything at all, if there were not pigments in nature which resembled the things imitated, and out of which the picture is composed?' " (*Cratylus* 434ab). The original elements which compose a word, the sounds, have some degree of resemblance to the objects of which the names are the imitation. The identification need not be total. This correspondence with nature enables names to resemble things actually existing. Thus, words, basically physical representations of physical objects, can take whatever form the artisan implants.

6

PERFECT AND IMPERFECT IMAGES

Although words unquestionably can have an honorable role in education, Plato takes, for the most part, a neutral position toward language. Knowledge may be found anywhere, not just in words. And quibbling about words just interrupts the interplay of ideas. True knowledge demands that all assumptions be examined:

> The method of dialectic is the only one which takes this course, doing away with assumptions and traveling up to the first principle of all, so as to make sure of confirmation there. When the eye of the soul is sunk in a veritable slough of barbarous ignorance, this method gently draws it forth and guides it upwards, assisted in this work of conversion by the arts we have enumerated. From force of habit we have several times spoken of these as branches of knowledge; but they need some other name implying something less clear than knowledge, though not so dim as the apprehension of appearances. "Thinking," I believe, was the term we fixed on earlier; but in considering matters of such high importance we shall not quarrel about a name. [*Republic VII* 533cd]

Glaucon agrees that any name which clearly expresses the thought of the mind is acceptable. This action of the intellect, unhindered by partial truths or the senses, has no need to dwell on verbal subtleties.

Just as Plato has refused to allow an interaction of sentences to establish a context for a poetic utterance, he denies any sentence in discourse the ability to present a unified assertion. Truth or falsity apply to a more minute level than the sentence. And meaning lies neither in the object nor in the language. Instead, it is the application of a word to what it purportedly represents that determines truth or falsity. Using an argument also found in the *Theaetetus* 193–94, Socrates states, "If I can assign names as well as pictures to objects, the right assignment of them we may call truth, and the wrong assignment of them falsehood. Now if there be such a wrong assignment of names, there may also be a wrong or inappropriate assignment of verbs; and if of names and verbs then of the sentences, which are made up of them" (*Cratylus* 431b). Truth cannot contain any element of falsehood. The noun is the first and most obvious element of consideration; other words have the same relation to nature. If each word is a statement about nature, examination of an entire sentence must come after an investigation of the individual components.

The words one assigns to any object may not be a perfect representation. A modern person must have at least as good a grasp of the principles of the name as the first namer had. "Primitive nouns may be compared to pictures, and in pictures you may either give all the appropriate colors and figures, or you may not give them all — some may be wanting; or there may be too many or too much of them" (431c). Plato then extends the analogy to language; the imitator will use syllables and letters to produce his imitation. By adding or subtracting, a maker will make a less than accurate image. Thus the word-maker who gives a complete representation gives a perfect picture or figure. Any addition to or subtraction from this standard will still give an image, but not a good one. The maker of names may be good or bad; this talented legislator can be judged by the same criteria as other artists.

Admitting that the maker of words can imitate well or badly, Cratylus tries to distinguish language from the other arts: "when by the help of grammar, we assign the letters α or β, or any other letters to a certain name, then, if we add, or subtract, or misplace a letter, the name which is written is not only written wrongly, but not written at all; and in any of these cases becomes other than a name" (431e–32a). Either the word corresponds to its object in every particular, or the word does not apply at all. Any variation of sound, even the slightest, nullifies all use of the word. Basically, he agrees with Socrates that language begins by a conscious imposition of meaning upon sounds and letters. But unlike Socrates, Cratylus puts an absolute and unreasoning faith in the mechanical faithfulness of language to nature.

Good images are neither the true creation by a god nor the superficial representation by a painter. Socrates believes that the statement of Cratylus may apply to numbers, which must be just what they are, or not be at all. For example, the number ten at once becomes other than ten if a unit be added or subtracted and so for any number. But this inflexibility does not apply to that which is qualitative or to anything which is represented under an image. If an image expressed an object with perfect fidelity, the copy would no longer be an image. The verbal copy must be a faithful imitation ($\mu\acute{\iota}\mu\eta\mu\alpha$), but it cannot be exact.

Some images, then, are more useful than the reality. Socrates suggests, "Let us suppose the existence of two objects: one of them shall be Cratylus, and the other the image of Cratylus; and we will suppose, further, that some god makes not only a representation such as a painter would make of your outward form and color, but also creates an inward organization like yours, having the same warmth and softness; and into this infuses motion, and soul, and mind, such as you have, and in a word copies all your qualities, and places them by you in another form; would you say that this was Cratylus and the image of Cratylus, or that there were two Cratyluses?" (432bc). Clearly, there would be two of him. Socrates implies that the real Cratylus consists of the exact physical and intellectual man as he is; there is no Form which this particular Cratylus embodies. Here again is Plato's dilemma: the imitation

of this man must either be exact — and therefore not an image —
or vary in some way from the reality and thus be imperfect.

Therefore, Plato will allow partial truths in man's language. As
an image, language must necessarily diverge from reality. Indeed,
no ultimate truth can abide in language, for language is a tool, not
an end. "If a man had all the nit-picking knowledge of words that
ever was, he would not be at all the wiser; he would only be able to
play with men, tripping them up and oversetting them with distinctions of words" (*Euthydemus* 278b). The names of things would
be ridiculous if they were exactly identical. Then word and object
would be doubles, and no one would be able to determine which
were the names and which the realities. Certainly, the word cannot
be taken for the reality.

Language can be useful even if name and thing do not correspond exactly. Socrates would ultimately judge language in terms
of absolute correctness or incorrectness, but language as commonly
used need not have its pristine relevance to truth. We should allow
people to use language in their own way, and not quarrel with
them about words. Instead, we should be thankful for whatever
truth is present (*Euthydemus* 285). Cratylus must "have the
courage to admit that one name may be correctly and another
incorrectly given; and . . . not insist that the name shall be exactly
the same with the thing; but allow the occasional substitution of
a wrong letter, and if of a letter also of a noun in a sentence, and
if of a noun in a sentence also of a sentence inappropriate to the
matter, and acknowledge that the thing may be named, and
described, so long as the general character of the thing which you
are describing is retained" (*Cratylus* 432e). Language has to give
only a rough approximation to the physical reality. Despite his
stature as a writer of prose, Plato expresses a complete disinterest in
stylistic details. If letters and words need not be respected, the
finer metrical points will have no merit at all.

Despite the imperfection and variability of specific words, language can convey at least partial truths. Even a loose approximation of truth will suffice for many situations. Language neither
expresses reality itself nor varies in a completely arbitrary fashion:

> When the general character is preserved, even if some of the proper letters are wanting, still the thing is signified; — well, if all the letters are given; not well, when only a few of them are given. I think we had better admit this, lest we be punished like travelers in Aegina who wander about the street late at night: and be likewise told by truth herself that we have arrived too late; or if not, you must find out some new notion of correctness of names, and no longer maintain that a name is the expression of a thing in letters or syllables; for if you say both, you will be inconsistent with yourself. [433ab]

Language in its present state does not accurately describe an object; in all secondary words only "the general character" need be preserved. Letters themselves contribute a discrete part to sketching in the object (like brushstrokes). By extension, sounds chosen for poetic devices such as alliteration, meter, or assonance are likely to introduce irrelevancy for the sake of language rather than any accurate statement of truth. Nevertheless, beauty may exist in language. A sloppy choice of letters can still result in an intelligible concept, "but there will be likewise an improper part which spoils the beauty and formation of the word" (433c).

But the word itself may not make its general meaning clear. At times, convention and custom provide the only explanation for the communication of sense. When a man makes a sound which he understands, another can somehow grasp his meaning. A fairly accurate indication of intent can come despite the use of sounds unlike what they represent. When this happens, one has made a convention with himself, and the correctness of a name comes from the convention. Through this human sanction, letters which are unlike their referent may indicate meaning as well as can those which are like. Both established custom and more or less arbitrary convention can contribute to the signification of words.

The example of number, previously cited, proves that custom and convention play an essential role in human communication. No one could ever find names to fit every figure in the infinity of numbers possible. Convention and agreement have almost sole authority here. Words should resemble things as far as possible.

But as Socrates states, "I fear that this dragging in of resemblance, as Hermogenes says, is a shabby thing, which has to be supplemented by the mechanical aid of convention with a view to correctness; for I believe that if we could always, or almost always, use likenesses, which are perfectly appropriate, this would be the most perfect state of language; as the opposite is the most imperfect" (435c). While convention contributes to the indication of thought, the applicability of word to thing remains the best criterion of judgment. But Plato does not discuss the extent to which, and in what manner, one can apply the mechanical aid of convention.

7

THE DANGERS OF LANGUAGE

While Plato does recognize good uses of language and the study of words, he is just as concerned about the dangers in this treacherous subject. The fascination of language engenders too much reliance on the medium of expression.[24] Since knowledge exists independently of language, name and thing are merely similar. One learns about words and objects in the same process. Because of the derived nature of much of language, inquiry into things is more likely to achieve certainty. Cratylus naïvely supposes that the name and thing are identical; to know the name is to know the thing. Thus, the information given by names is the best and only form of knowledge. Cratylus would confine all methods of inquiry and discovery to those of instruction in language. Socrates, on the other hand, sees that the first name-giver gave them according to his conception of the things which they signified. Thus, if the original con-

---

[24] Even Socrates admits (ironically) to a fascination with discourse that leads him to opinions which later reflection deems incorrect: "I was thrilled by it. And it was you, Phaedrus, that made me feel as I did: I watched your apparent delight in the words as you read. And as I'm sure that you understand such matters better than I do, I took my cue from you, and therefore joined in the ecstasy of my right worshipful companion" (*Phaedrus* 234d). If Socrates can be mistaken, the masses are certainly susceptible.

ception was erroneous, names given accordingly will be even more deceiving to us as followers.

The consistency of language does not prove its truth. Cratylus thinks that all uttered words have a common character and purpose. But even if he is right, Plato thinks that truth depends on original correctness, not consistent following:

> For if he did begin in error, he may have forced the remainder into agreement with the original error and with himself; there would be nothing strange in this, any more than in geometrical diagrams, which have often a slight and invisible flaw in the first part of the process, and are consistently mistaken in the long deductions which follow. And this is the reason why every man should expend his chief thought and attention on the consideration of his first principles: — are they or are they not rightly laid down? and when he has duly sifted them, all the rest will follow. Now I should be astonished to find that names are really consistent. [436cde]

There seems to be no consistent principle in letters representing rest and motion. The original giver of names probably did not himself know the truth. The majority of letters do seem to indicate rest, but mechanical counting of such examples cannot be trusted as a guide to certainty.

Since knowledge of an object precedes the application of its name, the name-giver first must understand nature in general. Only then can he work with the materials of his craft. The creation of names does not perpetuate itself; one must continuously investigate the correspondence of word to object. The acquisition of knowledge may come about in either of two ways, personal discovery or instruction from without. Discovery, being related to recollection, can be trusted more than authority. If knowledge could come from names alone, the origin of knowledge would become problematical. The application of names to objects comes at a specific time rather than developing gradually. Man comes upon eternal knowledge at a particular moment in time; from this encounter comes the name.

Because men rather than gods made language, confusion is inherent in its use. If the giver of names were an inspired being or a god, he would not have contradicted himself. As *Laws IV* 719 suggests, the complexity of human language implies contradiction and uncertainty. Two separate words or sentences cannot point to a common truth, for truth lies behind, not between, assertions. Only knowledge can give certainty amid the conflicting claims of language. "If this is a battle of names, some of them asserting that they are like the truth, others contending that *they* are, how or by what criterion are we to decide between them? For there are no other names to which appeal can be made, but obviously recourse must be had to another standard which, without employing names, will make clear which of the two are right; and this must be a standard which shows the truth of things" (*Cratylus* 438d). The standard cannot reside in language itself. The natural and correct (ἐικός τε καὶ δικαιότατον) way to know things is through their relationships to one another and by themselves; words are too loosely attached to things to be useful.

Even names rightly given are only intermediaries between man and the truth. The study of the underlying reality of these images profits less in all areas than an examination of the truth itself. The dialectical skill of the intelligent man requires knowledge of minute details of human existence. The endeavor of the dialectic is:

> to know what is and is not kindred in all arts, with a view to the acquisition of intelligence; and having this in view, she honors them all alike, and when she makes comparisons, she counts one of them not a whit more ridiculous than another; nor does she esteem him who takes the general's art for an example of hunting in any way more decorous than another who cites that of the vermin-destroyer. The former would be only the greater pretender. And as to your question concerning the name which was to comprehend all these arts of purification, whether of animate or inanimate bodies, the art of dialectic is in no wise particular about fine words, if she may be only allowed to have a general name for all other purifications, binding them up together and separating them off from the purification of the soul or intellect. For this is the purification at which she wants to arrive, and this we should understand to be her aim.

> [*Sophist* 227bc]

Only the soul deserves special attention. The wise man looks without distinction at all arts; words tend to make human a divine quest. As in the *Republic*, man has no faculty to reject corrupting impressions before they sink into the soul. The intellect is infinitely responsive to all physical influences; complete acquisition of things of the senses can only impede the proper action of the soul.

One can learn more about the accuracy of the verbal reproduction by looking directly at the truth. But Plato cannot state a method for this direct approach: "How real existence is to be studied or discovered is, I suspect, beyond you and me. But we may admit so much, that the knowledge of things is not to be derived from names. No; they must be studied and investigated in themselves" (*Cratylus* 439b). Since names are derived from things, one should go back to the sources. Plato insists on an immediate grasp of these realities, unhindered by the screen of words, which may or may not be reliable. Given the ambiguity naturally present in language, Plato will not accept the partial truth inherent in this human tool.

Not only has their human origin tainted words, but the whole fabric of language may be dangerously corrupt. Socrates' analysis of verbal sounds has indicated more change than stability in many words. Since knowledge must be fixed to exist at all, words grounded in motion have no substantial truth. But even lacking truth, these false words masquerade as truth along with the correct. The fault goes back to a sincere but mistaken opinion of the name-givers. Their error has a powerful tendency to infect all subsequent users of the words. Appeal to reason shows that flux cannot exist on a basic level. Since true beauty is always beautiful, the absolute existence of beauty need not be long doubted. Any instability in the essence of beauty would be transferred completely to the word. If beauty were constantly changing, its substance would be created, uttered, and destroyed while the word was being uttered.[25]

Nevertheless, despite his vigorous restatement of his thought on permanence, Plato refuses to accept dogmatically that there is an

---

[25] Cf. *Theaetetus* 157.

eternal nature in things. Heraclitus and his followers could possibly be right about flux. On the other hand, words with pleasant connotations suggest stability, thus supporting the Eleatic position. So whatever limited truth these rival philosophies may have, "no man of sense will like to put himself or the education of his mind in the power of names: neither will he so far trust names or the givers of names as to be confident in any knowledge which condemns himself and other existences to an unhealthy state of unreality; he will not believe that all things leak like a pot, or imagine that the world is a man who has a running at the nose. This may be true, Cratylus, but is also very likely to be untrue; and therefore I would not have you be too easily persuaded of it" (440cd). Socrates would not have Cratylus too quickly accept anything. And the skillful arrangement of words and sentences reduces the soul's awareness of the tentative stature of all language. The path to knowledge through sifting true from false words is arduous, if not impossible.

In short, Plato's strictures on language parallel those on poetry. All human representations — whether poetically of man's actions or verbally of things — fall short of reality itself. Bound by the common inadequacies of humanity, both poet and name-giver make physical imitations. Their products fall in the public domain and must be judged for their encouragement of excellence. No one class of men may enjoy a pleasure forbidden to others. There is no assurance that an abomination for the ignorant will be a blessing for the wise. Both word and poetry (the word writ large) have the same power as any other beautiful physical artifacts to inspire harmony in the beholder. But the unreconciled mingling of truth and falsity in human words makes the use of the beauty in language particularly dangerous.

VII

Static Beauty
and
Living Thought

A poem should be palpable and mute
As a globed fruit,

Dumb
As old medallions to the thumb,

Silent as the sleeve-worn stone
Of casement ledges where the moss has grown —

A poem should be wordless
As the flight of birds.

Archibald MacLeish, "Ars Poetica" 1–8

Plato has undercut the value of language as a guide to truth and beauty. Reality lies beyond language, not within. The *Cratylus* has shown the dangers of various approaches to language. First, convention mingles with truth, making language an untrustworthy repository for knowledge. Second, while recognizing some value in etymologies, Plato feels that caprice and ignorance play a large part in the vulgar attitude toward the study. If language is only a social convention, knowledge is impossible. Moreover, the study of language cannot substitute for the direct examination of truth. Lan-

[173]

guage should be an intelligent imitation of nature. Knowledge thus exists as independently of language as of society. The word-maker acts consciously, yet he can be mistaken. Only the dialectician, the one using the words currently, can judge the worth of the artisan who makes the words. In common usage, convention plays an important, but unspecified, part. Both the original confusion and the present convention render language unworthy of serious philosophical consideration.

With poetry thus eviscerated of its verbal organ, the reasons become clear for Plato's consistent refusal to admit poetry as a legitimate expression of human values. The "poetry" of language obscures its truth. The sophists, poets, and rhapsodes emphasize style at the expense of meaning. Plato, on the other hand, denies any worth whatsoever to the form of discourse. Utterances so brief as to be formless are best; the continuity of thought must not be obscured by the continuity of speech. Plato saw that human art — like physical nature — tends to be amoral. Man responds to beauty with his entire soul. His reaction to earthly beauty consists of either nonproductive pleasure or pain. The proper response to higher beauty is the total rapture of philosophy. And as noted in Chapter II, Plato's distinctions between the two sorts of total inspiration are subtle indeed.

Thus, on one hand, Plato admits only straightforward didactic discourse into his noble commonwealth. On the other, he never restricts himself to this narrow range of discourse. The profound thought, the drama, the wit of the dialogues argue that Plato has expended his energies to a serious end. His continual attention to style shows him to be well aware of the necessity of being effective. At the same time he resents the false effectiveness of the sophists. Didactic poetry has the same end, if not the same means, as his dialogues. All discourse must turn man's attention toward the Good. Didactic verse can thus be an integral part of the perfect state.[1]

---

[1] R. G. Collingwood, in "Plato's Philosophy of Art," focuses on *Republic X* 595–608, which he feels typical of Plato's thought elsewhere. He states, "If it is asked why Socrates permits certain forms of art to be retained in the ideal state instead of consistently banishing them all alike, the answer is

All discourse — including the dialogues — in a less-than-perfect state must be judged by its imitation of the beautifully pure didactic.

1

DIALOGUE AND THE WINGĒD WORD

All language as we know it, especially poetry, is liable to misinterpretation. Paul Friedländer argues that Plato intends his dialogues to be an example of the "art" allowed in the Republic. The drama does not lend itself to the portrayal of a temperate and self-contained character. "But did not Plato represent, always and everywhere, precisely this type of man in Socrates? In the *Phaedo*, when Socrates sends away the women dissolved in sorrow and admonishes and cheers the weeping friends? In the *Symposium*, when the *Logos* defeats the danger of cosmic disorder and humiliation? . . . Thus it is even more clear than before that he claimed for himself the very place he asked the tragic poets to vacate." [2] But one might object that Plato has elsewhere specifically banished lamentations. The dialogues present far more than sketches of Socrates; Plato may express contradictory opinions or even praise immorality, as shown by Callicles' speech in the *Gorgias*. Each dialogue falls under precisely the same judgment that literature does. Therefore, the *Phaedo*, moving as it is, must suggest the truth lying beyond the physical scene, or Plato would insist that this dialogue too must be banished.

While Plato certainly regarded his dialogues as more suitable for the good commonwealth than most contemporary poetry could be,

---

surely obvious: these are, in the opinion of Socrates, the forms which art will take in the hands of men who understand its true nature" (pp. 156–57). With Collingwood's reasoning one could argue, however, that one can cheerfully accept an injection of the Black Death if he has sufficient streptomycin in his system.

[2] See *Plato: An Introduction*, p. 121. In "Plato's Concept of *Mimesis*," Leon Golden concludes, "Plato's own practice in writing the dialogues shows how necessary the use of *mimesis* is in the search for ultimate reality. It must, however, be handled carefully and above all it must never be confused with true reality" (p. 130).

he would never have wished to take the poets' place. The fault in Greek poetry is that the beauty of the language tends to discourage thought. Indeed, Havelock stresses that Plato's fundamental objection to art is that poetry in Athens represented a social consciousness rather than the individual thought that Plato demands. Rather than questioning the meaning behind poetry, the Greeks were overwhelmed by its beauty. Just as Socrates continually probes beyond the physical world, Plato insists that the dialogues be points of departure for thought, not works of art in themselves.

To Plato, language is a living body of thought since philosophy is possible only in the dialectic seeking of truth. Poetry errs in seeming to fix knowledge in order to pass it down from age to age. Drama and epic, as written and established by the beloved ancients, interfere with the process of reasoning, for the beauty of language tends to obscure the beauty of thought. Precisely because of the dual role of language as the vehicle of thought and as the source of mere pleasure, the poet in Plato struggles constantly against the philosopher. "Again and again Plato's written work is mimesis; but it struggles against being nothing but mimesis. And where it seems to represent most strongly a pure work of art, it must not be read as such, but as an 'existential' document, that is, with the constant reminder *tua res agitur*." [3] The gifted literary style of the dialogues shows that Plato, like the sophists, was aware that philosophy must be effective. But Plato will not compromise the truth in any way for the sake of mere effectiveness. Didactic verse is permitted in the Republic because such language is not poetry at all. Like the bad verse he seems to sanction in the *Laws*, literature in the Republic must never sacrifice truth on the altar of pleasure and emotional appeal.

As Havelock suggests, poetry and language had a different role in Athenian society from that which art plays in our own.[4] Rhetoricians such as Isocrates and Alcidamus debated the proper uses of the written language. In Greece the written word did not have the

[3] Friedländer, *Plato: An Introduction*, p. 124.

[4] Eric Havelock, *Preface to Plato*, pp. 3–19.

authority which such established language now possesses.[5] Our attention to static language derives in part from the Hebraic tradition of veneration of sacred writings. The Judeo-Christian emphasis on the fixed language of revelation redirects man to his own inadequacy. Plato's focus on the transcendent suggests that all discourse must encourage man to escape his earthbound existence.

A modern person usually lacks this mingled respect for and frustration with language. A literary critic or a linguist will focus on minute nuances of style or syntax rather than on the meaning lying beyond the words. The poetry of Greece, on the other hand, was essentially oral and, for the most part, intended for a wide audience. The *Republic* itself was probably composed as "a matter of oral teaching in the school." [6] For Plato, the written word therefore follows from the heat of discourse. To use a phrase of Toynbee, the dialogues of Plato resemble a typescript, the basis for "wingèd words."

Both the written word and the language of poetry would, for Plato, have the property of fixing the *Logos*, of establishing the idea rather than letting thought range freely. In illiterate societies, memory takes the place of writing, and words such as those of Homer can be transmitted with great accuracy for generations. Thus Plato questions the worth of any language, written or orally recited, not immediately involved with philosophical reasoning. This probing extends to his own dialogues. "There is no doubt that Plato, in his earlier and even in his later years, was conscious of the problematic nature of all writing and that he did not believe he had said the most serious things in his written work, that is, in what has come down to us and what we are often inclined to regard as his greatest creation, and perhaps the greatest achievement of Greek genius." [7] In the *Second Letter*, Plato states, "The best safeguard is to avoid writing and to commit things to memory. For when a thing has once been committed to writing, it is impossible to pre-

[5] See Arnold Toynbee, *Civilization on Trial*, pp. 47–54.

[6] Gilbert Murray, *Greek Studies*, p. 37.

[7] Friedländer, *Plato: An Introduction*, p. 118.

vent it from gaining publicity. It is for this reason that I myself have never written anything on these subjects. There is not, and there never will be, a written treatise of Plato's. Those that are called his are really the teaching of Socrates restored to youth and beauty" (314bc).[8] Plato, of course, took his dialogues seriously. But precisely because of his seriousness, he feels that language is a poor vehicle to describe his vision of the Good. This sensitivity to the gulf between language and thought explains part of Plato's great effectiveness: his use of myths to suggest meaning that words cannot reveal.[9]

[8] *The Platonic Epistles*, trans. J. Harward, p. 103. See Herman L. Sinaiko, *Love, Knowledge, and Discourse in Plato*, pp. 3–10.

[9] The myths of Plato are subject enough for several books. He obviously feels myths are useful. In the *Gorgias*, Socrates tells Callicles that he will regard his account as a fable; he, Socrates, regards it as reasonable (523), Similarly, the *Phaedo* states that myths deal with the most likely or probable (114). J. Tate in "Plato and Allegorical Interpretation," p. 146, reemphasizes this point. Plato himself comments on what he regards as the proper interpretation of a myth. Phaedrus brings up the myth in which Boreas is said to have carried off Orithyia from the banks of the Ilissus. Socrates comments that,

> I should be quite in the fashion if I disbelieved it, as the men of science do: I might proceed to give a scientific account of how the maiden, while at play with Pharmaceia, was blown by a gust of Boreas down from the rocks hard by, and having thus met her death was said to have been seized by Boreas: though it may have happened on the Areopagus, according to another version of the occurrence. For my part, Phaedrus, I regard such theories as no doubt attractive, but as the invention of clever, industrious people who are not exactly to be envied, for the simple reason that they must then go on and tell us the real truth about the appearance of Centaurs and the Chimaera, not to mention a whole host of such creatures, Gorgons and Pegasuses and countless other remarkable monsters of legend flocking in on them. If our sceptic, with his somewhat crude science, means to reduce every one of them to the standard of probability, he'll need a deal of time for it. I myself have certainly no time for the business: and I'll tell you why, my friend: I can't as yet "know myself," as the inscription at Delphi enjoins; and so long as that ignorance remains it seems to me ridiculous to inquire into extraneous matters. Consequently I don't bother about such things, but accept the current beliefs about them, and direct my inquiries, as I have just said, rather to myself, to discover whether I really am a more complex creature and more puffed up with pride than Typhon, or a simple, gentler being whom heaven has blessed with a quiet, un-Typhonic nature. [229c–30a]

Herman L. Sinaiko, in *Love, Knowledge, and Discourse in Plato*, refers to the importance of this myth for understanding the entire *Phaedrus* (p. 13).

Plato's comments on the interpretation of poetry apply as well to the way he intends his dialogues to be regarded. Superficially, the *Republic* seems to have all the qualities he condemns in poetry. Not only does the dialogue contain allegories, myths, dramatic situations, and the presentation of contrary opinions, but immediately after Plato's attack on imaginative literature comes the Myth of Er. This flight of fancy does not make Plato a poet, for myths in his writings never stop with their literal statements.[10] The myths claim no more authority for themselves than does Socrates in his famous profession of ignorance. Praises of the gods and of noble men are allowed in the state because they are not poetry, poetry being beautiful in itself. Plato accepts any language which teaches the soul to ascend the ladder of the dialectic. Platonic dialogues or encomia may serve this purpose. The *Republic* would be allowed in the well-run state until someone mistakenly turned to study the dialogue as a repository of beauty and knowledge rather than as a vehicle of wingèd words.

2

THOUGHT AND THE WRITTEN WORD

Plato's contempt for the written word shows his perplexity over communication. Both the written word and the fixed language of poetry are ways of extending thought beyond the individual. Neither necessarily involves the listener or the reader in active philosophical response. Without this critical participation in the process of creating philosophy, the individual gives himself over totally and mindlessly to the enchantment of language. But, more dangerous, repeated exposure to uncritical language will deaden the listener to the truth lying behind language.

The *Phaedrus* states that far too much faith was originally placed in writing. Books separate language from the thought living

[10] Ludwig Edelstein, in "The Function of Myth in Plato's Philosophy," distinguishes between the ethical myths which are an addition to rational knowledge and the historical and scientific myths which serve where such knowledge does not exist (p. 473).

in the soul. The originator of letters, Teuth, advanced his discovery as a branch of learning, an easy approach which would make the people wiser and improve their memories. But his king, Thamus, knew that the ones who use devices are better judges of the tools' worth than the creators. Similarly, Socrates in the *Republic* feels that a man's creations lead him to excessive regard for the external: "The makers of fortunes have a second love of money as a creation of their own, resembling the affection of authors for their own poems, or of parents for their children" (*I* 330c).[11] Thus, Teuth's exaggerated regard for his offspring, writing, has led him to declare the very opposite of its true effect. Thamus states:

> If men learn writing, it will implant forgetfulness in their souls: they will cease to exercise memory because they rely on that which is written, calling things to remembrance no longer from within themselves, but by means of external marks; what you have discovered is a recipe not for memory, but for reminder. And it is no true wisdom that you offer your disciples, but only its semblance; for by telling them of many things without teaching them you will make them seem to know much, while for the most part they know nothing; and as men filled, not with wisdom, but with the conceit of wisdom, they will be a burden to their fellows. [*Phaedrus* 275ab]

Again, Plato chooses myth to advance his more tentative reasoning. Clearly, the semblance of knowledge, fixed in writing, is dead and useless. Having data encoffined in this manner causes man to let his memory atrophy, and, for Plato, perception of the Forms comes from recollection. Memory and reminiscence have little in common. The former gives access to the truth, the latter only a shadow of

---

[11] Usually, fame should be despised: "You are aware that the greatest and most influential statesmen are ashamed of writing speeches and leaving them in a written form, lest they should be called sophists by posterity" (*Phaedrus* 257e). On the other hand, some creations may bring fame without stigma: "Who, when he thinks of Homer and Hesiod and other great poets, would not rather have their children than ordinary human ones? Who would not emulate them in the creation of children such as theirs, which have preserved their memory and given them everlasting glory?" (*Symposium* 209cd).

reality. The love of wisdom requires involvement. Bookish dis-course, like poetry, can idly involve the attention without calling forth an active response. Moreover, access to this source of fact would allow a man to presume to unmerited honor and knowledge. Plato's attack on both sophist and poet comes from his hatred of presumption.[12] Poets flatter the appetite; sophists abuse the intellect.

Besides softening the fiber of the mind, the written word lacks substance and permanence. Both writer and reader engage in a futile attempt to grasp the flux of this world. The maker leaves the written manual behind him; the words lie empty of the soul which would seek living truth. Only the simpleminded would trust writing to provide something reliable and permanent. Just as knowledge precedes the application of discourse, speech precedes the literary embodiment. Written words can do nothing more than remind one who has previously known the subject of the writing. The proper interpretation of writing — like that of poetry — requires a preexisting knowledge. And he who already understands does not need these external reminders. Writing will thus be neces-sarily inferior to knowledge and recollection of the same matters.

In a real sense, for Plato both painting and writing are silent, for they cannot respond with immediate thought. Etymologically, Plato has justification for this identification. The word ζωγραφία (painting) literally means a drawing of living creatures. This word has an obvious relationship to the Greek word γραφή (writing). As in the *Republic X*, Plato earnestly presents his argument that dis-course and painting can be analogous:

> The painter's products stand before us as though they were alive: but if you question them, they maintain a most majestic silence. It is the same with written words: they seem to talk to

[12] Sophists, like the rhapsodes, claim all sorts of knowledge. Socrates states, ironically, "Here are two wise men, Euthydemus and Dionysodorus, Cleinias, wise not in a small but in a large way of wisdom, for they know all about war, — all that a good general ought to know about the array and command of an army, and the whole art of fighting in armor. And they know about law too, and can teach a man how to use the weapons of the courts when he is injured" (*Euthydemus* 273c).

you as though they were intelligent, but if you ask them anything about what they say, from a desire to be instructed, they
go on telling you just the same thing for ever. And once a thing
is put in writing, the composition, whatever it may be, drifts all
over the place, getting into the hands not only of those who
understand it, but equally of those who have no business with it;
it doesn't know how to address the right people, and not address
the wrong. And when it is ill-treated and unfairly abused it
always needs its parent to come to its help, being unable to
defend or help itself. [*Phaedrus* 275de]

Such written statements impose a false stability on the complexity of
life; a set discourse can make only one answer. Basically unintelligent, such compositions wander about making their single statement indiscriminately. Wisdom cannot be separated from the originator; the creator of the work must be present to defend his
offspring.

Skill in speaking can ravish the hearers, but true communication depends on an immediate and active interchange of ideas.
Earlier, the long and eloquent speech of Protagoras has thrown
Socrates into a trance, a nonintellectual stupor. But when Protagoras stops, Socrates' doubts return:

If a man were to go and consult Pericles or any of our great
speakers about these matters, he might perhaps hear as fine a
discourse; but then when one has a question to ask of them, like
books, they can neither answer nor ask; and if anyone challenges
the least particular of their speech, they go ringing on in a long
harangue, like brazen pots, which when they are struck continue
to sound unless someone puts his hand upon them; whereas our
friend Protagoras cannot only make a good speech, as he has
already shown, but when he is asked a question he can answer
briefly; and when he asks he will wait and hear the answer;
and this is a very rare gift. [*Protagoras* 329ab]

A speech and a poem should be interpreted in the same way.
Extended discourse draws the soul of man away from its seeking of

knowledge, whereas brief passages or statements of poetry can be grasped and assimilated.[13]

The danger in written language stems from the superficial resemblance between ordinary language and philosophical discourse. Written language and speech are brothers. Yet spoken discourse alone not only possesses an unquestioned legitimacy, but is inherently superior and more effective. This discourse is "the sort that goes together with knowledge, and is written in the soul of the learner: that can defend itself, and knows to whom it should speak and to whom it should say nothing" (*Phaedrus* 276a). The *Philebus* expresses a similar attitude toward external impressions on the soul. Here Socrates analyzes the relationship between opinion, memory, and perception. When a man sees a distant object, the soul receives the impress of opinion just as a book does. "Memory and perception meet, and they and their attendant feelings seem to me almost to write down words in the soul, and when the inscribing feeling writes truly, then true opinion and true propositions which are the expressions of opinion, come into our souls — but when the scribe within us writes falsely, the result is false" (39a). Plato then makes his familiar analogy of writing to poetry. After the scribe has done his work, the painter puts the writing into images. The mind does not proceed to work with the words, but rather transforms them into images: "A man, besides receiving from sight or some other sense certain opinions or statements, sees in his mind the images of the subjects of them" (39b). Thus, the soul will create false or true images corresponding to true or false opinions and words received. Each external impression must be immediately and

---

[13] Plato knows the rules for good rhetoric. Lysias, on the other hand, begins at what properly should be the end. Socrates observes, "And to pass to other points: doesn't his matter strike you as thrown out at haphazard? Do you find any cogent reason for his next remark, or indeed any of his remarks, occupying the place it does? I myself, in my ignorance, thought that the writer, with a fine abandon, put down just what came into his head. Can you find any cogent principle of composition which he observed in setting down his observations in this particular order?" (*Phaedrus* 264b). Still, brief passages are best (*Protagoras* 342–43). Plato develops only the second of these two positions.

correctly inscribed by some faculty under the direction of memory; the internal painter depends almost entirely on the internal scribe.[14]

Living speech is the original of the written word. Separated from the individual, the written, dead discourse can be only an inferior image. Socrates would implant intelligent words in the soul of the hearer. These words truly live — they respond actively to the rational element of the soul and have the power to place themselves in new contexts for their own defense. These words may be living bits of traditional wisdom, but only if the sayings evoke an intelligent reaction in the present. These living words are autonomous of the individual's perception. A word either speaks or is silent, is living or dead. The written word, then, provides an image, the dangerous sort of image Plato has generally condemned.

But writing need not be condemned completely. A man may provide himself with an amusement for when his real powers fail. Plato recognizes human failings, but he never admits them as excuses. He uses an image of a farmer sowing seeds to extend his concept of words as living, responding entities. Like the farmer, a thinker may legitimately seek amusement. But he will not seriously write them in water or that black fluid called ink, for his pen would sow words which cannot either speak in their own defense or present the truth adequately. The written word can refresh but not replace the human memory: "He will sow his seed in literary gardens, I take it, and write when he does write by way of pastime, collecting a store of refreshment both for his own memory, against the day 'when age oblivious comes,' and for all such as tread in his footsteps; and he will take pleasure in watching the tender plants grow up. And when other men resort to other pastimes, regaling themselves with drinking parties and such like, he will doubtless prefer to indulge in the recreation I refer to" (276d). Even old men may want to exchange ideas. These writings will provide a worthwhile recreation when the man has lost the power of active thought. Else-

[14] Ray L. Hart, in "The Imagination in Plato," astutely observes, "That Plato did not elaborate an explicit doctrine of the imagination is owing less to his only slightly developed psychology than to his appreciation of the ontological complexity of such a doctrine" (p. 436).

where, Plato says "A man may sometimes set aside meditations about eternal things, and for recreation turn to consider the truths of generation which are probable only; he will thus gain a pleasure not to be repented of, and secure for himself while he lives a wise and moderate pastime" (*Timaeus* 59cd). Certainly the written monuments to one's own past thought are more noble than idle banqueting. But one should not confuse innocent pastimes with the search for the eternal verities.

The writing of discourses about justice and other noble topics can be an acceptable pastime. But these individual amusements are useless as far as real philosophy is concerned. Nor can these recreations be shared; even in play a man keeps to himself. The serious treatment of great issues requires the art of dialectic. "The dialectician selects a soul of the right type, and in it he plants and sows his words founded on knowledge, words which can defend both themselves and him who planted them, words which instead of remaining barren contain a seed whence new words grow up in new characters; whereby the seed is vouchsafed immortality, and its possessor the fullest measure of blessedness that man can attain unto" (*Phaedrus* 276e–77a). Plato attributes great power to the properly applied word. As in the *Cratylus*, the dialectician is the true and effective user of language. He responds to a waiting spirit and fills it with these forceful words. The very act of giving the words aids the giver as well as the receiver. These words have a social value; they do not exist in a vacuum. Moreover, they possess the animate property of reproduction; the seed lies within the word and, given proper treatment, will respond immortally. Human words are static and need their creator to defend them. But words implanted by the dialectic pass from one soul to another.[15]

[15] The *Symposium* 209a also suggests a wordless conception: "Souls which are pregnant — for there certainly are men who are more creative in their souls than in their bodies — conceive that which is proper for the soul to conceive or contain. And what are these conceptions? Wisdom and virtue in general. And such creators are poets and all artists who are deserving of the name inventor. But the greatest and fairest sort of wisdom by far is that which is concerned with the ordering of states and families, and which is called temperance and justice." The state of mind is all-important to the

Plato now brings his discussion back to the immediate reason for the argument. A rhetorician must know the audience, his subject matter, and all the applicable rules of logic, particularly when he commits his idea to writing. Lysias' speech is condemned, not because of his evil praise of lust, but because of his muddy thinking and inept execution. The deliberate composition and delivery of speeches is not necessarily a matter of reproach, but his conclusions "have shown that any work, in the past or in the future, whether by Lysias or anyone else, whether composed in a private capacity or in the role of a public man who by proposing a law becomes the author of a political composition, is a matter of reproach to its author (whether or not the reproach is actually voiced) if he regards it as containing important truth of permanent validity. For ignorance of what is a waking vision and what is a mere dream-image of justice and injustice, good and evil, cannot truly be acquitted of involving reproach, even if the mass of men extol it" (277de). Popularity can no more justify bad writing than applause can vindicate bad poetry. Indeed, presenting one's ideas to the masses increases the danger of being swayed by vulgar adulation. Certainty and clarity of discourse depend on knowledge, not on techniques of style.

Thus, Plato identifies writing with eloquent speaking; both tend to be superficial persuasion. All language must inspire criticism and instruction; fixed language is frivolous: language is either believed or criticized, not simply enjoyed. A written discourse on any subject must necessarily contain much frivolous material. Indeed, written verse or prose merits little serious attention. The same strictures apply to the set speech. Declamation usually is mere persuasion without any questioning or exposition. Such compositions are at best a means of reminding those who know the truth already.

On the other hand, Plato realizes that some communication is not only necessary but desirable; yet he ignores the medium altogether. The true speaker first establishes the truth within himself.

---

outward expression: "Since there has been shown to be false speech and false opinion, there may be imitations of real existence, and out of this condition of the mind an art of deception may arise" (*Sophist* 264d).

His discourses are then legitimate children, creatures with lives of their own (264c, 277c–78a). This act of creation must be reinforced by correct instincts. With the proper purpose, a statement on justice, honor, goodness, or such topics can have a noble lucidity and seriousness. These spiritual children do not enter into another. Rather, it is their sons and brothers that go into the souls of other men (278b). There, the good discourse is engraved correctly, thus encouraging the listener to paint true images in his mind. Clearly, oral communication is far superior to its imitation in the written word. Only through personal contact can discourse be truly graven on another's soul. Personal, living knowledge must immediately precede all forms of discourse; writing can be only a faint echo of living speech.[16]

3

THE SILENCE OF POETRY

The subordinate status of writing can be extended to the spoken word of poetry. A man may write well or badly, but no matter what his skill, he cannot convey knowledge to his hearer directly. Plato's readiness to link truth with visual images may explain why poetry cannot contain more than its surface texture will hold.[17] Perception comes from envisioning reality, not from understanding language. The *Phaedrus* recognizes that man can aspire to the highest heaven, a realm no earthly poet can properly describe. Yet, motivated by the high subject matter, Plato boldly makes the attempt through his metaphors of flight and vision. "In the place beyond

[16] G. R. Levy, in his introduction to J. A. Stewart's *The Myths of Plato*, states that "Plato's whole plan for the dissemination of philosophy in writing was a continuation of personal relationships, not the perpetuation of doctrine" (p. 5).

[17] John Warry correctly states in *Greek Aesthetic Theory*, "It is worth remembering that the word for 'seeing' in Greek is etymologically germane to that which denotes 'learning,' and the same is true in other Indo-European languages. If pressed to name the second 'clearest' sense, Plato would hardly have done other than name that of hearing, for after the eye the ear is indisputably the finest minister to the intellect" (p. 29).

the heavens, true Being dwells, without color or shape, not susceptible to touch. Reason alone, the soul's pilot, can behold it, and all
true knowledge is knowledge thereof. Now even as the mind of a
god is nourished by reason and knowledge, so also is it with every
soul that has a care to receive her proper food; wherefore when at
last she has beheld Being she is well content, and contemplating
truth she is nourished and prospers, until the heavens' revolution
brings her back full circle" (*Phaedrus* 247cd). During the travels
of the soul, she perceives the very essence of justice, temperance,
and knowledge. In rapture the soul rises above the knowledge,
which, as neighbor to Becoming, varies with man's unintelligent
perception of various objects. "And when she has contemplated
likewise and feasted upon all else that has true being, she descends
again within the heavens and comes back home. And having so
come, her charioteer sets his steeds at their manger, and puts
ambrosia before them and draught of nectar to drink withal"
(247e). The soul which has seen the most of Being becomes a philosopher; less vision makes a poet or other imitative artist. As in
the *Republic VII* 517–18, Plato has the inspired soul return to the
lower world. But the return does not necessarily result in effective
work in this world of shadows.

Most people have lost the memory of the holy things they once
saw. Some had the vision only for a moment; others have forsaken
the "holy objects of their vision." The process of forgetting is like
sight fading. "Few indeed are left that can still remember much:
but when these discern some likeness of the things yonder, they are
amazed, and no longer masters of themselves, and know not what
is come upon them by reason of their perception being dim. Now
in the earthly likenesses of justice and temperance and all other
prized possessions of the soul there dwells no luster; nay, so dull are
the organs wherewith men approach their images that hardly can a
few behold that which is imaged" (*Phaedrus* 250ab). True rapture
makes a man gaze around like a bird. On the other hand, a partial
vision may result in the dulled response of ignorant amazement.
Any man whose senses are not dead can respond, but he cannot
understand his own reaction. The perception involves some effort

on the part of the individual. Images of reality can enrapture, but few people have the power to rise above this nonintellectual rapture to see the truth itself.[18]

The metaphor of eye as soul evokes a corresponding image of beauty as wisdom. The eye of the mind of course has a far greater power than that of the body, but both are windows of perception. The soul before imprisonment in the body had an unblemished vision of all sorts of revelations: "Now beauty, as we said, shone bright amidst these visions, and in this world below we apprehend it through the clearest of our senses, clear and resplendent. For sight is the keenest mode of perception vouchsafed us through the body; wisdom, indeed, we cannot see thereby — how passionate had been our desire for her, if she had granted us so clear an image of herself to gaze upon — nor yet any other of those beloved objects, save only beauty; for beauty alone this has been ordained, to be most manifest to sense and most lovely of them all" (250d). Plato could easily have allowed beauty of all sorts to lift man to a vision of true beauty. And indeed, artifacts and beautiful humans can serve this function. But art first calls attention to itself as a physical object and does not necessarily stimulate further vision. Earthly beauty causes not true rapture but selfish pleasure. Wisdom cannot be seen in this mundane existence, for the mere sight would be overwhelming.

Language can create only the basic condition for man's achieving this vision of absolute wisdom and beauty. The quest for truth does not begin from nothing; the mind must interact with tradition.[19] The sayings of the ancients have grace and beauty, and these

[18] Douglas Morgan, in *Love: Plato, the Bible and Freud*, states, "Seeing is sometimes believing, but believing is never knowing. What we see, we do not know. What we know, we do not see. This is the first and fundamental law of Plato's philosophy. It seems odd only to men whose understanding is beclouded by their senses, and who by habit close the eye of the mind to see only with the eye in the head" (p. 15).

[19] But even good information — laws, sayings, customs — is more antidote than treasure:

Of all kinds of knowledge the knowledge of good laws has the greatest power of improving the learner; otherwise there would be no meaning

bits of lore contain an important inactive wisdom. Respect for the traditional runs throughout the dialogues — usually expressed as deference to the ancients or by allusions to poetry. As noted earlier, Plato's inquiry often begins from a word of the ancients. The *Phaedrus* illustrates this principle: " 'Not to be lightly rejected,' Phaedrus, is any word of the wise; perhaps they are right: one has to see. And in particular this present assertion must not be dismissed" (260a). But often great modifications and restrictions must be applied, for here Phaedrus has just advanced a widespread belief that "the intending orator is under no necessity of understanding what is truly just, but only what is likely to be thought just by the body of men who are to give judgment; nor need he know what is truly good or noble, but what will be thought so; since it is on the latter, not the former, that persuasion depends" (259e–60a). So the sayings are only stable points for departure; one moves away from them, not toward them.[20] The word must challenge rather than grip the soul.

Socrates' disclaiming of merit almost always accompanies his eloquence. Deferential references to the ancients abound when he waxes poetic. By removing his own personality from his speech, he reaffirms — in accordance with his identification of soul and true discourse — the tentative nature of his words. Socrates declares that if Phaedrus goes "as far as that I shall find it impossible to agree with you; if I were to assent out of politeness, I should be confuted by the wise men and women who in past ages have spoken and written on this theme" (235b). Socrates characteristically cannot remember who, but he knows that "there is something welling up within my breast, which makes me feel that I could find something

---

in the divine and admirable law possessing a name akin to mind (νοῦς, νόμος). And of all other words, such as the praises and censures of individuals which occur in poetry and also in prose, whether written down or uttered in daily conversation, whether men dispute about them in the spirit of contention or weakly assent to them, as is often the case — of all these the one sure test is the writings of the legislator, which the righteous judge ought to have in his mind as the antidote for all other words. [*Laws XII* 957cd]

[20] Cf. *Meno* 81.

different, and something better, to say. I am of course well aware it can't be anything originating in my own mind, for I know my own ignorance; so I suppose it can only be that it has been poured into me, through my ears, as into a vessel, from some external source; though in my stupid fashion I have actually forgotten how, and from whom, I heard it" (235cd). Elsewhere Plato has stated that true discourse originates only in the soul of the speaker, yet Socrates declares his emptiness. His eloquence, the flowing outward of a speech earlier poured into his ears, merits no respect. But the images thus stimulated in the soul of another are the true offspring of the philosopher. Irony, that language which constantly refutes its direct statement, helps keep Plato's audience from passively absorbing doctrine.

4

Doctrine Versus Artistry in the Dialogues

Plato has explicitly denied worth to others' imaginative language and implicitly rejected the seriousness of his own dialogues. But the consummate artistry of his prose belies his casual dismissal of all but philosophical conversation. The example of the dialogues runs startlingly counter to the strictures both on creations of the imagination and on written words. Adherence to Plato's strictures on art would certainly demand a repudiation of the dialogues in any good state.[21] But the tentative nature of the dialogues saves them from the damning dogmatism of other forms of discourse. Phaedrus should convey a message to composers of speeches:

[21] Carleton Lewis Brownson states in *Plato's Studies and Criticisms of the Poets* that when Plato

> pronounces his final judgment against the poets, he seems to forget or disregard the significance which he has given to μίμησις in X. For he banishes not all poetry which is mimetic in the wider sense of X, but preeminently that which is mimetic in the narrower sense of III. Hymns to the gods and encomia upon good men are admitted to the state. They might well have been excluded as mimetic by the argument of X; they are not mimetic, however, if one adheres to the definition of III. The conclusion of X is consistent, therefore, with the premises of III, but not fully consistent with the premises of X. [pp. 93–94]

Do you now go and tell Lysias that we two went down to the
stream where is the holy place of the Nymphs, and there listened
to words which charged us to deliver a message, first to Lysias
and all other composers of discourses, secondly to Homer and all
others who have written poetry whether to be read or sung, and
thirdly to Solon and all such as are authors of political compositions under the name of laws: to wit, that if any of them
has done his work with a knowledge of the truth, can defend his
statements when challenged, and can demonstrate the inferiority
of his writings out of his own mouth, he ought not to be designated by a name drawn from those writings, but by one that
indicates his serious pursuit. [278bc]

Socrates will not call these authors possessors of wisdom, for only
gods always have knowledge. Instead, he who can create and
defend his creation will be called a lover of wisdom or a philosopher.[22] Through his use of irony, Plato has already recognized the
inferiority of the dialogues to true personal discourse. By patterning
his work as closely as possible upon the interchange of ideas, he has
set up attack and defense within the dialogues themselves.[23]

For Plato, speech is more plastic than wax or other such media.[24]
Thus, he has only contempt for stylists, those who spend hours on
phrases, twisting them around, pasting them together and pulling
them apart. Such men, clearly seeking popular recognition, should be
contemptuously called poets or speech-writers or law-writers. Literary
craftsmanship, Plato thinks, consists of unintelligent word games.
Obviously polished phrases do not attend to truth itself, but rather
show that their creator has been manipulating mere words.[25]

[22] Cf. *Laws IX* 858–59.

[23] Paul Shorey, in *Platonism, Ancient and Modern*, states, "In Plato dia-
lectics simply means discussion, argument; and the skill with which Plato in
his dialogues makes the written word perform the function of the spoken
word, is, in this respect, one of the chief though least often recognized values
of the study of Plato. . . . At its best, Plato's realistic reproduction of argu-
mentative conversation is a real verification of, and check upon, the processes
of thought" (pp. 37–38).

[24] See *Republic IX* 588, *Laws IV* 712, *V* 746.

[25] Socrates always claims a plain, awkward style. He would ask a question, "and if I do this in a very inartistic and ridiculous manner, do not laugh

The *Timaeus* makes a similar distinction between the lovers of truth and the lovers of language. A man may certainly admire the nobility of his discourse, but this love must not lead to sterile complacency. Indeed, out of frustration comes further inquiry. The description of the perfect state, the dialogue *Republic*, gives Plato a certain measure of satisfaction: "I might compare myself to a person who, on beholding beautiful animals either created by the painter's art, or, better still, alive but at rest, is seized with a desire to see them in motion or engaged in some struggle or conflict to which their forms appear suited; this is my feeling about the State which we have been describing" (*Timaeus* 19bc). A painter can create beautiful works just as a philosopher can leave behind noble examples of his thought. But both creations are inferior to real animate creations or to the real philosophic process.[26] Plato would like to see his creation in existence, performing in its proper way. But just as a painting gives only a momentary glimpse of true being, a dialogue can only suggest the Form for the state.

Plato does not claim authority for his teaching, nor does he approve of anyone else such as the poets or sophists making such claims.[27] The poets are the self-appointed and generally recognized teachers. But their art has no more permanence than Plato's, and

---

at me, for I only venture to improvise before you because I am eager to hear your wisdom: and I must therefore ask you and your disciples to refrain from laughing" (*Euthydemus* 278de).

[26] There is some justification for D. R. Grey's paradoxical statement in "Art in the *Republic*," that "there is, properly, *no* place for art in the *Republic*, because the whole philosophical, political, and metaphysical conception is aesthetic from beginning to end" (p. 302). Plato allows the rulers of the Republic only the greatest of arts — statecraft (see *Republic I* 342 and *Euthydemus* 291). Statecraft is like coloring sculpture (*Republic IV* 420d), like painting (*Laws VI* 769, *Republic VI* 484), and like composing a tragedy (*Laws VII* 817).

[27] G. R. Levy, in the introduction to Stewart's *Myths of Plato*, states that "for every Myth he is accustomed to use a different means of introducing the break in the dramatic dialogue, and of disclaiming it as his own creation. 'I am not good at inventing stories,' says his spokesman Socrates. Stewart has gathered a bunch of these impersonal openings, whose diversity may hide a subjective, and therefore, perhaps a universal, origin" (p. 7).

their dogmatism discourages any intelligent response. The poets inescapably imitate human actions; they set both real and ideal deeds in the province of the old humanity. Bound by natural human limitations, no man can speak directly, yet significantly, to the human situation. Plato says, "Now I, Critias and Hermocrates, am conscious that I myself should never be able to celebrate the city and her citizens in a befitting manner, and I am not surprised at my own incapacity; to me the wonder is rather that the poets present as well as past are no better — not that I mean to depreciate them; but every one can see that they are a tribe of imitators, and will imitate best and most easily the life in which they have been brought up; while that which is beyond the range of a man's education he finds hard to carry out in action, and still harder adequately to represent in language" (*Timaeus* 19cd). Poets tend to imitate without personal involvement or philosophical evaluation. They lie passively in their environment; their limited imagination does not allow them to improve upon what society has given them. And language proves more recalcitrant to meaningful expression than do actions. An action or thing may participate in some way in its corresponding Form. But there is no Form for language to resemble. Language can suggest all Forms, while being none of them truly.

The earlier tentative statements about the role of the dialogues become more definite in the *Laws*. The dialogues are indeed to be regarded as true poems, not the gripping poetry of conflict, but a serene embodiment of truth and beauty. Almost as an afterthought, the Stranger recognizes some merit in his long discourse:

> I think that I am not wholly in want of a pattern, for when I consider the words which we have spoken from early dawn until now, and which, as I believe, have been inspired by Heaven, they appear to me to be quite like a poem. When I reflected upon all these words of ours, I naturally felt pleasure, for of all the discourses which I have ever learnt or heard, either in poetry or prose, this seemed to me to be the justest, and most suitable for young men to hear; I cannot imagine any better pattern than this which the guardian of the law who is also the director of education can have. He cannot do better than advise the teachers to teach the young these words and any which are of a

like nature, if he should happen to find them, either in poetry
or prose, or if he come across unwritten discourses akin to ours,
he should certainly preserve them, and commit them to writing.

[*VII* 811cde]

Even here Plato does not claim authority for his creation. First, the
words of the dialogue are to be used in conjunction with the personal direction of a teacher. And second, the principles and laws
are not recommended outright for the world where the Athenian
reasons with Cleinias and Megillus, but rather for the state set up
by the dialogue. So in the second-best state, fallible men may need
the aid of the written word. True poetry of the soul comes through
a god-like communion with the eternal, but when the inspiration
is not present, preserved discourses may give some direction to
education.

Anyone who deals with the mere transmission of facts and customs must submit to the authority of one who truly knows, here the
lawgiver. The teachers Plato envisions in the *Laws* primarily trans-
mit sayings or discourses rather than ideas. For this reason, good
discourses are of great importance. The teachers must learn and
approve the dialogues. Those who will shall be employed; those
objecting will be dismissed. But Plato carefully declares that the
Athenian's ideas do not stem from a personal whim. The source of
inspiration is the same for philosophy and for poetry. Good words
are always inexplicable — they come from heaven. The seriousness
of his intent and the intensity of his lifelong dedication to philosophy lead Plato to admit that his dialogues, being just, are suitable
for the consideration of young men. But even here, his customary
modesty leads him to suggest that the dialogue is only a fanciful tale.

In addition to their role in education, written laws can help
guide the state in its ordinary functions. Whatever its inadequacies,
written discourse does have the advantage of allowing even the
slowest man to absorb its meaning. The value of such discourse still
comes from its being tested for contemporary relevance. Cleinias
receives the approval of Megillus and the Athenian when he says
that "the greatest help to rational legislation is that the laws when

once written down are always at rest; they can be put to the test at any future time, and therefore, if on first hearing they seem difficult, there is no reason for apprehension about them, because any man however dull can go over them and consider them again and again; nor if they are tedious but useful, is there any reason or religion, as it seems to me, in any man refusing to maintain the principles of them to the utmost of his power" (*X* 890e–91a). The state described in the *Laws* lacks the absolute order of the world set up by the *Republic*. The Athenian knows that heretical discourses have been scattered throughout the realm. The legislator himself must compose counterarguments. Thus, toward the end of his life, Plato begins to recognize that a wise man must fight error by some more direct method. The philosopher must not only bring down the dazzling vision of truth to this world, he must clear away the murk of human ignorance as well. Nevertheless, Plato will not illumine and cleanse with the same instrument. To the last, the philosopher rejects this dangerous compromise.

VIII

Sense
and Sensitivity:
A Conclusion

> Once out of nature I shall never take
> My bodily form from any natural thing,
> But such a form as Grecian goldsmiths make
> Of hammered gold and gold enamelling
> To keep a drowsy Emperor awake.
>
> William Butler Yeats,
> "Sailing to Byzantium," 24–29

Plato has thrown his challenge in the teeth of the lovers of Mistress Poetry. Her champions must plead in prose or in verse that she is no mere source of pleasure but a benefit to society and human life. Plato himself seems to make several attempts to defend her honor; his doctrines of inspiration, love, and beauty testify to this Siren's charm. But these lustrous philosophic gems only emphasize the dialogues' view of art as a dark temptation. The brazen voice of poetry speaks with unwarranted authority, seducing the entire soul by an appeal to the emotions. The larger subject of poetry is man, a particular artisan, in action. The representation either deceives the intellect or corrupts the emotions. Moreover, all language inescapably imitates reality. While good imitations are as possible as inferior, the imitation must never be exalted over the imitated. Although harmonious physical objects or beautiful people

[197]

can suggest their correspondence with the ultimate, language retains the defilement of its association with an unphilosophical society. The beautiful language of poetry turns man toward man, not to the eternal Forms. Art captures rather than liberates beauty.

The dialogues are hammered gold, a human attempt to escape the bonds of nature. But their self-contained majesty scorns any audience of real or even ideal men. A recapitulation of the argument of this study of Plato may help bring the issues into clearer focus. First, no one passage will express more than a fragment of his aesthetics. The philosopher does not give us a work devoted solely to art. Plato refines his thought about poetry in the fire of an immediate concern for man and society. He could not — even if he had so desired — treat poetry as a thing irrelevant to truth and to human excellence. He has fought his battle with the human and divine beauty of art; he insists that we fight ours. Rather than make a conclusive — and therefore dead — statement on poetry, he forces us to seek truth in his partial statements. Only this insistence on further thought keeps the dialogues themselves from receiving Plato's condemnation as works of art. The dialogue form does not lend itself to dogmatism, and his irony reinforces the intellectual tension.

While a unity does exist amid the diversity of Plato's comments on poetry, a superficial consistency obviously has less importance than relevance, profundity, or beauty. Some change is to be expected. Plato's career covers a span of more than fifty years, part of which was spent under the influence of Socrates. Moreover, Plato addresses a great variety of problems; each approach will influence one's view of his theories of poetry. The incredible expanse of Plato's thought almost demands that a critic seize upon one limited segment of his aesthetics. Thus, like their great master, the followers of Plato fight their tournaments not with lances but with bludgeons. Plato encourages this vigorous partisanship. On one hand, throughout the dialogues he casually gives high praise to the poets and their wisdom. The declarations concerning inspiration seem endorsements of amoral beauty. At times he even seems to identify the poet with the philosopher. On the other hand, his direct examination of poetry usually reveals a deep mistrust. Excerpts of poetry only may be invaluable sources of traditional wisdom, and although divine enthusiasm seizes the poet completely, Plato does not explain how inspiration leads to the production of poetry. Whatever his feelings about poetic inspiration, Plato finds human language an inferior teacher to the true and wordless poetry of knowledge.

His profoundly beautiful theory of inspiration describes man's aspiring toward the eternal. But he gives us little material here on which to build a psychology of poetic creation. The *Ion* has shown that the creation and criticism of poetry evoke the same sort of rapture. Every man but the poet has a clearly delineated skill. The very fact that Plato assigns the immediate source of poetry to the Muses or to the gods suggests that he believes no humans past, present, or future can create acceptable poetry on their own.

The total rapture of poet and philosopher reaffirms Plato's contempt for any reserve in embracing truth. Both the true poet-philosopher and the divinely possessed man are completely under a benign influence outside themselves. And both types of poets are filled with great beauty as a result of their vision. Yet neither poet can contribute actively to the creation of further beauty. Plato admits no craft to the poet, no way for him to improve his skills. Increasing his knowledge merely leads him further in his vision of the absolute. The wise poet leaves poetry behind on his journey toward understanding, while the possessed poet simply channels sayings away from the source of wisdom.

The theory of communication arising from this emphasis on individual inspiration denies poetry a legitimate role. Man cannot communicate directly with his fellows. A truly wise man will create children of the soul; somehow these offspring will enter the soul of another. Speech is so personal, so basic to humanity, that no language separated from its speaker can have much worth. Poetic language, however, has a dangerous, inhuman beauty. The *Ion* has shown that a chain of influence extends from Muse to poet to rhapsode to audience; at no point can the intellect interrupt this flow of beauty. Neither poet nor philosopher can stand between the man and his personal aspiring after wisdom; they can only encourage indirectly. The search is too much a matter for the individual. In particular, as a social statement of truth, poetry cannot advance an individual's personal vision of transcendent reality.

Even while recognizing beauty to be an integral part of poetry, Plato insists upon judging imaginative language against his standards for all discourse. Human beings either make nonsensical sound or they make sense. No merely pleasurable discourse exists. Thus, poetry teaches — either for better or for worse. Plato considers poetry and language only within an immediate social context. In both the *Republic* and the *Laws*, all poetry not contributing to society must be banished from it. His most serious consideration of the content of poetry comes in *Republic II* and the first part of *III*. Here he discusses the value of poetry as moral instruction in elementary education. Admissible excerpts directly and unambiguously exhort the youth to excellence. He concludes that young minds are incapable of understanding gross tales of the gods and of men. And Plato never goes beyond this point to allow poetry to those whose minds *are* prepared for it.

Plato has considered in this part of the *Republic* only poetry which presents models for conduct — tales about gods and heroes. Guides to virtue must be virtuous in every respect; no human failings can be added as contrast to the good. He leaves poetry about ordinary men until later; but while leaving open the possibility of poetic treatments of human beings, he concludes first that the focus on a particular man exalts the temporal, and second, that the dramatic art cannot present a moderate and wise man. The *Laws* puts into explicit form the theories set forth in the *Republic*. Throughout this last dialogue of Plato's career, poetry represents such a danger that only wise men should be allowed to create and judge it. In both the *Republic* and the *Laws*, dramatic poetry evokes a vision of man's body in particular actions, never man's soul in search of truth.

If Plato wished to recognize poetry, he could have done so in his discussion of the Guardians' amusements in *Republic III*. The wisest in the state, if anyone, should certainly have the ability to respond properly to beauty in words. But Plato denies even these men the faculty to reject portrayals of evil. Excellence must be instilled at every moment. Poetry is irrelevant for the wise. Private, thoughtful readings are not a possibility; the Guardians would witness poetry only together. Moreover, the Guardians are to become the actors and present all poetry dramatically. And in their capacity as rhapsodes and actors, they must utter only virtuous words. As in the *Ion*, he who delivers a poetic speech becomes so intensely involved with the language that he loses himself in the character portrayal.

Poetry tends to present human values directly and concretely. Any response therefore involves some degree of attention to this world. But Plato would emphasize the prior necessity of establishing one's own identity. If Socrates declares that he does not know himself, less gifted mortals can hardly claim more self-awareness. The poetic experience causes a total loss of identity. Since humans lack complete knowledge, the sympathy engendered by art introduces a dangerous disorder into the soul. Moreover, this personal confusion would extend into society. According to his abilities, each person has one specific function in the state. The Guardians must not play insane men, women or slaves, for no one can profit by seeking a correspondence with humanity in all its ignorance and passion. The understanding of truth is far more important than the perceiving of degenerate humanity. The Guardians must have knowledge of all other people, but they themselves stand aloof rather than participating in human struggles.

Plato's censure of dramatic presentations stems partly from his fear of evil's infiltrating the defenses of the soul. Lacking the critical objectivity we would allow the wise today, even the knowledgeable will find corruption in the repetition of immoral or trivial actions. Elementary education should establish truths vital to the proper growth of the rulers, and the same principles of excellence should extend throughout their later training. Constant reinforcement of the good is necessary, for the path to knowledge constantly runs athwart human weakness. Even the rulers are not above temptation, and Plato does not allow man a faculty for eliminating evil once it is implanted in his soul.

The banishment of poetry, then, follows from his discussions of both elementary education and mature entertainment. He has circumscribed the poetry he knew to the point where he no longer considers poetry — beautiful verbal creations — useful at all. The argument in *Republic X* is neither sophistical nor ironic. Intellectually, poetry deceives by confusing the real with the imaginary. Any artistic presentation of a human being or of an object imitates an imitation. Attention to a particular thing of this world only emphasizes the physical. And Plato does not grant the viewer a faculty for generalizing, for making the data relevant to himself and to the higher truth which a scene embodies.

His second charge, that poetry arouses the lower desires, has been debated more extensively in later aesthetics. Where Aristotle proposes a catharsis — the arousal and relaxing of the emotions — Plato would have man turned steadily toward the truth and beauty. To him, Aristotle's catharsis would make as much sense as plunging the philosopher back down into the cave periodically so that the light of knowledge will dazzle him more thoroughly. Plato insists that the emotional part of men can be useful only when the rational part maintains complete control. All dramatic and epic poetry that grips the spirit therefore stands condemned. Natural beauty subtly suggests the beautiful Forms which underlie all nature; artistic beauty blatantly demands attention to the particular. Total involvement may begin with an individual or with a single object, but the rapture must not end there.

Although denying it to be poetry, Plato recognizes one legitimate area for beautiful language. Praises of gods and famous men shall be welcome in the Republic; this immediately didactic language provides the same function as did the excerpts and myths and stories in *Republic II* and *III*, yet Plato does not specify which stories can be so treated. Friedländer conjectures that Plato regards dialogues themselves as poetry. But this is to accuse Plato of confusion, for the dialogues are filled with the things for which Plato has just condemned Homer and Hesiod. And one can hardly deny that Plato thinks he has condemned poetry — Homer and Hesiod who earlier provide good excerpts are banished in *Republic X*, and no one is advanced to take their place. The panegyrics permitted in the *Republic* certainly fall outside any poetry Plato knew or expected to know.

The condemnation of past, present, and future art in *Republic X* stands as the capstone of his theory of poetry. His other statements on aesthetics are neither as extensive nor as coherent. But one should not ignore the buttresses which support his explicit aesthetic statement. Both painting and poetry are ultimately excluded, but he applies his strictures more consistently to the verbal art. Words — being earlier created by the name-giver — already imitate reality; the beauty of poetic language thus calls attention to a mere imitation. Even if Plato wished to make the poet a skilled verbal artisan, the material of this craftsman would still be a dangerous combination of the true and the conventional, the original and the derived.

His contempt for word-play legislates against his recognition of the value of poetry. Plato does not allow art to imitate the good. Language cannot embody the ultimate vision. Words have lost much of their pristine correspondence to truth; the ignorant usages of society and the passage of time have obscured meaning. Language, like all physical objects, can be judged in terms of its correspondence to a higher reality. The mind must go beyond the words to the meanings which language suggests. The lawgiver looks to nature to assign sounds to words. The knower — the dialectician — best judges the use of language. This separation of maker and user denies any craft to the poet, an arranger of words and sentences. The clear grounding of language in truth has been deteriorating since the word was first established. Because Plato would find truth in each sound of each word of each sentence, no fresh combination is likely to embody or to suggest truth.

Plato's comments on language apply directly to his poetics. His philosophy stresses the dynamic interchange between minds, the ceaseless moving toward truth. That which is static in human beings is dead; the written word — like the fixed word of poetry — is always suspect. A word separated from its speaker lacks its necessary defender. Philosophy demands a yearning for truth, not the acquisition of sterile fact. Socrates abjures long speeches, for the flow of words breaks up the movement of thought. Long speeches, books, or poetry do not admit challenge. When words are fixed in a more or less permanent form, the expression begins to take precedence over the content. It is the interchange of thoughts rather than of words that makes philosophy live.

We must not forget, however, the context of Plato's attack on art. The public, then as now, exaggerates poetry's function in moral and intellectual instruction. (If exposure to poetry could truly fill a man with sweetness and light, departments of English everywhere would have the loveliest people possible.) Plato would not allow even a philosophic man to assume the title of teacher. Knowledge is so personal that no person can communicate truths directly to another. A man learns truly by recollection, and while this process can be aided, one draws out rather than instills wisdom. Memorization of the poets was fundamental to Greek education, and this mandatory recollection of words interrupts the true recollection of Forms.

But Plato's dialogues are not the negative satires of a frustrated nihilist. Rather, they are the diary of a soul, a perpetual challenge rather than a temporal statement. He would not want his words to be the new dogmatism. A true genius, he desired no recognition — desire for fame being the last infirmity of noble mind. Much of the Socratic gadfly remains in Plato. And while he may ask to speak to us through his dialogues, he defies anyone to rest mindlessly in the broad reaches of his thought. Poets and critics have tried to make his dialogues examples of good, ethical poetry. They cite Plato's descriptions of decorous action, his exhortations to virtue, his condemnations of vice. But this sort of misreading, the finding of dogmas, only justifies Plato's clear-sighted contempt for those who embrace the literal word. With brilliant irony flashing like aureate lightning in the background, the dialogues disavow themselves at the very moment of statement. The concrete situations of the dialogues at times show Plato to be confused, contradictory, or unjustly polemic. In other words, the dialogues speak with a personal human voice. Various characters live in the dialogues — and even they do not always speak in their own voices. Socrates relates the speech of Diotima, Phaedrus recites the speech of Lysias, and entire dialogues are set within a narrative framework. And like the poet of *Laws VII*, Plato cannot or will not say what utterances are correct.

Plato, therefore, leaves us a perplexing statement of aesthetics. This master goldsmith seeks no apprentices. His love of poetry is probably greater than ours, his conviction undoubtedly greater. Filled with passionate intensity, he hammers out before our eyes his honest reaction to poetry. The condemnation of poetry in *Republic X* simply extends his attack on empty rhetoric and misguided literary criticism. His statements about inspiration and the ethical uses of poetry, while historically important, do not substantially lessen the force of his attack. Plato loved beauty, and especially the beauty of poetry. Nevertheless, poetry — an enchanting verbal art — had to be banished from the well-run state for its ethical as well as for its intellectual abuses.

Rather than term his aesthetics inconsistent, one should call into question Plato's assumptions concerning the soul. His psychology creates conditions unfavorable to any actual poetry. In his analysis of the tripartite soul, Plato largely denies the importance of the lower elements. The spirited and the appetitive parts must always be subordinate to the rational. He knows well that poetry appeals powerfully to the emotions. But the passions may corrupt as well as ennoble. Plato nowhere allows poetry to strengthen the rational element through the direction of the well-disciplined spirited element. In the *Phaedrus* 253–54, the white horse, or the spirited part, does not guide the charioteer, the rational element. Similarly, in the *Republic V* 434–41, the spirited element should help the rational to subdue the appetite. But Plato does not show how this partnership is to be formed and strengthened.

Plato might admit that poetry may ideally present its own golden world, but he would insist that in the world of philosophic questioning poetry gives us charm rather than truth. The lover of wisdom seeks only the beauty of virtue and knowledge, not the lesser beauty of language. This vision, as Diotima describes it in the

Symposium 210, is ineffable; she doubts that even Socrates can reach this height. But Plato must still wrestle with the almost insurmountable problem of what means one can use to describe the realm. Poetry is an important battleground for Plato's divergent approaches to beauty and knowledge, but his treatment of poetry is too personal, too fragmented to be fully resolved by us or even by Plato himself. The scraps scattered throughout the dialogues only whet the appetite. His aesthetics shows us not a banquet of thought but a hunger.

Selected
Bibliography

TEXTS, TRANSLATIONS, AND COMMENTARIES

Bloom, Allan, trans. *The Republic of Plato*. New York and London: Basic Books, 1968

Burnet, John, ed. *Platonis Opera*. 5 vols. Oxford: Clarendon Press, 1905–13.

Cornford, Francis M., trans. *The Republic of Plato*. 1941; rpt. New York and London: Oxford University Press, 1966.

Hackforth, Reginald, trans. *Plato's Examination of Pleasure*. Cambridge: Cambridge University Press, 1945.

————. *Plato's Phaedrus*. Cambridge: Cambridge University Press, 1952.

Harward, J., trans. *The Platonic Epistles*. Cambridge: Cambridge University Press, 1932.

Jowett, Benjamin, trans. *The Dialogues of Plato*. 4th ed. 4 vols. Oxford: Clarendon Press, 1953.

Plato in Twelve Volumes. Various translators. Loeb Classical Library. 1914–26; rpt. London: William Heinemann and Cambridge Mass.: Harvard University Press, 1961–67.

Taylor, A. E., trans. *The Laws*. London: J. M. Dent, 1960.

BOOKS AND ARTICLES

Allan, D. J. "The Problem of Cratylus." *American Journal of Philology*, 75 (1954), 271–87.

Anderson, Daniel E. "Socrates' Concept of Piety." *Journal of the History of Philosophy*, 5 (1967), 1–13.

Anderson, Warren D. *Ethos and Education in Greek Music: The Evidence of Poetry and Philosophy.* Cambridge, Mass.: Harvard University Press, 1966.

Ardley, Gavin. "The Role of Play in the Philosophy of Plato." *Philosophy,* 42 (1967), 226–44.

Atkins, J. W. H. *Literary Criticism in Antiquity.* Cambridge: Cambridge University Press, 1934.

Bambrough, Renford. "Plato's Modern Friends and Enemies." *Philosophy,* 37 (1962), 97–113.

―――. *New Essays on Plato and Aristotle.* London: Routledge and Kegan Paul, 1965.

―――. "The Disunity of Plato's Thought Or: What Plato Did Not Say." *Philosophy,* 47 (1972), 295–307.

Barker, Sir Ernest. *The Political Thought of Plato and Aristotle.* 1906; rpt. New York: Dover, 1959.

Barrow, Robin. *Plato: Utilitarianism and Education.* London and Boston: Routledge and Kegan Paul, 1975.

Battin, M. Pabst. "Plato on True and False Poetry." *Journal of Aesthetics and Art Criticism,* 36 (1977), 163–74.

Beardsley, Monroe C. *Aesthetics from Classical Greece to the Present: A Short History.* New York: Macmillan, 1966.

Beck, Frederick A. G. *Greek Education: 450–350 B.C.* New York: Barnes and Noble, 1964.

Bolgar, R. R. *The Classical Heritage.* New York: Harper and Row, 1964.

Bosanquet, Bernard. *A History of Aesthetic.* 1892; rpt. London: S. Sonnenschein, 1910.

Boyd, John D. *The Function of Mimesis and Its Decline.* Cambridge, Mass.: Harvard University Press, 1968.

Bréhier, Émile. *The Hellenic Age.* Translated by Joseph Thomas. Chicago: University of Chicago Press, 1963.

Brownson, Carleton Lewis. *Plato's Studies and Criticisms of the Poets.* Boston: R. G. Badger, 1920.

Brumbaugh, Robert S. *Plato on the One.* New Haven: Yale University Press, 1961.

―――. *Plato for the Modern Age.* New York: Crowell-Collier, 1962.

Burnet, John. *Early Greek Philosophy.* 1914; rpt. London: A. and C. Black, 1948.

—————. *The Socratic Doctrine of the Soul.* Proceedings of the British Academy, Vol. 7. Oxford, 1916.

Carter, Robert Edgar. "Plato and Inspiration." *Journal of the History of Philosophy,* 5 (1967), 111–21.

Cavarnos, Constantine. *Plato's Theory of Fine Art.* Athens: Astir Publishing Company, 1973.

Collingwood, R. G. "Plato's Philosophy of Art." *Mind,* n.s. 34 (1925), 154–72.

—————. *The Principles of Art.* Oxford: Clarendon, 1938.

Cornford, Francis M. "Psychology and Social Structure in the *Republic* of Plato." *Classical Quarterly,* 6 (1912), 246–65.

Crocker, Richard L. "Pythagorean Mathematics and Music," *Journal of Aesthetics and Art Criticism,* 22 (1963–64), 189–98, 325–35.

Crombie, I. M. *An Examination of Plato's Doctrines.* London: Routledge and Kegan Paul, 1962.

Cross, R. C., and A. D. Woozley. *Plato's Republic: A Philosophical Commentary.* 1964; rpt. London: Macmillan, 1971.

Cushman, Robert Earl. *Therapeia: Plato's Conception of Philosophy.* Chapel Hill: University of North Carolina Press, 1958.

Demos, Raphael. *The Philosophy of Plato.* New York: Charles Scribner, 1939.

Dodds, Eric Robertson. *The Greeks and the Irrational.* Berkeley: University of California Press, 1951.

Dorter, Kenneth. "The *Ion*: Plato's Characterization of Art." *Journal of Aesthetics and Art Criticism,* 32 (1973), 65–78.

—————. "The Significance of the Speeches in Plato's *Symposium*." *Philosophy and Rhetoric,* 2 (1969), 215–34.

Edelstein, Ludwig. "The Function of Myth in Plato's Philosophy." *Journal of the History of Ideas,* 10 (1949), 463–81.

—————. *Plato's Seventh Letter.* Leiden: E. J. Brill, 1966.

Else, Gerald F. " 'Imitation' in the Fifth Century." *Classical Philology,* 53 (1958), 73–90.

Elyot, Sir Thomas. *The Boke Named the Governour.* Edited by H. H. S. Croft. 2 vols. London: C. Kegan Paul, 1883.

—————. *The Defence of Good Women.* Edited by Edwin J. Howard. Oxford, Ohio: Ohio University Press, 1940.

Field, G. C. *Plato and His Contemporaries: A Study in Fourth Century Thought.* 1930; rpt. New York: Haskell House, 1974.

————. *The Philosophy of Plato*. 2d ed. London and New York: Oxford University Press, 1969.

Findlay, John N. *Plato: The Written and Unwritten Doctrines*. New York: Humanities Press, 1974.

Frazer, Sir James G. *The Growth of Plato's Ideal Theory*. London: Macmillan, 1930.

Friedländer, Paul. *Plato: An Introduction*. Translated by Hans Meyerhoff. 1954; rpt. New York: Harper and Row, 1964.

————. *Plato: The Dialogues, First Period*. Translated by Hans Meyerhoff. New York: Pantheon Books, 1964.

————. *Plato: The Dialogues, Second and Third Periods*. Translated by Hans Meyerhoff. 1960; rpt. Princeton: Princeton University Press, 1969.

Gadamer, Hans-Georg. *Dialogue and Dialectic: Eight Hermeneutical Studies on Plato*. Translated by P. Christopher Smith. New Haven and London: Yale University Press, 1980.

Gauss, Hermann. *Plato's Conception of Philosophy*. London: Macmillan, 1937.

Gilbert, Allan. "Did Plato Banish the Poets or the Critics?" *Studies in Philology*, 36 (1939), 1–19.

————, ed. *Literary Criticism: Plato to Dryden*. 1940; rpt. Detroit: Wayne State University Press, 1962.

Gilbert, Katherine E. "The Relation of the Moral to the Aesthetic Standard in Plato." *Philosophical Review*, 43 (1934), 279–94.

Gilbert, Katherine E., and Helmut Kuhn. *A History of Esthetics*. 1939; rpt. Bloomington, Ind.: Indiana University Press, 1953.

Golden, Leon. "Plato's Concept of *Mimesis*." *British Journal of Aesthetics*, 15 (1975), 118–31.

Gosson, Stephen. *The Schoole of Abuse*. Edited by Edward Arber. London: Alexander Murray and Son, 1868.

Gould, Thomas. *Platonic Love*. New York: Free Press, 1963.

Greene, William Chase. "Plato's View of Poetry." *Harvard Studies in Classical Philology*, 29 (1918), 1–75.

Grey, D. R. "Art in the *Republic*." *Philosophy*, 27 (1952), 291–310.

Gross, Barry, ed. *The Great Thinkers on Plato*. New York: Capricorn, 1969.

Grube, G. M. A. "Plato's Theory of Beauty." *Monist*, 37 (1927), 269–88.

————. *Plato's Thought.* 1935; rpt. Boston: Beacon Press, 1966.

Gulley, Norman. *Plato's Theory of Knowledge.* London: Methuen, 1962.

————. *The Philosophy of Socrates.* London: Macmillan, 1968.

Hackforth, Reginald. "The Modification of Plan in Plato's *Republic.*" *Classical Quarterly,* 7 (1913), 265–72.

Hall, Robert W. *Plato and the Individual.* The Hague: Nijhoff, 1963.

————. "Plato's Theory of Art: A Reassessment," *Journal of Aesthetics and Art Criticism,* 33 (1974), 75–82.

Hall, Vernon, Jr. *A Short History of Literary Criticism.* New York: New York University Press, 1963.

Hamlyn, D. W. "*Eikasia* in Plato's *Republic.*" *Philosophical Quarterly,* 8 (1958), 14–23.

Harriott, Rosemary. *Poetry and Criticism Before Plato.* London: Methuen, 1969.

Hart, Ray L. "The Imagination in Plato." *International Philosophical Quarterly,* 5 (1965), 436–61.

Havelock, Eric A. *Preface to Plato.* Cambridge, Mass.: Harvard University Press, 1963.

Jaeger, Werner. *Paideia: The Ideals of Greek Culture.* Translated by Gilbert Highet. 3 vols. 1939; rpt. New York: Oxford University Press, 1969.

Joseph, Horace W. B. *Knowledge and the Good in Plato's "Republic."* London: Oxford University Press, 1948.

Karelis, Charles. "Plato on Art and Reality." *Journal of Aesthetics and Art Criticism,* 34 (1976), 315–21.

Keyt, David. "Plato's Paradox That the Immutable Is Unknowable." *The Philosophical Quarterly,* 19 (1969), 1–14.

Kirk, G. S. "The Problem of Cratylus." *American Journal of Philology,* 72 (1951), 225–53.

Kitto, H. D. F. *Poiesis: Structure and Thought.* Berkeley and Los Angeles: University of California Press, 1966.

Koyré, Alexandre. *Discovering Plato.* Translated by Leonora Rosenfield. New York: Columbia University Press, 1945.

Kraut, Richard. "Egoism, Love and Political Office in Plato." *The Philosophical Review,* 82 (1973), 330–44.

Lodge, Rupert C. *Plato's Theory of Ethics.* New York: Harcourt, Brace, 1928.

————. *Plato's Theory of Education.* New York: Harcourt, Brace, 1947.

————. *Plato's Theory of Art.* London: Routledge and Kegan Paul, 1953.

————. *The Philosophy of Plato.* London: Routledge and Kegan Paul, 1956.

McKeon, Richard. "Literary Criticism and the Concept of Imitation in Antiquity." *Modern Philology,* 24 (1936), 1–35.

More, Paul E. *Platonism.* 3d ed. Princeton: Princeton University Press, 1931.

Morgan, Douglas N. *Love: Plato, the Bible, and Freud.* Englewood Cliffs, N. J.: Prentice-Hall, 1964.

Morrison, J. S. "The Origins of Plato's Philosopher-Statesman." *Classical Quarterly,* n.s. 8 (1958), 198–218.

Mountford, J. F. "The Musical Scales of Plato's *Republic.*" *Classical Quarterly,* 17 (1923), 125–36.

Mueller, Gustav E. *Plato: The Founder of Philosophy as Dialectic.* New York: Philosophical Library, 1965.

Murphy, N. R. *The Interpretation of Plato's Republic.* Oxford: Clarendon Press, 1951.

Murray, Gilbert. *Greek Studies.* Oxford: Clarendon Press, 1946.

Nehring, A. "Plato and the Theory of Language." *Traditio,* 3 (1945), 13–48.

Nettleship, Richard L. *Lectures on the Republic of Plato.* 1897; rpt. London: Macmillan, 1964.

————. *The Theory of Education in the Republic of Plato.* Chicago: University of Chicago Press, 1906.

Oates, Whitney J. *Plato's View of Art.* New York: Charles Scribner's Sons, 1972.

————, ed. *Basic Writings of Saint Augustine.* 2 vols. New York: Random House, 1948.

Partee, Morriss Henry. "Plato's Banishment of Poetry." *Journal of Aesthetics and Art Criticism,* 29 (1970), 209–22.

————. "Sir Thomas Elyot on Plato's Aesthetics." *Viator,* 1 (1970), 327–35.

————. "Inspiration in the Aesthetics of Plato." *Journal of Aesthetics and Art Criticism,* 30 (1971), 87–95.

————. "Plato's Theory of Language." *Foundations of Language*, 8 (1972), 113–32.

————. "Plato on the Criticism of Poetry." *Philological Quarterly*, 52 (1973), 629–42.

————. "Plato on the Rhetoric of Poetry." *Journal of Aesthetics and Art Criticism*, 33 (1974), 203–12.

Paton, H. J. "Plato's Theory of ΕΙΚΑΣΙΑ." *Proceedings of the Aristotelean Society*, n.s. 22 (1922), 69–104.

Peck, Arthur L. "Plato Versus Parmenides." *Philosophical Review*, 71 (1962), 159–84.

Pieper, Josef. *Enthusiasm and Divine Madness*. Translated by Richard and Clara Winston. New York: Harcourt, Brace, 1964.

Plockmann, George K. "Plato, Visual Perception, and Art." *Journal of Aesthetics and Art Criticism*, 35 (1976), 189–200.

Quimby, Rollin W. "The Growth of Plato's Perception of Rhetoric." *Philosophy and Rhetoric*, 7 (1974), 71–79.

Randall, John. *Plato: Dramatist of the Life of Reason*. New York: Columbia University Press, 1970.

Ranta, Jerrald. "The Drama of Plato's *Ion*." *Journal of Aesthetics and Art Criticism*, 26 (1967), 219–29.

Rau, Catherine. *Art and Society: A Reinterpretation of Plato*. New York: R. R. Smith, 1951.

Raven, J. E. *Plato's Thought in the Making*. Cambridge: Cambridge University Press, 1965.

Ritchie, David G. *Plato*. Edinburgh: T. and T. Clark, 1902.

Ritter, Constantin. *The Essence of Plato's Philosophy*. Translated by Adam Alles. New York: The Dial Press, 1933.

Robinson, Richard. *Plato's Earlier Dialectic*. 2d ed. Oxford: Clarendon Press, 1953.

Robinson, T. M. *Plato's Psychology*. Toronto: Toronto University Press, 1970.

Rosen, S. H. "Collingwood and Greek Aesthetic." *Phronesis*, 4 (1959), 135–48.

Rosenmeyer, T. "Gorgias, Aeschylus and *Apate*." *American Journal of Philology*, 76 (1955), 225–60.

Ross, Sir David. *Plato's Theory of Ideas*. Oxford: Clarendon Press, 1951.

————. "The Date of Plato's *Cratylus.*" *Review of Philosophy,* 9 (1955).

Ryle, Gilbert. *Plato's Progress.* Cambridge: Cambridge University Press, 1966.

Rucker, Darnell. "Plato and the Poets." *Journal of Aesthetics and Art Criticism,* 25 (1966), 167–70.

Sayre, Kenneth. *Plato's Analytic Method.* Chicago: University of Chicago Press, 1969.

Schaper, Eva. *Prelude to Aesthetics.* London: Allen and Unwin, 1968.

Schipper, Edith W. *Forms in Plato's Later Dialogues.* The Hague: Nijhoff, 1965.

Sesonske, Alexander, ed. *Plato's Republic: Interpretation and Criticism.* Belmont, Calif.: Wadsworth, 1966.

Sesonske, Alexander, and Noel Fleming, eds. *Plato's Meno: Text and Criticism.* Belmont, Calif.: Wadsworth, 1965.

Shorey, Paul. *The Unity of Plato's Thought.* Chicago: University of Chicago Press, 1903.

————. "On Plato's *Cratylus* 389d." *Classical Philology,* 14 (1919), 85.

————. *What Plato Said.* Chicago: University of Chicago Press, 1933.

————. *Platonism: Ancient and Modern.* Berkeley: University of California Press, 1938.

Sidney, Sir Philip. *The Prose Works of Sir Philip Sidney.* Edited by Albert Feuillerat. 4 vols. Cambridge: Cambridge University Press, 1963.

Sinaiko, Herman L. *Love, Knowledge, and Discourse in Plato.* Chicago: University of Chicago Press, 1965.

Sontag, Frederick. "The Platonist's Conception of Language." *Journal of Philosophy,* 51 (1954), 823–30.

Steven, R. G. "Plato and the Art of His Time," *Classical Quarterly,* 27 (1933), 149–55.

Stewart, John Alexander. *The Myths of Plato.* Edited by G. R. Levy. 1905; rpt. New York: Barnes and Noble, 1970.

————. *Plato's Doctrine of Ideas.* Oxford: Clarendon Press, 1909.

Tate, J. " 'Imitation' in Plato's *Republic.*" *Classical Quarterly,* 22 (1928), 16–23.

————. "Plato and Allegorical Interpretation." *Classical Quarterly*, 23 (1929), 142–54, and 24 (1930), 1–10.

————. "Plato and 'Imitation.'" *Classical Quarterly*, 26 (1932), 161–69.

————. "On Plato: *Laws X* 889cd." *Classical Quarterly*, 30 (1936), 48–54.

Taylor, A. E. *The Mind of Plato*. 1922; rpt. Ann Arbor, Michigan: University of Michigan Press, 1964.

————. *Plato: The Man and His Work*. 1927; rpt. New York: Meridian Books, 1960.

————. *Platonism and Its Influence*. New York: Cooper Square, 1963.

Thayer, H. S. "Plato: The Theory and Language of Function." *Philosophical Quarterly*, 14 (1964), 303–18.

Tigerstedt, Eugene N. *Plato's Idea of Poetical Inspiration*. Commentationes Humanarum Litterarum. Helsinki: Societas Scientiarum Fennica, 1969.

Toynbee, Arnold. *Civilization on Trial*. New York: Meridian Books, 1958.

Verdenius, W. J. *Mimesis: Plato's Doctrine of Artistic Imitation and Its Meaning to Us*. Leiden: E. J. Brill, 1949.

Versenyi, Laszlo G. "Plato and His Liberal Opponents." *Philosophy*, 46 (1971), 222–37.

Vlastos, Gregory. *Platonic Studies*. Princeton: Princeton University Press, 1973.

————, ed. *Plato: A Collection of Critical Essays*. 2 vols. Berryville, Va.: Doubleday, 1971.

Vries, Gerrit Jacob de. *A Commentary on the Phaedrus of Plato*. Amsterdam: Adolf M. Hakkert, 1969.

Warry, John G. *Greek Aesthetic Theory*. New York: Barnes and Noble, 1962.

Webster, T. B. L. "Greek Theories of Art and Literature Down to 400 B.C." *Classical Quarterly*, 33 (1939), 166–79.

Wild, John. *Plato's Theory of Man*. Cambridge, Mass.: Harvard University Press, 1948.

Wilson, J. R. S. "The Argument of *Republic IV*." *The Philosophical Quarterly*, 26 (1976), 111–24.

Wimsatt, William K., and Cleanth Brooks. *Literary Criticism: A Short History*. New York: Knopf, 1964.

Dialogue Index

Index of Subjects
and Authors

Design and Composition
by Donald M. Henriksen